Strategic Stu

DISJOINTED WAYS, DISUNIFIED MEANS: LEARNING FROM AMERICA'S STRUGGLE TO BUILD AN AFGHAN NATION

Lewis G. Irwin

May 2012

The views expressed in this report are those of the author and do not necessarily reflect the official policy or position of the Department of the Army, the Department of Defense, or the U.S. Government. Authors of Strategic Studies Institute (SSI) publications enjoy full academic freedom, provided they do not disclose classified information, jeopardize operations security, or misrepresent official U.S. policy. Such academic freedom empowers them to offer new and sometimes controversial perspectives in the interest of furthering debate on key issues. This report is cleared for public release; distribution is unlimited.

*****

This publication is subject to Title 17, United States Code, Sections 101 and 105. It is in the public domain and may not be copyrighted.

*****

Comments pertaining to this report are invited and should be forwarded to: Director, Strategic Studies Institute, U.S. Army War College, 45 Ashburn Drive, Bldg. 47, Carlisle, PA 17013-5046.

*****

All Strategic Studies Institute (SSI) publications may be downloaded free of charge from the SSI website. Hard copies of this report may also be obtained free of charge while supplies last by placing an order on the SSI website. SSI publications may be quoted or reprinted in part or in full with permission and appropriate credit given to the U.S. Army Strategic Studies Institute, U.S. Army War College, Carlisle Barracks, PA. Contact SSI by visiting our website at the following address: *www.StrategicStudiesInstitute.army.mil*.

*****

The Strategic Studies Institute publishes a monthly e-mail newsletter to update the national security community on the research of our analysts, recent and forthcoming publications, and upcoming conferences sponsored by the Institute. Each newsletter also provides a strategic commentary by one of our research analysts. If you are interested in receiving this newsletter, please subscribe on the SSI website at *www.StrategicStudiesInstitute.army.mil/newsletter/*.

ISBN 1-58487-528-3

*****

For the dedicated professionals of America's joint, interagency national security team.

*****

CONTENTS

Preface vii

About the Author xvii

Introduction xix

Part I: The Challenge of Afghanistan 1

1: Defining the Afghan Problem 3

2: The Scope of Irregular Warfare
   and "Nation-Building" 55

3: Evolving U.S. Strategic Interests,
   Options, and Risks 83

Part II: Disjointed Policies and
         Organizational Structures 123

4: Disjointed Policies, Strategies,
   and Objectives................................125

5: A Clash of Organizational Cultures
   and Resources 173

6: Disunified Interagency Structures,
   Processes, and Effort 215

7: The Unsurprising and Uneven
   Results.......................................259

Part III: Potential Solutions 289

8: Commonly Proposed Solutions
   and Faulty Assumptions 291

9: Essential Elements of Any Feasible and
   Effective Solution..327

10: A Way Ahead — The NSC, Combatant
    Commands, and USRADCOM 345

A Brief Epilogue: Contemplating the
Context and Future of "Nation-Building".....385

Bibliography..395

Acronyms and Abbreviations 413

PREFACE

From August 2007 until February 2008, I served with the U.S. Army in Afghanistan as the leader of an ad hoc interagency group assigned the mission of designing and implementing a nation-wide reform of the Afghan National Police. This extensive police reform initiative, dubbed "Focused District Development," represented a major shift in focus for the U.S. agencies charged with developing the Afghan security forces and their corresponding Afghan governmental institutions—tasks clearly at the heart of any successful irregular warfare effort. Coalition and Afghan leaders alike deemed the mission to be of central importance to the ongoing counterinsurgency and, accordingly, the Afghan police development mission received enhanced resources and concentrated senior leader attention, as "Focused District Development" moved forward in its design, operational planning, and eventual execution.

In spite of these natural advantages, however, the development, coordination, and implementation of this high-profile initiative revealed to me major shortcomings in U.S. Government systems for coordinating and integrating the resources and effort of its agencies, at least at the operational level of activity. It was also becoming increasingly clear then that the North Atlantic Treaty Organization (NATO) mission was falling well short of achieving its other major nonmilitary objectives, despite the hard work of so many. Given the central importance of U.S. contributions to the broader coalition effort, I began to wonder about the root causes of the interagency shortfalls I had observed, as well as about the potential reforms that might enable the U.S. Government to achieve true interagency "unity of effort." In short, how could we realize the genuine "whole of government" approach needed to achieve our complex national security objectives more effectively, efficiently, and directly?

As I prepared to return home at the end of my tour of duty, a series of fundamental questions remained unanswered:

- With so many talented people working so hard to achieve "success" in Afghanistan, why were the results falling so far short of the goal?
- Was the notion of "nation-building" in Afghanistan reasonable in the first place? Or was there something about Afghanistan that predestined "nation-building" to likely failure there, given the basic requirements of nationhood?
- Had the administration's strategic guidance for Afghanistan been clearly defined and feasible? Did the capabilities, priorities, and effort of the various agencies match the requirements of this complex irregular warfare and "nation-building" mission?
- What specific shortcomings in the U.S. Government interagency processes were contributing to these shortfalls? Did these problems stem from structural or procedural deficiencies at the strategic, operational, or tactical levels of the national security apparatus, or perhaps from some combination of the three?
- Were there reforms of our national security structures and systems underway already that might reasonably be expected to solve these interagency problems?
- What elements would any national security reforms need to feature in order to be successful, given the practical realities of the agencies' ex-

isting mandates, core expertise, organizational cultures, comparative resources, and career incentives?
- What specific national security reforms might address those requirements directly, while overcoming likely practical and political obstacles to their implementation?
- What were the broader implications of these lengthy, resource-intensive irregular warfare, and "nation-building" missions for U.S. national security in general?

After returning home and continuing this line of inquiry, I quickly realized that the challenges I had discovered for myself were already commonly recognized by most practitioners and observers concerned with U.S. national security. In fact, these obstacles to unified agency and departmental effort were acknowledged to extend much further than any one operational theater or any one reform initiative. As a result, while my own operational-level interagency experience served as the initial impetus for my research, this book is not intended merely to recount my own experiences or to focus solely on the operational-level shortfalls in the U.S. Government interagency processes. Instead, the goal of this analysis is to carry out a much broader and more systematic review of our government's strategic and interagency performance in Afghanistan to date, using the Afghan case as the vehicle for an investigation into the nature and root causes of the interagency problems I observed firsthand. I then use this analysis to frame potential corrective measures that can be applied to future irregular warfare and "nation-building" missions in particular and American national security affairs more generally.

Put another way—and into the Army's vernacular—most military officers will recognize this book as an attempt at a thorough strategic-level "in-progress review." Like any other review, the basic objectives are to facilitate a constructive dialogue while helping the participants get the answers right—and to help the United States to succeed in Afghanistan and in the other irregular warfare or "nation-building" missions likely to arise in the future. At the same time, I am also hopeful that some of these findings and recommendations can be applied outside the realm of national security to improve the articulation of strategic guidance and to strengthen other U.S. interagency relationships. Taken together, these are the primary goals of this book.

In many ways, the questions that have driven this research run in parallel with the American public's growing unease with our goals, methods, and prospects for success in Afghanistan. The reader will have to judge whether or not my answers to these questions are compelling or satisfying, but collectively, they represent the truth as I have come to see it. As the title of the book suggests, my experience, research, and reflections on the U.S. effort in Afghanistan point toward fundamental shortcomings in America's strategic processes and products at the national level—coupled with structural deficiencies in the U.S. Government systems for coordinating and integrating the efforts of its various agencies—as the primary culprits in explaining the major shortfalls in the U.S. mission in Afghanistan over its course. In essence, I will argue that a risky combination of disjointed ways and disunified means has resulted in adverse effects that begin at the strategic level of national security activity, before subsequently trickling down to cause corresponding problems at the operational and tactical levels of effort. I will also argue that if these proximate causes of our struggles in Afghanistan are left unresolved, this dangerous combination of disjointed ways and disunified means will pose serious risks for the future of U.S. national security. Furthermore, real change will not come easily, but instead, will require much heavy lifting, practically and politically.

With all of these assertions in mind, however, this book is intended neither as a "gotcha" exercise nor as some "tell-all." On the contrary, I have a deep respect and abiding affection for the talented and hard-working members of the joint, interagency, and intergovernmental partnerships trying to realize success in the pursuit of remarkably difficult national security objectives in the face of equally difficult circumstances. At the same time, the evidence clearly suggests that the articulation of U.S. strategy by our leadership and our existing interagency processes for national security have fallen far short of what is needed for our nation to succeed in these incredibly complex and resource-intensive irregular warfare and "nation-building" operations. Putting this idea into Army terms as well, to this point there has been no comprehensive strategic-level "troop-to-task" analysis, or any honest effort to match our national objectives with available capabilities. Nor has there been any serious attempt to mandate cooperation among agencies and departments. We can and must do better.

In terms of its structure, the book begins with an introductory section that briefly outlines the primary arguments that will follow, in the manner of an executive summary. The remainder of the book is then divided into three major parts, with individual chapters that aim to address the various questions posed earlier in this preface. Part I of the book, "The Challenge of Afghanistan" and its three chapters, offers an analysis of the scope and depth of the challenges confronting the coalition in the Afghan theater of operations, as well as an examination of relevant U.S. interests, options, and risks. This part of the book begins with a chapter that considers the numerous social, political, economic, demographic, and historical factors that make Afghanistan a remarkably difficult candidate for irregular warfare and "nation-building" in the first place. As an extension of that theme, Chapter 2 describes the broad scope and extraordinary complexity of irregular warfare and "nation-building" missions. Chapter 3 considers the shifting nature of U.S. national security interests in Afghanistan and the region, while also offering a sketch of the varied motives and interests of other key national and transnational actors holding their own stakes in the outcome.

The second part of the book, "Disjointed Policies and Organizational Structures," consists of four chapters, which present an analysis of the root causes of our strategic and interagency difficulties in meeting the challenges described in Part I. While Chapter 4 critically examines and assesses the U.S. Government's national-level strategic guidance for Afghanistan, Chapter 5 analyzes the predominant organizational cultural norms, existing core competencies, and comparative resources of the key U.S. agencies charged with meeting the demands of that guidance. Chapter 6 looks directly at the shortfalls of the U.S. Government's interagency doctrine, structures, and processes for integrating agency effort as they apply to the case of Afghanistan. Building on these findings, Chapter 7 concludes this section of the book by cataloguing the corresponding unfavorable and largely unsurprising results of this strategic disjointedness and disunity of effort, all placed within the context of a truly challenging set of Afghan circumstances.

The third part of the book, "Potential Solutions," considers commonly proposed potential remedies to our strategic and interagency problems, examines their prospects for success, and proposes an alternate set of organizational recommendations. Specifically, Chapter 8 examines frequently proposed solutions to the interagency problem, while also identifying a host of faulty assumptions implied by these potential solutions that render them unlikely to succeed. Chapter 9 lists a set of characteristics that any feasible solution to the U.S. Government's strategic and interagency challenges will need to feature, in order for those solutions to be able to overcome the likely practical and political obstacles that any attempt at major organizational change will face. Chapter 10 concludes this third section of the book, by offering a set of potential reforms that could meet those standards. The book closes altogether with a brief epilogue, which contemplates the future of irregular warfare and "nation-building" missions and their broader practicality.

By way of my own background, I am both a long-serving military officer and a professional political scientist, and I have applied both perspectives in this analysis. This "dual-hat status" was especially useful, given my particular duties in Afghanistan, since those duties provided me with the rare opportunity to interact with key leaders — ranging from the most-senior leaders of the coalition, the Afghan government, and the international community — all the way out to leaders at the "tip of the spear." With this background in mind, the book also benefited from numerous U.S. Army War College seminars, U.S. Joint Forces Command training activities, Joint Forces Staff College discussions, academic conferences, interviews, and other research activities that took place subsequent to my return from the operational theater. Likewise, this book also represents the extension of a series of op-ed pieces and journal articles that I wrote, which helped to frame and refine these arguments. In that vein, I am especially grateful to the editors of the National Defense University's *Joint Force Quarterly* and the U.S. Army War College's *Parameters* for their willingness to allow me to incorporate into this larger effort the ideas that I had first expressed in those excellent journals.

Finally, while authors routinely offer the caveat that their works are possible only because of the efforts of others, I am confident that in my case this qualification applies to an even-greater extent than for most. During my comparatively brief tour of duty in Afghanistan, I benefited from the opportunity to work for a particularly gifted set of senior leaders and with selfless comrades who truly served the public interest. Among others, I developed great respect for then-Major General Robert Cone, Brigadier General Andrew Twomey, and U.S. Ambassador William Wood, as well as then-Afghan Deputy Minister for Security Lieutenant General Mohammad Munir Mangal—serving as the acting Afghan Minister of the Interior as of this writing. These leaders could shift effortlessly from the military aspects of the operations in Afghanistan to the political, economic, and sociological dimensions of the mission. They were equally conversant about the individual Afghan and coalition players and their strengths, weaknesses, and likely actions or reactions. The American people and our Afghan partners have been remarkably well served by these key leaders.

Along the same lines, U.S. Army Colonels Pete Foreman and Mike McMahon provided much of the creative thinking and force of will that were central to the genesis of the police reform initiative that I worked to develop. Other comrades whom I counted upon heavily for friendship and mission support included U.S. Marine Corps Colonels Howard Parker and Mark Goldner, the European Union Police's William Morrell, U.S. Aid for International Development's (USAID) Barbara Krell, the State Department's Merry Miller and Brent Hartley, Afghan interpreter Mattiulah Mati Sohawk, British Army Leftenant Colonel Dickie Winchester, the Afghan Ministry of the Interior's Colonel Wakil, Navy Petty Officer Pete Wirebaugh, DynCorp's Tony Campagna, MPRI's Jim Lee, and U.S. Army comrades including Major Jesse Pooler, Major Matt Prohm, Lieutenant Colonel Brett Rypma, Colonel Mike Glenn, Major McKinley Cunningham, and Major Chris Crary. A special acknowledgment goes to Colonel Mike Haerr, a Soldier whose diligence and passion on the behalf of the Afghan people was unmatched in my experience. These comrades exemplify the concept of selfless service.

Lastly, the arguments that follow are mine alone, and they are not intended to represent the views of the Department of Defense or any other organization with which I am affiliated. Among those organizations, I would like to thank my colleagues at Duquesne University for their habitual forbearance during my absences for military duty, as well as the faculty and colleagues at the U.S. Army War College and my comrades at U.S. Joint Forces Command and in the U.S. Army Reserve. I would also like to offer special thanks to Mike McMahon, Trey Braun, and Randy Boyer for their meticulous and insightful comments on earlier drafts, and to Douglas Lovelace and Dallas Owens of the Strategic Studies Institute for the great energy and enthusiasm they brought to the project. As always, however, my most heartfelt thanks go to Marcia, Mary Tristan, Eva, and Andrew for their affection and support.

Lewis G. Irwin

ABOUT THE AUTHOR

Lewis G. Irwin is a Colonel in the U.S. Army Reserve and an Associate Professor of Political Science and Public Policy at Duquesne University, jointly appointed to the Department of Political Science and the Graduate Center for Social and Public Policy. In the Army Reserve, Colonel Irwin commands the 926th Engineer Brigade, and has served in a wide variety of assignments during more than 25 years of service in the U.S. Army. These assignments have included tours of duty in Afghanistan, Iraq, Saudi Arabia, Kuwait, and Germany, including service with the 101st Airborne Division, the 1st and 3rd Armored Divisions, West Point's Department of Social Sciences, and the U.S. Joint Forces Command, among others. From August of 2007 until February of 2008, he served with the U.S. Army in Afghanistan as the leader of an ad hoc interagency team assigned the mission of designing and implementing a nation-wide reform of the Afghan National Police, then known as "Focused District Development." That effort continues today. An Army Reserve Adjunct Professor for Research at the Strategic Studies Institute of the U.S. Army War College, Colonel Irwin is the author of *The Chill in the House* (SUNY Press, 2002) and *The Policy Analyst's Handbook* (M. E. Sharpe, 2003), in addition to numerous journal articles and other publications. Colonel Irwin holds a bachelor's in civil engineering management from the U.S. Military Academy at West Point, a master's in strategic studies from the U.S. Army War College, and a Ph.D. in political science from Yale University.

DISJOINTED WAYS, DISUNIFIED MEANS: LEARNING FROM AMERICA'S STRUGGLE TO BUILD AN AFGHAN NATION

INTRODUCTION

The International Community, including NATO, is helping the Afghan Government enhance security, improve governance and step up reconstruction and development. Progress in all three areas is essential in helping Afghanistan establish itself as a secure, stable country that poses no threat to itself or the International Community.

> NATO's *Afghanistan Report 2009*, Foreword[1]

Remarkably ambitious in its audacity and scope, the North Atlantic Treaty Organization's (NATO) irregular warfare and "nation-building" mission in Afghanistan has struggled to meet its nonmilitary objectives by most tangible measures. Put directly, the alliance and its partners have fallen short of achieving the results needed to create a stable, secure, democratic, and self-sustaining Afghan nation, a particularly daunting proposition given Afghanistan's history and culture, the region's contemporary circumstances, and the fact that no such country has existed there before. Furthermore, given the central nature of U.S. contributions to this NATO mission, these shortfalls also serve as an indicator of a serious American problem as well. Specifically, inconsistencies and a lack of coherence in U.S. Government strategic planning processes and products, as well as fundamental flaws in U.S. Government structures and systems for coordinating and integrating the efforts of its various agencies, are largely responsible for this adverse and dangerous situation.

As a rationally ordered expression of the ways and means to be applied in the protection of vital national security interests, strategy is supposed to represent a careful analysis and prioritization of the particular interests at stake. In turn, these interests are linked to feasible methods and the resources that are available for their protection, all placed within the context of competing global security demands and a serious consideration of risk. In the case of Afghanistan, however, U.S. Government strategic guidance has been disjointed--or inconsistent and lacking coherence--while interagency efforts have been "disunified," with agency outputs too often fragmented, inadequate, or internally at odds with one another. As a result, U.S. strategic supervision of the Afghan operation has been muddled and shifting at best, even as our government's interagency processes and available agency capabilities have fallen far short of what is needed to carry out the complex and broad requirements of irregular warfare and "nation-building." Given the breadth, length, and expense of the U.S. commitment in Afghanistan, these strategic and operational shortfalls also carry with them potentially dire consequences for U.S. national security interests around the globe, considering potential first- and second-order effects and other associated risks. U.S. Government disjointed ways, coupled with a corresponding disunity of means, represent the proximate cause of our struggles in Afghanistan, and these deficiencies must be addressed if this mission and other similar future endeavors are to succeed.

Applying a finer resolution to the problem, these setbacks can be largely attributed to four related causes, each of which can be traced back to corresponding shortcomings at the national strategic level of planning and decisionmaking. As a first root cause, our struggles in Afghanistan stem at least in part from the immense challenges that Afghanistan poses as a candidate for nation-building and irregular warfare in the first place. These challenges include significant economic, sociological, demographic, political cultural, geographic, and even anthropological impediments that continue to stand in the way of any successful nation-building in Afghanistan. Compounding these obstacles is the fact that there are both internal and external actors who regard the notion of a stable, secure, democratic, and self-sustaining Afghanistan as a potent threat to their own vital interests. Furthermore, these enormous challenges seem to have been largely underestimated, misunderstood, or ignored by national-level decisionmakers as the United States commenced irregular warfare operations in the region and subsequently expanded the effort to encompass Afghan nation-building. All in all, the public record yields little evidence of any frank acknowledgment or systematic analysis of these major obstacles as the United States added nation-building to the original combat mission.

As a second root cause of our difficulties, the U.S. Government has also failed to articulate and maintain a set of clear, consistent, and feasible national security objectives in Afghanistan. Nor have we linked those objectives to practical methods for achieving them that match the realities of the situation on the ground or the agency resources and capabilities available to execute them--failing to link strategic ends, ways, and means. Exacerbating this lack of strategic coherence, only in recent years has the United States defined the compelling national security interests at stake in

Afghanistan and the region in a conclusive way. As a result, the justifications and desired end states for this mission have shifted and drifted over the years that the United States was engaged in irregular warfare and nation-building. Compounding this strategic drift, mismatched instruments of national power have been misapplied in the pursuit of two vague and possibly infeasible broader national security strategies. Reviewing the evidence then, the United States appears to have backed into nation-building in Afghanistan with little serious analysis of the likely costs, duration, or of the feasibility of the mission. There is also little evidence of any clear-headed sense of what the second-order effects of this "mission creep" might be for other U.S. strategic interests around the globe. In sum, the process of strategy formulation has clearly fallen short of what it is supposed to be at the national level.

Partly as a result of this strategic disjointedness, the third and fourth root causes of U.S. difficulties in Afghanistan represent natural extensions of these deficiencies in strategic planning and mission guidance at the national level. As a third root cause of our struggles in Afghanistan, there is a clear mismatch between the existing organizational cultures, core competencies, and available capabilities of the key U.S. agencies involved in the mission and the demands and requirements of irregular warfare and nation-building operations. In particular, the Department of Defense (DoD), the State Department (DoS), and the U.S. Agency for International Development (USAID) serve as the "key three" U.S. agencies with roles and responsibilities in irregular warfare and nation-building, with the U.S. Central Intelligence Agency (CIA) in the mix as a shadowy fourth. For a host of reasons, however, none of these three organizations or the others charged with roles and responsibilities in these operations is well-suited to the particular tasks required of them by these expansive and complex missions.

Lastly, the fourth root cause of the U.S. Government's checkered performance in Afghanistan has been its consistent failure to apply the full weight of its various instruments of power to achieve the desired goals. This problem is largely due to the inability or unwillingness of these various agencies to agree upon the operational-level ends, ways, and means needed to prosecute the mission successfully. This operational-level disunity of effort also stems from structural deficiencies in the mechanisms for facilitating interagency coordination and integration, and this deficiency has contributed directly and significantly to the broader shortfalls in the Afghan mission.

While these shortcomings in the interagency coordinating structures and processes are commonly recognized by participants and observers alike, there is no consensus regarding the corrective actions needed to solve this critical concern. Furthermore, the remedies applied to correct this problem to date have been more cosmetic than substantive in nature. So although there are many very talented people working hard to achieve "success" in Afghanistan, the efforts of U.S. agencies have been disunified in many cases and actually counterproductive in some others. Given the realities of major resource disparities, missing capabilities, and weak interagency integrating mechanisms, the United States turned to DoD as a stop-gap substitute for those missing capabilities. The United States also turned to DoD as a substitute for the actual robust "whole of government" interagency structures needed to meet the major challenges associated with irregular warfare and nation-building operations.

Having settled upon this approach for reasons that are justifiable in some respects and questionable in others, the evidence illustrates that this method has brought with it some advantages but also major and distinct disadvantages--and generally poor results. Accordingly, the U.S. effort in Afghanistan must serve as more than a mere cautionary reminder of T. E. Lawrence's sage observation that even in the best of circumstances, irregular warfare is "messy and slow, like eating soup with a knife," as thinker and practitioner John Nagl famously quoted in his seminal book on counterinsurgency.[2] Instead, we must learn the right lessons from our experience in Afghanistan, including the realization that achieving success in Afghanistan and in other similar national security challenges in the future will require more than simple, cosmetic changes to our national security apparatus. We must first improve our structures and processes for generating strategic analysis, plans, and guidance to achieve strategic coherence. Then we must reorganize the U.S. Government processes and systems for coordinating and integrating agency and departmental effort, if we are to realize the genuine unity of effort that will be vitally important in an era of constrained resources and emerging new threats.

ENDNOTES - INTRODUCTION

1. James Appathurai, *Afghanistan Report 2009*, Brussels, Belgium: NATO, 2009, Foreword.

2. John A. Nagl, *Learning to Eat Soup with a Knife: Counterinsurgency Lessons from Malaya and Vietnam*, Chicago, IL: University of Chicago Press, 2005 Ed., p. xii.

PART I

THE CHALLENGE OF AFGHANISTAN

The first stage of the war verified the lesson proven over the centuries that Afghanistan is not such a difficult country to invade. . . . The bulk of the ad hoc Afghan army melted away, while individual fighters waited patiently for a better opportunity to resist this new wave of feringhees (foreigners). . . . The fighting took on the most brutal aspect of guerrilla war as the British in Afghan territory could not always tell for sure who was the enemy.

> Historian Stephen Tanner's account of the failures of the British "Army of Retribution" in the Second Anglo-Afghan War of 1877-80[1]

In Afghanistan, we must deny al-Qa'ida a safe haven, deny the Taliban the ability to overthrow the government, and strengthen the capacity of Afghanistan's security forces and government so that they can take lead responsibility for Afghanistan's future. . . . First, our military and ISAF partners are targeting the insurgency, working to secure key population centers, and increasing efforts to train Afghan security forces. . . . Second, we will continue to work... to improve accountable and effective governance . . . focusing assistance on supporting the President of Afghanistan and those ministries, governors, and local leaders who combat corruption and deliver for the people. . . . This will support our long-term commitment to . . . a strong, stable, and prosperous Afghanistan."

> The National Security Strategy of the United States of America, May 2010[2]

CHAPTER 1

DEFINING THE AFGHAN PROBLEM

> The goal of our statecraft is to help create a world of democratic, well-governed states that can meet the needs of their citizens and conduct themselves responsibly in the international system. This is the best way to provide enduring security for the American people.
>
> The National Security Strategy of the
> United States of America, March 2006[3]

In aiming to create a "democratic, well-governed state" in Afghanistan, the United States chose an extremely difficult candidate for nationhood or "nation-building" assistance. In fact, in many respects one would be hard-pressed to identify a less-suitable candidate for nation-building than Afghanistan, regardless of the specific meaning intended by that often used, but nondoctrinal term. At its most basic level, a modern nation must comprise a people, a functioning government, a recognized territory, and an economic base. Even when compared against that modest standard, the case of Afghanistan is problematic.

However, when one carefully considers Afghanistan's history, as well as its geography, demographics, tribalism, warlordism, existing political cultural norms, drug trade, crime, and history of ineffective governance and corruption—among other unfavorable factors and conditions—it becomes abundantly clear that there are major obstacles standing in the way of the North Atlantic Treaty Organization's (NATO) ambitious goals of effective democratic governance and nationhood. So the United States could not have chosen a more difficult nation to build, even setting aside for the moment the fact that it is not clear exactly what variety of "nation" the United States is trying to realize. Dimming these prospects further, there are a number of domestic, international, and transnational actors who are working just as hard to undermine this nation-building effort.

AFGHANISTAN'S VIOLENT HISTORY

Afghanistan has long been known as a crossroads of empires, but in spite of the dramatic violence and persistent warfare that have characterized its past, the country has held little real influence or significance in world events over the centuries. Instead, the various Afghan tribes have remained largely isolated from external events, global trends, and one another. In fact, for most of its history, the territory now known as Afghanistan was not even considered to be a single country, either by the countries that bordered the land or by the Afghan tribesmen themselves.[4] Consistent with this view, the focus of daily life among the various Afghan peoples has always remained at the tribal level, with the warriors of the assorted tribes and other ethnic groupings more than willing to fight one another when not working together to repel the frequent foreign invasions. The Afghan tribesmen have always fought and lived independently, remaining largely ungoverned outside their tribal structures and honing their martial skills by fighting among themselves when not fighting foreign aggressors.[5] The U.S. involvement there today is just the latest chapter in a long history of foreign invasions and interventions.

Viewed holistically, Afghanistan's military history, its culture, and its political development have all been shaped to a great extent by its topography.

Afghanistan has no natural geographic borders, with the exception of brief stretches like the Amu Darya River in the north. Its harsh terrain consists largely of the Hindu Kush mountain range and the bleak deserts surrounding it, making for a land that is easily invaded but difficult to conquer. In the rugged and mountainous central regions of Afghanistan, there are numerous tribes living independently of one another and governed on a feudal basis. These tribes in the highlands have maintained their independence for thousands of years, even as the more sedentary villages on the transit routes have been routinely invaded and conquered many times over. In its essence then, most of recorded Afghan history reads as a long series of periodic, vicious wars between the Pashtun majority of Afghanistan's south and east and a variety of foes, among them the Persians to the west, the Indians to the east, and the nomadic warrior tribes of the northern steppes.[6]

Emerging as a byproduct of Britain and Russia's Great Game, Afghanistan was formally created only a few centuries ago, but the earliest written use of the word "Afghan"—ironically meaning "unruly" or "ungovernable"—is found as far back as the 3rd century. British historian Mountstuart Elphinstone visited the country in 1809, and he noted that while others called the country Afghanistan, the Afghan people themselves did not.[7] In forming the modern geographical and political entity of Afghanistan at the end of the 19th century, European surveyors chose Afghanistan's largely arbitrary borders not with the territory's various tribal structures in mind, but rather in order to create "the best possible buffer state between British India and the inexorable tide of Russian annexations in Central Asia."[8] As part of this opportunistic mapmaking, the sliver of Afghan land that borders China was imposed upon Afghanistan by the British to ensure that no part of Russia would touch then-British India. In fact, the famous Durand Line, which delineates the Afghan-Pakistan border, splits the influential Pashtun ethnic faction roughly in half. Some historians believe that the division of this key ethnic group was done intentionally, to limit Pashtun power and to ensure that Afghanistan would forever be a weakly governed state.

Serving as another similar but natural barrier to potential Pashtun influence, the Hindu Kush mountain range physically separates several Afghan ethnic groups that do not normally choose to associate with one another. Throughout Afghan history, the Uzbeks, Tajiks, and Turkmen of the north have resisted being governed by the dominant Pashtuns of the south, most often by force of arms. The Pashtun tribesmen represent about 40 percent of the overall Afghan population, making them the largest single ethnic group in the country, and they hold a disproportionate influence over Afghan affairs. However, they have never been able to impose any consistent control over the other ethnic or tribal factions within the Afghan borders, and as a result, Afghanistan has suffered a state of nearly constant civil war throughout its history. Adding further fragmentation and divisiveness to this warlike society, is the fact that even the various tribes themselves are not unified or homogenous, since there are numerous animosities at work inside each ethnic grouping as well. And whether categorized by broader ethnic group or by tribe, these animosities are persistent and remembered, often serving as the basis for sustained armed conflict and as enduring impediments to any potential reconciliation or political compromise.

Afghanistan has been routinely invaded, occupied, and abandoned by a long series of foreign powers throughout its existence. Greek historian Herodotus recorded the earliest known events in the territory; appropriately, these are accounts of fighting in the area in 520 BC.[9] In the 4th century BC, Afghans found themselves fighting Alexander the Great and his Macedonian armies, then the world's preeminent military power. This conflict began the trend of numerous major powers invading over subsequent centuries. Conquerors from Babur to Genghis Khan to Tamerlane all failed to subdue the Afghan tribes, as each was able to seize or destroy the larger cities but unable to overpower the Afghan tribesmen in the mountains. Alexander himself eventually realized that he would not be able to defeat the mountain tribesmen, so he chose instead to employ them as mercenaries in his own empire-building, basically putting them on the payroll to prevent them from cutting his lines of supply.[10]

For centuries after Alexander's eventual withdrawal, little of real significance to history took place in the territory now known as Afghanistan, as various foreign invaders came and went while largely leaving the mountain and rural tribes to themselves. Elements of Islam were introduced to Afghanistan as early as 642 AD, and like other developments in Afghan history, this religious development came about as part of a foreign invasion. This invasion was quite similar to the others in that the invading armies successfully occupied Afghan territories, only to be resisted and ultimately expelled by the Afghan tribes.[11] But even as Islam was introduced and took root among the assorted Afghan ethnic groupings, the Afghan territory remained a largely provincial, ungoverned, and relatively unimportant corner of several larger and more influential empires.

Afghanistan's relative insignificance did not mean that its frequent wars were not vicious, however. The extreme violence and harsh brutality in warfare that has been typical of Afghanistan throughout its history is rooted at least as far back as the early-13th century. In that century, the Mongol hordes under Genghis Khan descended upon what is now Afghanistan to lay waste to Balkh, Herat, and other cities, typically executing most citizens in any town that resisted or rebelled.[12] In their wake, the Mongols left a major swath of destruction still visible today and inflicted upon the tribesmen a calamitous series of events that caused a severe setback for Afghan society, while indelibly shaping Afghan culture. After the Mongol invasion, a succession of Tajik, Turkmen, and other Asian conquerors alternated in exerting loose control over Afghanistan during the next few centuries. This list of subsequent invaders includes the Kart Dynasty of the Tajiks in the 13th century, as well as the Turko-Mongol invader Tamerlane in the 14th century. Tamerlane adopted the terroristic tactic of stacking the skulls of his many victims in pyramid-shaped piles to discourage resistance.[13] Afghans are no strangers to brutality.

In the 16th century, the rising Persian empire of the Safavids and then the Uzbeks and Ottomans took turns occupying what is now Afghan land. Following these and other subsequent foreign invasions, the country that is now known as Afghanistan was created in 1747 after the assassination of a Persian ruler. In response to the opportunity presented by this assassination, the Afghan tribal leaders chose Ahmad Khan Durrani as "Shah" for the Pashtun-speaking tribes in and around Kandahar.[14] Often referred to as the Durrani Empire, Ahmad Shah presided over more of a confederation than an empire, after consolidating the disparate tribes into one kingdom. The kingdom came to be called Afghanistan, and the confederation clearly had a distinctive Sunni and Pashtun cast to it. In a recurring theme of Afghan history, within 50 years of Ahmad Shah's death, the country had again collapsed into civil war among its various ethnic and tribal factions.[15]

In the 19th century, Afghanistan became a focal point for the Great Game between the British and Russian empires and, as a result, Afghan leaders learned the practice of utilizing foreign benefactors as a substantial source of income. Likewise, revealing a willingness to change sides quickly when their interests changed, after turning on the British presence in the country, the Afghans committed remarkably brutal atrocities in massacring more than 16,000 British troops, family members, and camp followers in late 1842 in the infamous British retreat from Kabul to Jalalabad.[16] Legend has it that the few individuals who survived the massacre were left alive intentionally by the Afghans, to allow them to recount the scope and brutality of the event to the British government. Foreshadowing decisions that would confront future invading armies, "The crucial question for the British became whether to risk further armies that might similarly be wiped out . . . in a land that offered no benefits or revenue but only blood and expense to the Crowne."[17] In response to the massacre, the British government dispatched the ill-fated "Army of Retribution," and this force suffered its own severe losses and ultimately retreated from the Afghan territory as well.

In 1877, the British embarked on another war in Afghanistan, this one having a punitive flavor as the British Army had not forgotten the events of 1842. Having entered the industrial age, the British enjoyed major technological advantages in comparison to the Afghans. The Afghan leader at the time was Sher Ali, a son of Dost Mohammad, another king who had seized temporary control of most of the Afghan territory. Sher Ali also sought to manipulate the Great Game between Russia and Britain to his and Afghanistan's advantage, although he was hindered in this attempt by the fact that the Afghan villagers' loyalties remained largely with their tribes rather than with any national Afghan identity.[18] Britain's second Afghan war ended much the same as the first, with the British formations absorbing major losses and ultimately leaving the country as quickly as they could disengage their forces.

After the British left once again, there were a number of significant internal attempts to centralize governing authority over the Afghan territory. However, while a few of these initiatives succeeded for relatively short periods of time, none succeeded in the long run. Abdur Rahman, known as the "Iron Emir," ruthlessly attempted to break Afghanistan's feudal tribal system with Russian support in the late-19th century, imposing a forced relocation of some tribes but meeting with limited success.[19] As successor to the throne, Abdur Rahman's son, Habibullah, used the limited centralized authority that his father had achieved to attack the British across the Indian border in 1919. This action ultimately led to an Afghan-British peace treaty, a reduction in British intervention in Afghan affairs, and some international recognition of Afghanistan as an actual country.[20] Within Afghanistan, the 20th century saw a succession of rulers seize power, but none of the leaders was able to centralize control over the country to any major degree. Of special note among these rulers, King Amanullah undertook another effort at broad political and social reform in 1927, an initiative aimed at modernizing Afghan society and weakening the tribal leaders' power while centralizing governing authority. This reform initiative was initially successful, but it failed when Amanullah tried to enforce reforms such as mandatory beard-shaving and women's education, unpopular changes that ran into stiff opposition from tribal leaders on conservative religious grounds.[21]

With the Bolshevik revolution unfolding about the same time as these events, the Russian government became the first country to recognize the new Afghan state. Further complicating any future potential Afghan unity, during the 1920s and 1930s thousands of Uzbek, Turkmen, and Tajik refugees crossed into northern Afghanistan while fleeing Russian encroachment in Central Asia. When Muslim Pakistan split from Hindu India in 1947, Afghanistan immediately requested that Pakistan redraw their mutual border to allow Afghanistan to encompass all of the Pashtun tribesmen. Pakistan refused, setting the stage for decades of strained relations over the so-called "Pashtunistan" issue. America began its own involvement in the region during this period, as the United States developed a strong relationship with Pakistan in the 1950s that included membership in the Southeast Asia Treaty Organization (SEATO) and the Central Treaty Organization (CENTO). This period also saw Afghanistan drift toward Russian influence as the country adopted Russian arms, doctrine, and advisers for its military.[22]

As a culmination of this drift toward Russia, the Communist Party of Afghanistan formed in 1977 and seized power over the central government in 1978, on the heels of the assassination of Daoud Khan. When the Soviet Army ultimately invaded Afghanistan in late 1979, within a matter of days the Russian Army was able to seize control of the major population centers and key infrastructure sites throughout the country. Soon afterward, however, Afghan religious leaders declared jihad across the country, and "the true fighting strength of Afghanistan began to respond."[23] Soviet planners had always considered Afghanistan, with its high rates of illiteracy, fractured feudalistic tribal culture, and subsistence farming economy, as the worst possible place for a "proletariat revolution," but this assessment was ignored in the decision to rescue the failing Communist regime.[24] Thousands of mullahs across Afghanistan declared jihad against the invading Soviets, and Afghanistan mobilized its strength in the rural, independent sections of Afghanistan, where the central government never could quite reach in the best of circumstances. These fighters, or *mujahedeen,* came to be called "freedom fighters" in the West, but the term actually means "soldiers of God."[25]

From the beginning of the conflict, both sides committed widespread atrocities, but as the Soviets failed to meet their objectives, they eventually embarked upon a scorched-earth policy. These infamous "destroy-and-search" tactics aimed to lay waste to the rural mujahedeen's vital center of strength in the countryside.[26] Confronted with the Soviets' clear superiority in technology and training, the mujahedeen came to rely upon raids, ambushes, and ultimately crude roadside bombs for their own attacks, as precursors to the asymmetric tactics and improvised explosive devices (IEDs) employed in the current war. Like many other wars through Afghan history, the Afghan resistance to the Soviets never really became centralized under any one leader, but rather consisted of decentralized leadership and execution in pursuit of a common, unifying goal.

During the Soviet war, the majority of the Afghan population was uprooted and forced to relocate as a result of the devastation in the countryside, with millions fleeing the country to Pakistan and many others moving into the Afghan cities to escape the rural destruction. If the Soviets had thought Afghanistan to be a difficult nation-building project before, it was now viewed as even more difficult, since most of the agricultural infrastructure of the country had been intentionally destroyed. Additionally, the Soviet Union repeatedly violated the Geneva Conventions by using nerve agents, mustard gas, and other chemical and biological weapons in the early years of the war.[27] The Soviets escalated these tactics in 1984 by beginning widespread carpet-bombing of the remaining mujahedeen strongholds not under Soviet control. A United Nations (UN) report in 1985 described "serious and widespread abuses" by Soviet troops, including "bombing villages, massacring civilians, and executing captured guerrillas," along with torture and "booby traps disguised as toys scattered around the countryside."[28] These brutal tactics resulted in countless civilian casualties but ultimately failed to subdue the tribes. Concluding that they had "lost the battle for the Afghan people," the Soviets finally abandoned Afghanistan in defeat in February 1989.[29] The Afghan tribesmen had repelled yet another foreign invader.

Upon successfully ousting the Soviet forces, the Afghans immediately returned to fighting among themselves, first by attacking their Afghan brethren in the Soviet-backed Afghan Army and next in a postwar power struggle among the seven Sunni factions that had fought together during the occupation. When powerful Uzbek warlord Abdul Rashid Dostum turned on the Afghan government early in 1991, the mujahedeen were then able to seize control of Kabul and the government, just after the collapse of the Soviet Union. As the Pashtun tribes lost control of Kabul, a vicious civil war ensued, and most of Kabul was ultimately destroyed, throwing the country further into chaos, privation, and disorder. This civil war, coming after the brutal Soviet occupation and preceding the Taliban's rise, is remembered by many key Afghan leaders today as having created the deepest scars on Afghan civil society, out of all the modern wars.[30]

At this point, the stage was set for the Taliban movement to emerge in 1994. It is noteworthy that the Taliban movement arose in southern Afghanistan around the historic Afghan capital of Kandahar and among the Pashtun people, who reached out to their Islamic leadership to establish law and order in a lawless and corrupt society dominated by warlords. A loosely controlled country even in the best of circumstances, it was during this same period that Afghanistan devolved wholly into an anarchic society and narco-state dominated by warlords, with illicit drug profits fueling the economy and the various ethnic, tribal, criminal, and warlord factions. Pursuing its own interests and ends, Pakistan reached out to the Taliban to assist in reopening southern Afghanistan as a trade route, bypassing the formal Afghan government in the process.[31] The close connections developed during this period between the leaders of the Taliban movement and the Pakistani government, and in particular with the Pakistani Inter-Services Intelligence Directorate (ISI), remain in place. These connections shape, and in many cases undermine, the relationship between Pakistan and Afghanistan's government today.

However brutal their methods—as evidenced by their original declaratory act of executing a rapist publicly—the Taliban initially found support among the beleaguered Afghan people because they offered a rough rule of law in a land dominated by criminals, corrupt government officials, and warlords. The Taliban, translated as "students" or "seekers" of Islam, attracted thousands of volunteers as the movement grew, including volunteers from the ranks of the native Pashtun, refugees, the homeless, the destitute, and the orphaned—all unified by the conservative Islamic ideology of the *madrassas*, the religious schools of the Pakistani refugee camps and the local tribes.[32] While some observers have argued that the Taliban were a Pakistani creation in the first place, it is without question that Pakistan openly supported the Taliban until September 11, 2001 (9/11). Since then, U.S. officials have asserted that Pakistan's covert support for the Taliban continued with ISI sponsorship for a long time after the public support ceased. It is also worth noting that some within the U.S. Government initially viewed the emergence of the Taliban and their draconian imposition of social order as a potentially positive development in Afghan affairs, in spite of allegations of Afghan complicity in the 1995 attack on the World Trade Center.

In any case, as the Taliban grew in strength and numbers, various other competing Afghan factions and the nominal Afghan government began to form a coalition in opposition. This opposition coalesced around Ahmed Shah Massoud of the northern tribes in the Panjshir Valley, and the group eventually came to be called the "Northern Alliance." The alliance consisted of nearly all of the non-Pashtun tribes of northern Afghanistan, as well as a few disgruntled Pashtuns, united in a desire to resist the Taliban's control of the country. Not surprisingly, once Ahmed Shah Massoud was perceived as a genuine potential threat to the Taliban and al Qaeda, he was targeted for assassination, like so many other leaders before him in Afghan history. Massoud's assassination, just prior to the 9/11 attacks on the United States, eliminated what some saw as a genuine opportunity for the creation of a unified Afghanistan. For their own part, the members of the Northern Alliance demonstrated similar brutality in the aftermath of their eventual U.S.-backed victory, as they were alleged to have herded several thousand Taliban prisoners into shipping containers—after which the prisoners were either shot to death or allowed to suffocate in the Afghan heat.[33] These events merely served to reinforce the violent, treacherous, and even Hobbesian nature of Afghan society, which has figured so prominently in the country's history from the earliest times.

Afghanistan's Physical and Human Terrain.

Afghanistan's terrain, both physical and human, makes the notion of building a cohesive, democratic, and self-sustaining nation every bit as difficult as does its violent history. Roughly the size of Texas, the Islamic Republic of Afghanistan contains over 250,000 square miles of territory and a population estimated at around 30 million, though there is little confidence in that number, since there has never been a systematic or comprehensive census of the various tribes and other smaller groupings.[34] Afghanistan is a remarkably poor country, whether measured by per capita income or per capita gross domestic product. In part because of its history of frequent invasion as well as its lack of any tradition of effective central governance, the country is variously included with the Middle East or South or Central Asia, depending on the context and its current political circumstances. Long an international pawn of other more powerful nations, Afghanistan has been noteworthy primarily for the frequency and violence of its conflicts and because it must be traversed in order to carry out trade and other commercial activities in Asia.

In order to survive, the tribes and the country's occasional central governments have often cultivated donor states throughout its history. The major destruction of agricultural resources and infrastructure associated with the Soviet invasion of the 1980s rendered the nation almost wholly dependent on donated aid for subsistence, except for the thriving drug and smuggling trades. Afghanistan has some recently discovered mineral resources, but these have remained largely untapped, due to the persistent conflicts and instability that make foreign investment too risky to contemplate. Afghanistan is a land-locked country with porous borders, essentially a huge mountain range surrounded by desert plateaus. The peaks of the eastern portion of the Hindu Kush—usually translated as "Hindu killer"— rise over 7,000 meters high, with the mountains extending west and dividing northern and southern Afghanistan with strategically important passes interspersed periodically along the chain.[35] The scarcity of paved roads, coupled with the difficult terrain, has made the country almost ungovernable from Kabul throughout its history.[36]

About half of Afghanistan's land mass lies above 2,000 meters in altitude, and there is little forestation across the country. Travel around the country, whether commercial or military, is therefore difficult, and the "ring road" is both the main source of trafficability for commerce as well as a main venue for corruption. Likewise, the harsh and variable climate adds to these economic infrastructural challenges. The mountain areas are largely barren, and although Afghanistan has enough water to support agriculture, the various major wars have seen the destruction of most of the irrigation infrastructure needed to support anything other than subsistence farming. Farming methods are primitive for the most part. Ironically, both Soviet and American engineers contributed to the construction of the original agricultural infrastructure, but what remains now is used primarily for the cultivation of the poppies that enable Afghanistan to dominate the world production of heroin—processed primarily in labs in Pakistan and the countries to the north.

Influenced greatly by this harsh terrain, Afghanistan's population is fragmented in very many ways. There are dozens of languages spoken in Afghanistan, including numerous local variations of Pashtu and Dari, a variant of Persian. These variations are significant enough that many tribes of the same ethnicity have difficulty communicating with each other, adding additional fault lines to the already fragmented nature of Afghan society. The primary identity for the average Afghan rests with the family and tribe rather than the Afghan nation, and the name "Afghan" is actually linked to the Pashtun language, since the Pashtuns are the dominant and most significant tribe politically. As noted, population estimates vary widely, with projections ranging from about 10 million people in the mid-1970s to a UN estimate of approximately 27 million in 2000.[37] Recent estimates place the figure at 28-30 million, with fewer than 25 percent living in urban areas.[38] These figures do not account for another estimated one million nomadic tribesmen who move in and out of the Afghan territory routinely, and the more recent population figures are even more unreliable—given the massive displacement caused by consecutive wars, including the Soviet conflict, the civil war, the overthrow of the Taliban, and the current insurgency. The Soviet destruction of rural areas in the 1980s also caused an extensive rural-urban migration, creating a concurrent increasing demand for urban social services and placing additional major burdens on already overtaxed Afghan civil institutions.[39]

Regarding the demographics of the Afghan society, there are no simple classifications of Afghan ethnic and linguistic groupings, mainly because these groupings are so diverse and numerous. Afghans identify their tribal and family linkages as the *qaum*, or a "complexity of affiliations (and) a network of families or occupations."[40] The *qaum* may also correspond to a geographic location in some Afghan usage, but more generally it refers to the genealogical and cultural connections of extended family, tribe, tribal confederation, and social world. Among the numerous tribes, most estimates place the Pashtun ethnic group at approximately 40 percent of the Afghan population, and although this tribe is generally located from the southwestern to eastern regions of Afghanistan, the Pashtuns traditionally hold the dominant place in Afghan society in terms of size and political influence. The Pashtuns are further divided into tribal groups, with the Durrani Pashtuns representing about 12 percent of the overall Afghan population and the Ghilzai group representing about 14 percent.[41] There are at least eight other major Pashtun tribes that combine with these two major tribes to encompass the Pashtun population in Afghanistan, further increasing the societal fragmentation.

Adding another layer to Afghanistan's demographic complexity, the Afghan Pashtuns represent only roughly half of the Pashtun tribesmen altogether, since the other half of this ethnic group are found across the Afghan-Pakistan border in the east and southeast. Other Sunni tribes include the Tajiks at about a quarter of the total Afghan population, as well as the Uzbeks, Turkmen, and Qizilbash tribesmen, each with less than 10 percent of the overall population of the country. The Hazaras, long discriminated against for their predominantly Shiite Muslim faith and their Mongol roots, are largely isolated in their mountainous territory and account for approximately 18 percent of the population.[42] There are also many other ethnic, tribal, or socio-cultural groupings in Afghanistan, among them the Aimaq (nomadic herders), the Sunni Arabs of the northeast and west, the Kirghiz, the Baluchs, the Nuristanis, and several other major groupings. The northern region of Afghanistan also includes transnational linkages between the ethnic Uzbeks, Turkmen, and Tajiks who trace their lineage to the countries across the northern border.

Even these numerous classifications miss much of the relevant demographic and ethnographic Afghan story, however, since each clan, tribe, and ethnicity has its own cross-group affiliations, cross-border transnational loyalties, tribal histories, and persistent animosities. This ethnic fragmentation is further complicated by the steady flow of nomads and refugees across the mostly uncontrolled Afghan borders, ebbing and flowing depending upon the seasons and the circumstances. In sum, the fragmented demography and topography of Afghanistan, combined with the anthropological implications that correspond to the challenges of the human and physical terrain, represent major obstacles to any attempt at coherent nation-building within the Afghan population.

The Impact of *Pushtunwali*, Islam, and Other Afghan Cultural Norms.

In addition to the basic linguistic and demographic impacts that Afghanistan's geographic location and its physical terrain have had on the population, the country's mountain peaks have also served to separate the various Afghan tribes culturally in many other ways. These effects are magnified, when one considers Afghanistan's porous borders and its proximity to other countries sharing ethnic and tribal ties. So even while the tribes hold certain key cultural values in common, the inhabitants of these different regions also take great pride in their own ethnic and cultural differences and their own tribal customs. Likewise, they also carry with them lengthy histories of tribal animosities and other conflicts that reinforce this separation. In an ironic twist, both the tribes' intercultural differences and their intracultural similarities tend to pull them apart from one another, rather than providing any basis for coherence as a people or the building blocks for successful nation-building.

Moreover, it is the family that is at the center of Afghan life, rather than any national Afghan identity, and the family also serves as the country's most important social institution. Adding to this fragmentation and isolation, Afghan families are routinely endogamous, marrying within their own lines; the extended family is the basis for most social and economic transactions.[43] Extended families typically live in geographic proximity. Running counter to most reform initiatives over the last century or so—including the current attempts at societal reform—the cultural norms of male superiority and decisionmaking dominance are deeply ingrained in Afghan society. Afghans venerate the elderly, and Afghan society is highly patriarchal. Similarly, women's activities are severely limited by the cultural norm requiring separate facilities and veiling, or *purdah* (seclusion).[44] These cultural norms are widely held, especially among the rural tribesmen, and are intertwined with the two major Afghan cultural forces of *Pushtunwali* and Islam.

Regarding the first of these major influences, Pashtun culture revolves around *Pushtunwali*, a tribal ethical and legal code that emphasizes the concepts of honor, hospitality, shame, and revenge, among other social values.[45] As noted, the Pashtuns are at the center of gravity of Afghan culture, though they are neither wholly dominant nor the only key players. Some of the main cultural characteristics of the Pashtun code include a "proud and aggressive individualism" and "obligations of revenge, hospitality, and sanctuary," placed within the context of a "familial and tribal society with predatory habits."[46] The Pashtun code, which has overlapped culturally into that of other Afghan tribes to a certain extent over the centuries, also allows for the private resolution of economic or political disputes—resulting in a culture that encourages personal vendettas and generalized conflict.[47] As an extension of this code, Afghans generally share a devotion to freedom as a societal norm and "will carry hospitality to embarrassing extremes but are implacable as enemies."[48]

In terms of the formal rule of law, there are three different types of legal authority recognized to varying degrees within Afghan society, including the Shariah (or Islamic law), the *jurga* (or local Afghan law), and the national constitutional authority (the statutory law of Afghanistan). Of the three, the local Afghan law is the most commonly observed, and Afghanistan in general suffers from a shortage of the components needed to support and enforce the national Afghan law. Even at this point in the Western intervention, there are still few formal courts, trained investigators, prosecutors, lawyers, or judges to sustain the Afghan national justice system. Additionally, there is a basic cultural mismatch at work in Afghanistan, since Afghans do not pursue justice in the Western sense of the word. Instead, the Afghans apply a standard of justice that is closer to the idea of "practical conflict-resolution."[49]

Bridging the large gaps in these social institutions, Islam is a major, pervasive force in the average Afghan's daily life. First introduced into the Afghan territory around 642 AD, Islam and the norms of Islamic culture also generally serve as common denominators across the Afghan tribes and Afghan society. Islam and Islamic normative values pervade Afghan society, including governmental, ritual, medical, juridical, and educational roles.[50] Furthermore, Islam extends well beyond the Western view of religion, since it pervades all aspects of daily life, including governing. There is no distinction between politics and religion under Islam, and religious leaders hold major influence over a wide variety of societal decisions.[51] For many Afghans, their only formal education comes through a religious school, or *madrassa*, or at the local mosque. Local religious leaders, or *mullahs*, are often appointed by the government, and they serve as local judges, arbitrators, and religious teachers, officiating at various ceremonies.[52] The *ulema* are the well-respected religious scholars, the body of men who interpret the Quran and issue binding religious edicts, while also applying and interpreting Shariah.[53] Amir Abdur Rahman attempted to elevate Shariah over customary Afghan law beginning in 1747, but there is still no one Afghan legal standard from tribe to tribe today.[54]

Given these weaknesses in Afghan governmental and social institutions, the preponderance of Afghan education and the transmission of cultural norms and values takes place primarily in the *madrassas*, the mosques, and at home.[55] While measures of educational attainment and literacy are sketchy at best, prior to the Soviet intervention in 1979, the literacy rate was estimated to be 11 percent, with males at approximately 19 percent and females at about 3 percent.[56] As one might expect, the literacy rates in the cities tend to be much higher than in rural Afghanistan, and most observers believe the literacy rate declined significantly during the Soviet war years.[57] More recent estimates of the literacy rate range from about 28 percent to 35 percent for adults, although this figure is not easily confirmed, given the lack of basic educational infrastructure throughout the country and the corresponding difficulty in measuring any social characteristics among the rural tribes.[58] In any event, the means of distributing information are very limited.

In terms of public health, Afghanistan has some of the highest infant mortality rates in the world, and its life expectancy is very low—about 44 years.[59] The healthcare infrastructure is extremely limited, and

Afghan tribesmen typically count upon local healers, barbers, and other makeshift workers for rudimentary healthcare procedures and healing, rather than any governmental assistance.[60] Adding to these public health woes, there are an estimated 10 million mines and other types of unexploded ordnance spread throughout Afghanistan as a result of the numerous wars, and these same wars have also resulted in millions of refugees and internally displaced persons (IDP).[61] As a further indicator of the harshness of the land and the martial culture of the people of Afghanistan, the country's national pastime is called *buzkashi*, a dangerous game with no explicit rules that involves players mounted on horseback competing to control the headless carcass of a goat, with the field often stretching over many miles of terrain.[62] So whether viewed from the perspectives of the dominant norms of Afghan culture or the absence of basic social services, Afghanistan once again presents an extraordinarily difficult case for achieving stability, security, or any Western-style quality of life and governance.

Afghan Political Culture: Dysfunction, Manipulation, and Corruption.

In addition to the challenges posed by entrenched Afghan tribal cultural norms and the weakness of existing Afghan social structures, the goal of building a democratic, well-governed state also runs counter to the dominant norms of Afghan political culture. In essence, the country has never had a national democratic tradition, nor has it ever had a central government that was truly powerful enough to direct the lives of most Afghan citizens outside of the cities. But while Afghanistan's central leaders have never proven adept at building effective governing institutions or providing basic services to the Afghan people, they have clearly and consistently shown the ability to manipulate foreign geopolitical interests in order to cultivate donations and to build personally lucrative relationships. Put simply, Afghans learned long ago how to survive as a recipients of international donations.

Accordingly, there are a number of key defining characteristics and dynamics within Afghan political culture that will have to be overcome in order to achieve any effective central governance where it has not existed before. For example, any successful reform effort will have to overcome the fragmentation and multiple, conflicting tribal and ethnic minorities that make up the population; the conflicting pressures of traditionalism and modernization; the difficulty of imposing (or superimposing) modern, sophisticated political methods and technologies on traditional tribal loyalties, norms, and structures; and achieving or creating a national Afghan identity that would trump local identities and loyalties.[63] Additionally, since much of Afghan culture revolves around the norms of *Pushtunwali*, any successful governmental reforms will also have to accommodate this aspect of Afghan life, one that runs counter to many elements of Western-style democracy.[64] Likewise, any centralizing governing reforms will also have to be able to overcome the focus of the average Afghan's daily life on tribal events rather than national ones. Successful transformations would also have to overcome the average Afghan's historical resistance to reform initiatives, efforts to impose changes in social norms, or attempts to exert external control. When coupled with the widespread norms and traditions of corruption and the common use of violence to resolve conflicts, the notion of affecting this kind of wholesale change in Afghan political culture represents a daunting task at best, if it is feasible at all.

Briefly reviewing Afghanistan's political history, the first Afghan king, Ahmad Shah Durrani, ruled from 1747 to 1773 after being selected to lead an Afghan confederacy—not a strong central government—by the various leaders of stronger, more influential tribes. He was chosen for this role precisely because he could not challenge the other stronger "khans" for control of their various factions, and as such, he was a safe choice that ensured that the various factions would retain the real power in Afghanistan.[65] Ahmad Shah Durrani essentially served as a "first among equals," with the twin goals of preventing anarchy in Afghan society while bringing the tribes together periodically to repel foreign invaders.[66] In general, the power and influence of Afghan monarchs has waxed and waned, depending upon the external threats and the particular monarchs' skills and ability at keeping the governing coalitions together. In Ahmad Shah Durrani's case, he used the technique of plundering neighboring countries and distributing the spoils of those raids as a means of keeping the tribes together.[67] Given the long memories among the peoples and countries of this region, his raids had the unintended consequence of making neighboring countries wary of a strong Afghanistan, a concern that persists today.

So even as the country of Afghanistan first began to take shape, the mutually reinforcing tendencies toward weak central governmental control and warlordism were already firmly established, characteristics that have continued to predominate without serious challenge over the course of modern Afghan political history. Upon Ahmad Shah's death, his sons and grandsons proved to be far less adept than he was politically, and the monarchy collapsed until Dost Muhammad reestablished the throne in 1826, governing until 1839 and the first British intervention in Afghan affairs.[68] The subsequent British disaster strengthened Dost Muhammad's reputation, resulting in his governing as the Afghan king after the expulsion of the British in 1842 until 1863.[69] This period also saw the rise of Afghan interaction with foreign powers, as Afghan leaders began to balance domestic political pressures against the intervention of foreign powers in Afghan affairs and the willingness of those powers to provide developmental and military assistance. Abdur Rahman, who governed as king or "amir" from 1880-1901, used this foreign assistance and ruthless practices such as hostage-taking to impose some central governmental control on the various tribes and factions across Afghan society.[70] Abdur Rahman's son, Habibullah, continued this system upon his father's death.

Beginning in the 1920s, Afghan monarchs periodically embarked upon major social-reform initiatives, most often aimed at increasing education, women's rights, or agricultural productivity.[71] Next in succession, King Amanullah ruled from 1919 to 1929, and embarked upon ambitious Western-style reforms after a brief war with the British that saw the Afghans win recognition as a sovereign state.[72] Amanullah was soundly rebuffed when his reforms ran contrary to conservative Muslim norms, and he eventually came under siege by tribal armies opposed to his educational and cultural changes.[73] Like other Afghan leaders before him, Amanullah was largely undone by resistance driven by his direct challenge to the authority of the tribal leadership, as well as by conservative Islamic backlash to the nature of his reforms. Among these social reforms were minimum age limits for marriage, monogamy for government employees, women's education, and Westernized clothing for women in Kabul.[74] The American governmental reform agenda in Afghanistan today is only the latest in a long history of attempts at Afghan social, governmental, and economic change.

Viewed broadly, there is a modest precedent in Afghan society for a form of democracy, the *shura* (local council) and its national counterpart, the *loya jurga* (great council). However, under the Taliban in particular and throughout Islam in general, there is a general distrust of democratic principles, as the *ulema* either exercise the decisionmaking functions *in toto* or do so in consultation with the appointed governmental leaders, rulers often appointed by the *ulema* themselves.[75] "The *ulema*'s attitudes toward local and international issues are central to governmental approaches," and typically they oppose reformist movements while maintaining "suspicion towards political, economic, and philosophical notions born and fostered in the West (including) democracy."[76]

More pointedly, over the years Islamic religious leaders in Afghanistan have equated modernizing reforms with direct attacks upon Islam and religious cultural norms.[77] In fact, the whole idea of democracy represents a direct challenge to the *ulema*, since government is supposed to be consistent with Allah's Divine Will and, under democracy, the ballot box serves to represent that Divine Will instead of the *ulema* themselves, the ones who fulfill that interpretive role in Afghanistan and other Islamic societies that merge the secular with the divine.[78] "Traditionalists emphatically deny Islam's preparedness to acknowledge the right of people to have the final say (over Allah's Divine Will and) the *ulema* do not compromise the Divine Voice of which they are the only lawful speakers."[79] Afghanistan attempted its first democratic reforms in 1964, after hundreds of years of autocratic and fragmented rule, but these reforms failed as a result of the numerous cultural and practical impediments.[80]

To put these features of Afghan political culture into a modern perspective, while many Muslims expressed outrage over the Taliban's alleged anti-Muslim behavior, many others "considered the Taliban's administration the embodiment of Islamic law and politics."[81] Furthermore, as noted previously, Afghanistan has three types of law at work within its borders. The central government and international community are attempting to build and impose a Western-style legal system in Afghanistan, but the Shariah and traditional common Afghan tribal laws are more commonly enforced and observed. In fact, some scholars hold that "religiously conservative countries will always have difficulty establishing Western style democratic institutions and believing in them."[82] Exacerbating this problem, judges are scarce, poorly paid, barely literate, and largely unfamiliar with the constitutional law being advocated by the Karzai government.[83] The other elements of the rule of law are still largely nonexistent.

As another facet of this challenge, in 2006 President Karzai appointed 13 former regional militia commanders as police chiefs, in spite of their ties to armed violence, organized crime, and the drug trade.[84] The results are not surprising: Afghanistan supplied about 92 percent of the world's heroin in 2004, a figure which has increased in the years since.[85] As one observer writes:

> Kept afloat by billions of dollars in American and other foreign aid, the government of Afghanistan is shot through with corruption and graft. . . . [P]eople at the highest levels of the Karzai Administration . . . including (his) own brother (since killed), are cooperating in the country's opium trade. . . . [H]ardly a public transaction seems to unfold that does not carry with it the requirement of a bribe.[86]

The Kabul neighborhood of Sherpur is a wealthy enclave, with average Afghans referring to its huge mansions as "poppy houses."[87] "Transparency International" rates Afghanistan as one of the most corrupt countries in the world, ranking it 117th of 159 countries evaluated in 2005.[88] Corruption is so pervasive in Afghan society that the Afghans speak of both "one-fisted" and "two-fisted" corruption, or corruption that benefits one's family or tribe as opposed to that which merely benefits the person perpetrating the fraud or abuse. Demonstrating a thorough misunderstanding of Afghan culture, many observers were shocked by the corruption that accompanied President Karzai's reelection "victory."

Along with this rampant corruption, the prospects for legitimate and effective governance in Afghanistan suffer directly from warlordism, as factional chiefs and warlords still hold the real power across Afghanistan.[89] Afghanistan is currently controlled by regional warlords who "have divvied up the land into personal fiefdoms and transformed central government institutions, including the police, into instruments of their will."[90] While President Karzai rationalizes the selection of these warlords for appointment as officials of his government on various grounds, there is no question that this strategy has slowed development within the country and has contributed directly to the corruption and the crisis of legitimacy that the government faces.[91] The average Afghan has no basis for comparison anyway, as the actual Afghan state government has done little for the Afghan people historically, whether in terms of development, education, security, or medical care.[92]

As a byproduct of this situation, weapons are prevalent throughout the country, and typically warlords or strongmen raise their own militias, based on personal or tribal loyalties.[93] Warlords and strongmen have included Gul Agha Shirzai in Kandahar, Mullah Aqib of the Alkozai, Aziz Sarqatib of the Ghilzais, Abdul Haleem of the Noorzais, and Haji Ahmad of the Achakzais, among many others.[94] These strongmen, having been legitimized by the U.S. Central Intelligence Agency (CIA), the U.S. military, and the Karzai administration, have used their positions within the state apparatus to consolidate their personal power by rewarding their followers with jobs and other positions of influence.[95] Through these appointments, these men have been able to achieve power over the national institutions, including at different times the Ministry of the Interior (MOI), the Ministry of Defense (MOD), and others, in addition to the provincial government organizations.[96] So after decades of war and the collapse of basic social services and governing institutions that were never strong in the first place, few Afghans even know "what right looks like."[97]

As another unintended consequence of these appointments, the warlords have been able to stymie a variety of national governmental reform initiatives, including reforms of the police, MOI, and other national governing institutions.[98] Without question, those in Afghanistan who threaten to use force tend to get what they want, as demonstrated early on in Kandahar by the U.S. backed Gul Agha Shirzai, a shady warlord with ties to Pakistan and the ISI.[99] As another example of the Americans' general misunderstanding of Afghan culture, on numerous occasions U.S. leaders would travel to meet at the homes or offices of appointed Afghan leaders. In Afghanistan, it is the superior who always hosts and takes care of his "subordinate" guests, so these well-intentioned but ill-advised gestures on the part of the Americans (and at times, Hamid Karzai) served to elevate the status and prestige of a number of dubious characters whose ultimate loyalties were still very much in doubt.[100]

In a simplified view, the national level of governance has always been the traditional nexus of corruption and abuse of authority in Afghanistan, with various strongmen vying for control of the instruments of power and absconding with donor countries' aid. The tribe, on the other hand, has been the traditional and historical focal point for actual governance and the center of gravity of Afghan social and economic institutions. Any successful reforms or development in Afghanistan would need to build upon the tribal-level strengths while finding a way to overcome the rampant corruption and abuse of authority commonly found at the national level of the government. Given the lack of democratic traditions or norms in Afghan political culture, and the dysfunctional nature of attempts at Afghan "democracy" to date, it must be acknowledged that any effort toward democracy in Afghanistan will be a long-term project. Furthermore, the reformers must also find a way to build upon the elements of Afghan society—such as the traditions of the *loya jirga* and the local *shura*—in order to achieve any realistic chance of success. Complicating the prospects for any effective, democratic governance further, different factions in Afghan society view each other as enemies and in some cases as "infidels."

Some observers have argued that the cases of Switzerland and Afghanistan are similar, in that the goal has been to meld together disparate ethnic groupings into one strong governing society. However, whereas the Swiss ultimately achieved success through their rigorous application of democratic principles at the grassroots level, the Afghan peoples never have embraced that approach.[101] Afghans have, however, matched the Swiss in their ability to provide mercenary fighters to various armies in the region. As a result, the inability of the Afghans to unite under one central government has long been viewed as a positive advantage to the other countries that border them, since they have been concerned about potential invasions by any centralized Afghan power. In sum, Afghans could rally to a strong national leader when there was good cause—such as an invading foreign army—but Afghans have typically resisted central governance, instead choosing to live as they have for centuries, with the tribe serving as the key component of governance in their daily lives.

Afghan Economics.

Unfortunately, the prospects for viable nationhood are not much better when viewed from an economic perspective. Afghanistan is one of the poorest countries in the world, with most of its inhabitants subsisting on the equivalent of a few dollars a day. The country ranked only 173rd of 178 countries in 2004 on the UN "Human Development Index."[102] In spite of the major influx of U.S. and international aid over the past 10 years, Afghanistan still ranked only 155th of

169 countries evaluated on the UN index as of 2010.[103] As a result of the focused influx of international aid over this decade, the legitimate Afghan economy has increased in size to about $27 billion in 2009 U.S. dollars, but this increase still leaves the country in 110th place, when economies are ranked by size among the countries of the world.[104] Afghanistan is primarily defined by its barrenness and poverty, and both of those characteristics have been exacerbated by the decades of warfare. Compounding these bleak economic prospects are the widespread desertification, deforestation, and soil degradation in Afghanistan—the economic progress that the country made as a result of Cold War-era developmental aid was almost completely erased along with its agricultural infrastructure as a result of the consecutive wars.[105] Reflecting these grim characteristics, Afghans still perceive their employment prospects as being low today in spite of the years of focused international assistance.[106]

The majority of Afghans engage in subsistence farming—with some sedentary and others nomadic—often switching between the two methods, depending upon local soil and environmental conditions.[107] This nomadic population has been variously estimated at between a half-million and 1.5 million people, though neither figure is reliable.[108] Nor do the nomadic farmers and herders seem to worry about crossing international borders, which are usually unmarked and unobserved anyway. As a broader measure of the economic privation, Afghan worker productivity lags drastically, even when compared against the standard of nearby countries. Afghan workers produced about $333 worth of output in 2007, compared to more than $10,000 for workers in Pakistan and more than $20,000 for workers in China.[109]

Over the course of the country's history, Afghan governments have typically relied upon three sources of revenue—pillage, tolls, and foreign subsidy.[110] Along these lines, Afghanistan has a long history of managing and manipulating foreign powers and donor states to achieve domestic political ends, and the country's leaders have usually been quite adept at playing these donor countries and organizations off against one another. In the 1960s, for example, about two-thirds of the funding for development of Afghanistan came from foreign sources, most notably the United States, the Soviet Union, and Germany. Writing about this situation in the mid-1960s, one observer noted, "The Afghans are almost certainly aware that it will greatly increase the volume of aid if they can keep Russia and America trying to outbid each other."[111] In the 1960s, for example, Communist and Western aid amounted to 80 percent of the total developmental expenditures in the country, and by 1970 there were more than 20 countries providing some type of assistance.[112] In that same period, customs taxes and tariffs represented 45 percent of all governmental revenues.[113] In the period between 1957 and 1978, Afghanistan received foreign aid totaling $750 million from the Soviet Union, $346 million from the United States, and 764 million DM from the West German government.[114] This dependence is even more pronounced today.

Projecting forward, there are significant mineral resources in Afghanistan that could serve as the basis for a legitimate economy, though constant civil war and other major conflicts have generally prevented the exploitation of this potential wealth. Furthermore, if past history serves as a guide, it is unclear exactly who will benefit from the development of those resources, given the tradition of corruption and exploitation.

Nevertheless, the types of natural resources found in Afghanistan include natural gas, copper, coal, uranium, beryllium, lithium, and other minerals.[115] Afghanistan also has great potential for hydroelectric power, though the wide seasonal variations in runoff and precipitation mean that it will take substantial infrastructure development to take advantage of this potential—with that infrastructure also remaining susceptible to insurgent attacks. Only about 12 percent of the land is arable, or able to be cultivated, but the majority of Afghans—about two-thirds—engage in farming or livestock management.[116] Any prospects for economic development are further dimmed by the widespread lack of education and the wholesale illiteracy of the people.

Other factors that adversely affect Afghan economic prospects include widespread soil degradation, deforestation, and desertification as a result of the years of war and civil strife.[117] The country was hit with the worst drought in over a generation in 2000, and it is believed that millions of the Afghan people continue to rely upon external aid and relief supplies in order to survive.[118] The problem of land mines is also acute, with some estimates claiming that there are nearly 10 million mines laid throughout the country.[119] The constant fighting in Afghanistan during the Soviet invasion created millions of Afghan refugees, many of whom fled to Pakistan, where they became indoctrinated by radical Islamist groups in the madrassas, which substituted for the overburdened Pakistani school system.[120] The most recent Department of Defense (DoD) assessment notes that while international efforts at economic assistance have led to some pockets of increased activity, growth remains slow or has not even been assessed yet in most of the country.[121]

Unfortunately, there is one economic activity that is remarkably successful in Afghanistan, and that is the drug trade. Poppy cultivation and opium production in Afghanistan accounted for 93 percent of the world's production in 2006-07.[122] The 2007-08 poppy activity involved an estimated 366,500 Afghan families, equal to roughly 2.4 million people, spread among 16 of Afghanistan's 34 provinces.[123] The exact measure is unknown, and a recent blight reduced the past year's crop significantly, but it is estimated that the economic value associated with this illegal activity may equal as much as 33 percent of the country's legal gross domestic product (GDP) in recent years.[124] Furthermore, the State Department's 2009 International Narcotics Control Strategy Report concludes that "the Afghan government has been unwilling or unable to fully implement [its national drug control strategy] and has failed to take serious steps to combat" the problem. The report goes on to assert that "many Afghan government officials are believed to profit from the drug trade," while "narcotics-related corruption is particularly pervasive at the provincial and district levels of government."[125] The country's porous borders, its tradition of smuggling and corruption, and its abject poverty combine to make any counternarcotics operations incredibly difficult.

Exacerbating these challenges further, Western efforts at economic development in Afghanistan run afoul of Islamic norms as they relate to economic life. First, Islam does not sanction the pursuit of profit merely for the sake of profit itself, but rather emphasizes the values of generosity, humility, and hospitality, which are contrary to the basic model of Western market capitalism. As one observer notes, "A totally materialistic approach is alien to the Islamic way of life and the historical tradition of the Muslim people."[126] Furthermore, there is a widely held belief among Muslims that "the western approach has been based on a disrespect, albeit not always explicitly articulated, for other cultures and social systems . . . (a sort of) cultural imperialism."[127] Representative of these claims, one Islamic observer from the region summarizes five reasons Western economic development models are at odds with Islamic cultural norms, or why Western economic developmental methods have not worked well in Afghanistan, asserting that:

1. The promotion of an imitative mentality is at odds with creativity and originality, creating an artificial demand for Western products in the process;

2. The application of the Western model has been highly divisive within Muslim societies, perpetuating colonial traditions and creating schisms in the Muslim societies;

3. This effort has been extremely wasteful, inefficient, and costly, and has created norms of high consumerism in societies where there is little to consume;

4. Western "hedonistic individualism" is at odds with the basic tenets of the Islamic faith, and this shift in norms has encouraged individual greed and corruption at the expense of strengthening the broad national economic base; and,

5. This approach has assumed that legitimate economic development can occur without concurrent development in political systems, social institutions, and the moral attitudes of the people.[128]

As a result, many Muslims have resisted the Western model of economic development, with Muslim scholars arguing that "the totality and integrity of the social system has been ignored" in the rush to impose (or adopt) Western models of economic development.[129] These scholars push for the development of Muslim economic systems that are consistent with the teachings of Islam, but this distinction appears to be lost on the Western organizations seeking to "redevelop" Afghanistan.

The Taliban and Other Threats to Security, Stability, and Democracy.

The active opposition of regional and transnational actors who see a viable Afghan state as a threat to their own interests adds another layer that further dims the prospects for a stable, secure, democratic, and self-sustaining Afghanistan. In addition to the Taliban, there are a number of other criminal and militant factions working to undermine the statutory Afghan government, among them *Hezb-e-Islami*, the *Haqqani Network*, foreign fighters, some local tribes, and smugglers and drug traders.[130] In his own analysis, former International Security Assistance Force (ISAF) Commanding General Stanley McChrystal identified three main insurgent groups, including Mullah Omar's *Quetta Shura Taliban* (QST), the *Haqqani Network* (HQN), and the *Hezb-e-Islami* movement headed by Gulbuddin Hekmatyar.[131] Hekmatyar's *Hezb-e-Islami* is an active militant organization that has historically received support from both Iran and Pakistan, as well as from the United States in the past—which is one indicator of the convoluted and intertwined nature of the threats to stability and security in Afghanistan.[132] There are also several other political and ideologically-driven resistance movements active in the region, including the militant *Jamiat-i-Islami* ("Islamic Association"), which has fought bitterly against Hekmatyar's *Hezb-e-Islami* ("Islamic Party"), in spite of the groups' common ideological beliefs.[133]

Not surprisingly, Afghanistan has a long history of transitioning governing authority, mainly through assassinations, power struggles, civil wars, coups, and intrigue. Ironically, the Taliban rose to power in large part because they were able to deliver some measure of security and law and order to the war-weary Afghan population, while the weak central government and the competing warlords could not.[134] The Taliban tapped directly into the ancient Afghan history as a warrior culture, and the movement was further shaped by the 1979 Soviet invasion and the example of the mujahedeen. The Taliban's rise was facilitated by the conditions of civil war and warlordism that prevailed in Afghanistan after the Soviet invasion, and the movement also sprang from the religious indoctrination taking place in *madrassas* in Afghanistan and Pakistan. Comprised primarily of Sunni Muslim Pashtuns, the Taliban were initially accepted by the Afghan people as potentially bringing peace, law and order, and stability.[135] The group eventually lost the support of the Afghan people and the international community as a result of its extreme application of the ultraconservative Wahhabist interpretations of Islam.[136]

In general, the Taliban have two primary strategic objectives: first, reasserting control over Afghanistan, and then, eventually extending their movement to establish an Islamic caliphate.[137] To further these broad goals, the Taliban aim to achieve four specific short-term objectives: (1) mobilizing the religious publics in Afghanistan and Pakistan to their cause; (2) rallying the Pashtun tribes using the *Pushtunwali* code and the influence of non-Pashtun ethnic groups in the Kabul-based government as motivators; (3) building up confidence in their own organization by providing a shadow government and basic services in the rural areas, while simultaneously undermining confidence in the Islamic Republic of Afghanistan government; and (4) expelling the Western "crusaders" in order to control eastern and southern Afghanistan as well as western Pakistan.[138]

To achieve these objectives, the Taliban's organization includes specialized cells with responsibility for the planning, resourcing, training, and the execution of diverse activities ranging from information operations, to suicide attacks, to intelligence, finance, improvised bomb-making, research and development, and operations.[139] A recent example of the Taliban's information operations included their campaign to highlight the fraud that accompanied Karzai's 2009 reelection. The Taliban are further organized into regional commands and other elements that carry out administrative, personnel, and logistical functions, and they are suspected of having a political wing as well.[140] The local cells or militias are typically self-generated at the lowest level, gaining the Taliban "franchise" designation and recognition from the central Taliban leadership once the cell has demonstrated its support and cooperation through tangible actions.[141]

Like the analogous al Qaeda cells, the Taliban's local cells and militias largely retain their freedom of movement and action, running their own intelligence gathering, logistics, and population control activities.[142] Taliban fighters are well known for their fanatical willingness to engage directly with better equipped forces, as in the words of one British Special Air Services officer who fought in Afghanistan, "Surrender was the last thing on their minds. . . . If they had a breath left in them, they would be trying to shoot you, so we had no choice but to kill."[143] The

Taliban "organization has been able to build on tribal kinship networks and a charismatic mullah phenomenon to mobilize a critical and dynamic rural base of support . . . buttressed by Talib reinforcements from Pakistan's tribal areas."[144]

The "neo-Taliban" movement that has emerged since the fall of the Taliban to coalition forces in 2001 is a more sophisticated force that is also more closely tied to the international jihadist movement.[145] The neo-Taliban militias have been more effective at command and control, logistics, and information operations among other core insurgent competencies.[146] The resurgent Taliban movement has grown in sophistication and effectiveness, and it is larger and stronger than the pre-2001 Taliban—while operating a parallel government in Afghanistan that is often more responsive to the basic needs of Afghan citizens than the actual government.[147] The Taliban claim to represent both the Islamic faith and the Pashtun code of *Pushtunwali*, giving them moral and cultural credibility, since those two moral codes serve as the common denominators of Afghan society.[148] The Taliban also continue to receive assistance from al Qaeda and the international jihadist movement.[149] Finally, while the Taliban constitute the most significant and direct threat to potential Afghan stability, security, and democracy, they do not represent the only threat to those goals. A variety of transnational criminals, individual tribal factions, splinter cells of other radical elements, and other nation-state actors all have an interest in undermining the prospects for Afghan security, stability, democracy, and economic prosperity. These actors are examined in more detail in Chapter 3.

The Bottom Line: An Extraordinarily Difficult Candidate.

In sum, Afghanistan's largely arbitrary borders contain within them a wide variety of major obstacles that confront any foreign power aiming to create a coherent, stable, secure, democratic, and self-sustaining nation-state. A wide variety of Afghan social, political, economic, demographic, and historical factors stand in the way of the successful execution of the coalition's mission, and these factors are severe enough to call into question whether the U.S. and NATO "nation-building" goals are even feasible or reasonable in the first place. Among other challenging aspects, Afghanistan encompasses discordant cultural and sociological factors, entrenched adverse political-cultural norms, a history of ineffective governance, tribal animosities, warlordism, corruption, economic privation, illiteracy, transnational crime, and a host of other elements that undercut Afghan prospects for success as a modern, conventional nation-state. In some respects, even the common denominators in the fragmented Afghan society, among them the moral codes of *Pushtunwali* and Islam, stand in opposition to the creation of any stable, democratic society founded upon the rule of law, as opposed to the rule of men.

When these factors are considered together, it becomes clear that Afghanistan represents a remarkably poor candidate for nationhood. Afghanistan's violent history, its fragmented tribal and ethnic structures, its numerous persistent tribal animosities, and the deep-seated conservative Islamic resistance to modernizing Western reforms are just the first-order obstacles to potential success. Just as significantly, Afghanistan's widespread illiteracy, its abject poverty, the country's weak or nonexistent civil institutions and social services, rampant corruption, and the prevalence and predominance of drug activity and smuggling all combine to make NATO's nation-building challenge that much greater. As if all of that were not hard enough, the prospects for success are further dimmed by the active opposition of a variety of domestic, international, and transnational actors who have a clear interest in thwarting the coalition's effort to build that modern nation. Taken together, these realities combine to make the creation of effective, democratic governance and the development of a national Afghan identity exceedingly daunting propositions, if they are even feasible at all.

ENDNOTES - CHAPTER 1

1. Stephen Tanner, *Afghanistan: A Military History from Alexander the Great to the Fall of the Taliban*, Cambridge, MA: Da Capo Press, 2002, pp. 206-207.

2. The President of the United States, *The National Security Strategy of the United States of America*, Washington, DC: U.S. Government, May 2010, pp. 20-21.

3. The President of the United States, *The National Security Strategy of the United States of America*, Washington: U.S. Government, March 2006, p. 1.

4. Tanner, *Afghanistan*, p. 109.

5. *Ibid.*

6. *Ibid.*, p. 6.

7. *Ibid.*, p. 5.

8. *Ibid.*

9. *Ibid.*, p. 10.

10. *Ibid.*, Chap. 2.

11. M. J. Gohari, *The Taliban: Ascent to Power*, Oxford, UK: Oxford University Press, 2000, pp. 3-4.

12. Martin Ewans, *Afghanistan: A Short History of Its People and Politics*, New York: HarperCollins Press, 2002, pp. 23-25.

13. *Ibid.*, pp. 24-25.

14. Gohari, *The Taliban*, p. 5.

15. Peter R. Blood, ed., *Afghanistan: Past and Present*, Los Angeles: IndoEuropean Publishing, 2007, p. 12.

16. Tanner, *Afghanistan*, Chap. 7.

17. *Ibid.*, p. 190.

18. *Ibid.*, pp. 204-205.

19. *Ibid.*, pp. 219-220.

20. *Ibid.*, pp. 218-219.

21. *Ibid.*, p. 222.

22. *Ibid.*, p. 226.

23. *Ibid.*, p. 238.

24. *Ibid.*

25. *Ibid.*, p. 244.

26. *Ibid.*, p. 255.

27. Jeffery J. Roberts, *The Origins of Conflict in Afghanistan*, Westport, CT: Praeger, 2003, p. xi.

28. Martin Ewans, *Conflict in Afghanistan: Studies in Asymmetric Warfare*, London, UK: Routledge, 2005, pp. 227-228.

29. *Ibid.*, p. 231.

30. Recounted to Colonel Mike McMahon by various senior Afghan leaders during his tenure as CJ-7, Combined Security Transition Command-Afghanistan (CSTC-A).

31. Tanner, *Afghanizan*, pp. 278-279.

32. *Ibid.*, pp. 278-280.

33. Robert D. Crews and Amin Tarzi, eds., *The Taliban and the Crisis of Afghanistan*, Cambridge, MA: Harvard, 2008, p. 320.

34. Blood, ed., *Afghanistan*, pp. 62-65.

35. *Ibid.*, pp. 56-57.

36. Shaista Wahib and Barry Youngerman, *A Brief History of Afghanistan*, New York: InfoBase Publishing, 2007, 1.

37. Blood, ed., *Afghanistan*, pp. 62-65.

38. Joseph J. Collins, *Understanding War in Afghanistan*, Washington, DC: National Defense University Press, 2011, 6-7.

39. Blood, ed., *Afghanistan*, pp. 62-65.

40. *Ibid.*, p. 64.

41. *Ibid.*, pp. 62-65.

42. *Ibid.*, p. 65.

43. Blood, ed., *Afghanistan*, pp. 86-88.

44. *Ibid.*, pp. 94-96.

45. *Ibid.*, p. 66.

46. Ewans, *Afghanistan*, p. 7.

47. *Ibid.*

48. *Ibid.*, p. 12.

49. Sarah Chayes, *The Punishment of Virtue: Inside Afghanistan After the Taliban*, New York: Penguin, 2006, p. 34.

50. Ewans, *Afghanistan*, pp. 7-8.

51. Blood, ed., *Afghanistan*, pp. 110-115.

52. *Ibid.*, p. 111.

53. *Ibid.*

54. *Ibid.*, p. 113.

55. *Ibid.*, pp. 117-120.

56. *Ibid.*, p. 118.

57. *Ibid.*, pp. 118-119.

58. Robert I. Rotberg, ed., *Building a New Afghanistan*, Cambridge, MA: World Peace Foundation (and Brookings Institution), 2007, p. 143. See also *CIA World Factbook: Afghanistan* available from *https://www.cia.gov/library/publications/the-world-factbook/geos/af.html*.

59. Blood, ed., *Afghanistan*, pp. 123-124.

60. *Ibid.*, p. 124.

61. *Ibid.*, pp. 124-125.

62. Wahib and Youngerman, *A Brief History of Afghanistan*, pp. 21-22.

63. J. C. Griffiths, *Afghanistan*, New York: Praeger, 1967, pp. 65-68.

64. Blood, ed., *Afghanistan*, p. 66.

65. Nancy Peabody Newell and Richard S. Newell, *The Struggle for Afghanistan*, Ithaca, NY: Cornell University Press, 1981, pp. 34-35.

66. *Ibid.*, p. 34.

67. *Ibid.*, p. 35.

68. *Ibid.*

69. *Ibid.*

70. *Ibid.*, pp. 35-36.

71. Robert D. Crews and Amin Tarzi, eds., *The Taliban and the Crisis of Afghanistan*, Cambridge, MA: Harvard University Press, 2008, p. 315.

72. *Ibid.*, p. 37.

73. *Ibid.*, pp. 38-39.

74. Ewans, *Afghanistan*, pp. 130-131.

75. Gohari, *The Taliban*, pp. 50-55.

76. *Ibid.*, p. 60.

77. Griffiths, *Afghanistan*, pp. 83-84.

78. Gohari, *The Taliban*, p. 61.

79. *Ibid.*

80. Griffiths, *Afghanistan*, p. 90.

81. Gohari, *The Taliban*, p. xi.

82. Rotberg, ed., *Building a New Afghanistan*, p. 5.

83. *Ibid.*

84. *Ibid.*, p. 7.

85. *Ibid.*

86. Dexter Elkins, "For Afghans, a Price for Everything," originally published in *The New York Times* and subsequently reprinted in *The Pittsburgh Post-Gazette* on January 2, 2009.

87. *Ibid.*

88. Rotberg, ed., *Building a New Afghanistan*, p. 7.

89. *Ibid.*, pp. 44-47.

90. Griff Witte, "To the Warlords Belong the Spoils," *The Washington Post National Weekly Edition*, June 22-28, 2006.

91. *Ibid.*

92. Ewans, *Afghanistan*, p. 11.

93. Chayes, *The Punishment of Virtue*, p. 18.

94. Antonio Giustozzi, *Koran, Kalashnikov and Laptop: The Neo-Taliban Insurgency in Afghanistan*, London, UK: Hurst, 2007, p. 16.

95. *Ibid.*, p. 17.

96. *Ibid.*

97. Colonel Trey Braun suggested this point.

98. Giustozzi, *Koran, Kalashnikov and Laptop*, p. 17.

99. Chayes, *The Punishment of Virtue*, p. 79.

100. *Ibid.*, p. 78.

101. Tanner, *Afghanistan*, p. 109.

102. Rotberg, ed., *Building a New Afghanistan*, p. 6.

103. "United Nations Human Development Index- 2010 Rankings," United Nations Development Program, available from *hdr.undp.org/en/statistics/*.

104. *CIA World Factbook: Afghanistan*.

105. Ewans, *Conflict in Afghanistan*, p. 294.

106. Department of Defense, *Report on Progress toward Security and Stability in Afghanistan*, Report to Congress of April 2010, p. 59.

107. Blood, ed., *Afghanistan*, pp. 83-84.

108. *Ibid.*, p. 82.

109. Rotberg, ed., *Building a New Afghanistan*, p. 143.

110. Chayes, *The Punishment of Virtue*, p. 85.

111. Griffiths, *Afghanistan*, p. 48.

112. Ewans, *Conflict in Afghanistan*, p. 159.

113. *Ibid.*, p. 161.

114. Crews and Tarzi, eds., *The Taliban and the Crisis of Afghanistan*, p. 315.

115. Gohari, *The Taliban*, pp. 84-85. In the summer of 2010, the Department of Defense also announced that geologists under contract to the U.S. Government had discovered major mineral and natural gas deposits.

116. *Ibid.*, p. 85.

117. Ewans, *Afghanistan*, p. 294.

118. *Ibid.*

119. *Ibid.*, p. 295.

120. *The 9/11 Commission Report, Official Government Edition*, Washington, DC: U.S. Government Printing Office, 2004, p. 63.

121. Department of Defense, *Report on Progress toward Security and Stability in Afghanistan*, Report to Congress of April 2010, p. 59.

122. Christopher M. Blanchard, *Afghanistan: Narcotics and U.S. Policy*, Washington, DC: Congressional Research Service, CRS 7-5700, August 12, 2009, p. 2.

123. *Ibid.*, p. 3.

124. *Ibid.*

125. *Ibid.*, p. 8.

126. Gohari, *The Taliban*, p. 69.

127. *Ibid.*

128. *Ibid.*, pp. 68-72.

129. *Ibid.*, pp. 70-71.

130. Seth G. Jones, *Counterinsurgency in Afghanistan*, Santa Monica, CA: Rand Corporation's National Defense Research Institute Press, 2008, p. xi.

131. Bob Woodward, "The Case for Afghanistan," *The Washington Post National Weekly Edition*, October 4, 2009, p. 7.

132. Jones, *Counterinsurgency in Afghanistan*, p. 41.

133. Ewans, *Conflict in Afghanistan*, p. 14.

134. *Ibid.*, p. 256.

135. Shahid Afsar, Chris Samples, and Thomas Wood, "The Taliban: An Organizational Analysis," *Military Review*, May-June 2008, pp. 58-59.

136. *Ibid.*, p. 60.

137. *Ibid.*, p. 64.

138. *Ibid.*

139. *Ibid.*, pp. 64-65.

140. *Ibid.*

141. *Ibid.*, p. 65.

142. *Ibid.*

143. Ewans, *Conflict in Afghanistan*, p. 173.

144. Thomas H. Johnson and M. Chris Mason, "Understanding the Taliban and Insurgency in Afghanistan, *Orbis*, Winter 2007, p. 71.

145. Giustozzi, *Koran, Kalashnikov and Laptop*, p. 13.

146. *Ibid.*

147. Pamela Constable, "A Modernized Taliban," *The Washington Post National Weekly Edition*, September 29-October 5, p. 12.

148. Ewans, *Conflict in Afghanistan*, p. 266.

149. Jones, *Counterinsurgency in Afghanistan*, pp. 61-62.

CHAPTER 2

THE SCOPE OF IRREGULAR WARFARE AND NATION-BUILDING

> I don't think the (British) government sees their way out of the terrible difficulty of setting up a decent government here at all.
>
> > British Colonel Frederick Rowcroft, in a letter written in 1879 while serving in Afghanistan during the Second Anglo-Afghan War[1]

Irregular warfare and nation-building operations are incredibly complex, broad, and expensive undertakings in the best of circumstances, and a variety of foreign powers can ruefully attest to the fact that Afghanistan represents a particularly tough prospect. Formally speaking, *irregular warfare* is defined as "a violent struggle among state and nonstate actors for legitimacy and influence over the relevant populations," as this type of warfare aims to "erode an adversary's power, influence, and will."[2] In our strategic approach to Afghanistan, the United States rapidly progressed from conventional combat operations at the outset of the conflict to irregular warfare operations, ultimately deciding upon nation-building and a full-blown counterinsurgency (COIN) effort as the key components of the strategy to deny a safe haven to al Qaeda. Most recently, COIN has been defined as the "comprehensive civilian and military efforts taken to defeat an insurgency and to address any core grievances."[3] In its essence, the United States and the North Atlantic Treaty Organization (NATO) have embarked upon a strategy for Afghanistan that requires the creation of a functional Afghan state in the midst of a protracted violent struggle with various nonstate actors. Or as the old saying goes, "We are building the airplane as we are flying it."

Irregular warfare operations generally require substantial commitments of money, manpower, and time, especially in the particular case of COIN operations. Furthermore, the nation-building effort that sits at the center of America's strategy for Afghanistan, and our two most recent U.S. national security strategies, strongly embrace the central tenets of liberal democratic peace theory. This is a theory that in its simplest form holds that democracies do not typically go to war with other nations without provocation. But while the empirical evidence related to the validity of liberal democratic peace theory is mixed, the evidence pertaining to the costs and difficulties of armed nation-building is conclusive. Nation-building is incredibly expensive and difficult, as it encompasses literally hundreds of complex and resource-intensive tasks, most entailing heavy costs. Even more troubling is the fact that the outcome of these expensive and difficult missions is never certain. Or, as another old Army saying goes, "The enemy always gets a vote."

In the case of our nation-building operations in Afghanistan, the creation of a viable nation and a functioning government requires nothing short of affecting wholesale change in the country's entrenched political culture, as well as constructing institutions needed for security; the rule of law; economic viability; and, local, provincial, and national governance. With these major requirements in mind, nation-building in Afghanistan is at least as much a social, political, and economic challenge as it is a military one. Nevertheless, in spite of America's relevant history of involvement in irregular warfare, stability operations, counterinsurgencies, and the other "small wars" of our nation's past, there is little evidence that the U.S. Government fully understood or acknowledged the scope and challenges of nation-building in Afghanistan prior to expanding the mission in that direction—or before deciding to embark upon a similarly difficult set of objectives simultaneously in Iraq. In any event, the United States clearly lacked the cultural awareness, civilian expertise, and military assets needed to set the conditions for success in irregular warfare and nation-building in Afghanistan at the outset of the mission.

THE GOALS AND METHODS IN AFGHANISTAN

Crafted a few years after the United States and NATO had already begun irregular warfare and nation-building operations in Afghanistan and Iraq, the *National Security Strategy of the United States of America* of 2006 offers a clear statement of the ultimate American strategic goals for Afghanistan. Strongly embracing democratic peace theory, the strategy identifies the promotion of "freedom, democracy, and human dignity" and the creation of "free nations" as the cornerstones of U.S. foreign policy.[4] Asserting that "free nations tend toward peace," the strategy declares that the United States had "aided a new, democratic government to rise" in Afghanistan, while "working to end tyranny, to promote effective democracies, and to extend prosperity" more generally.[5] The document goes on to claim that "Afghanistan and Iraq have replaced tyrannies with democracies," citing the ratification of a constitution and the creation of an elected legislature in Afghanistan as successes toward that strategic end.[6] This strategy then offers a direct definition of the national security goal of "promoting effective democracies," describing as the objective states that feature Western-style freedoms, the maintenance of order, responsive and effective governance, "independent and impartial systems of justice," political participation, a resistance to corruption, and the protection of private property.[7]

Although they did not start out this way, by 2006 the United States and NATO had settled upon two methods for achieving these strategic ends in Afghanistan, including the two separate but mutually reinforcing ways of irregular warfare and nation-building. Ironically, even as President Obama clearly backed away from the nation-building rhetoric in major speeches on Afghanistan and Pakistan in March and December 2009, his decision to commit increased civilian and military resources in Afghanistan in support of a full-blown COIN only served to reinforce and expand this status quo.[8] A few months later, in May 2010, the Obama administration published a complementary *National Security Strategy of the United States* that superseded the Bush-era national security guidance, with the new strategic guidance placing far less emphasis upon achieving a Western-style democracy in Afghanistan. Instead, the new strategic guidance offered a more general call for a "strong, stable, and prosperous Afghanistan."[9] As noted, however, the President's accompanying strategic decisions have actually served to reinforce and expand the two strategic methods currently being applied, including irregular warfare—or in particular, COIN—and the concurrent effort to build an Afghan nation.

U.S. national-level goals for Afghanistan are contained within the *Strategic Plan for Fiscal Years 2007-*

2012, published by the U.S. State Department and U.S. Agency for International Development (USAID).[10] In February 2010, the State Department published the *Afghanistan and Pakistan Regional Stabilization Strategy*, a document in which State's Office of the Special Representative for Afghanistan and Pakistan outlines ongoing and proposed initiatives in support of viable Afghan nationhood, among them: "Rebuilding Afghanistan's Agricultural Sector"; "Strengthening Afghan Governance"; "Enhancing Afghan Rule of Law"; and, "Building an Economic Foundation for Afghanistan's Future," among others.[11] Former International Security Assistance Force (ISAF) Commanding General David Petraeus reinforced this approach, though perhaps scaling down the specific objectives somewhat, as the ISAF Campaign Strategy includes:

1. "Protecting the population";
2. "Enabling the Afghanistan National Security Forces (ANSF)";
3. "Neutralizing malign influences" (including corruption);
4. "Supporting the extension of governance"; and,
5. "Supporting socio-economic development."[12]

Without question, the U.S. and NATO goals remain ambitious.

Furthermore, it is especially interesting to note that although the President and Secretary of State may have backed away rhetorically from the goal of a Western-style nation-state as the primary desired end-state for the mission in Afghanistan, the agencies, departments, and other executive arms of the U.S. Government have not yet changed their operational objectives to reflect that intent. Viewed from a practical perspective, however, perhaps the reality is that they cannot. That is, from one perspective, the conflation of the methods of COIN and nation-building in Afghanistan makes perfect sense, given that the United States and NATO cannot achieve the basic goals of irregular warfare and COIN without the existence of a legitimate and effective host-nation government to serve as the beneficiary or focus of that effort. Viewed from a different perspective, however, this dynamic represents a bit of circular logic, in the sense that the strategic methods are at least partly dictating the strategic ends, instead of the other way around — or the way it is supposed to be. In any case, the current U.S. strategic goals and methods require the creation of a viable Afghan state.

SO WHAT TYPE OF "NATION" ARE WE BUILDING?

While U.S. policymakers have focused on the functional processes of governance in defining prospective nationhood for Afghanistan, there is no consensus among scholars regarding the conventional definitions of the terms *nation*, *state*, or *nationality*. Defined by Webster's, a *nation* is "a stable, historically developed community of people with a territory, economic life, distinctive culture, and language in common . . . united under a single government."[13] The root word *nation* itself is originally derived from the Latin word for birth, though variations in the definition over history have included some that have emphasized the elements of common ethnicity and language, while others highlight the aspect of living under the same political system or governing arrangements.[14] Along these same lines, *nationality* usually refers to some subset of a group identity, while the term *state* has been defined as "the power or authority represented by a body of people, especially an independent government (and) political organization constituting the basis of civil government."[15] In its simplest form, then, the word *nation* refers to a "sovereign government ruling a particular territory."[16] Even when compared against these most basic definitions, the raw material of Afghanistan poses major challenges for nationhood.

Applying a finer resolution, sociologists, political scientists, and other social scientists have added texture and depth to these basic definitions. In these disciplines, the elements of common ethnic origins among a population, an accepted national identity, the exercise of sovereignty within recognized borders, and functional state institutions have all moved in and out of the definition of *nation* over the last century. At the same time, in most modern definitions of a *nation* or *nation-state*, the "modern civic national identity" has come to predominate, as opposed to more traditional ethnic models of nationality.[17] "Civic nationality" refers to the model of nationhood in which "the people of a society are bound together in common loyalty to the public institutions of a particular territory," a loyalty that "typically arises because the people perceive the government as committed to serve their interests without reference to particular ethnic considerations."[18] Based upon the relevant U.S. and NATO goal statements, this civic model is the brand of *nation* and *nationality* that the coalition seeks to achieve in Afghanistan, or one that is based upon civil governing institutions with a basis in the rule of law, serving the people without regard to tribal or ethnic origins. Given Afghan demographics, this is a tall order.

Refining this model further, this state-centered model of the modern nation-state must feature "ministries, departments, agencies, and a range of related bodies, (with each) reflecting a degree of institutional development within a polity."[19] This type of state must also achieve *legitimacy* to go along with this ministerial *capacity*.[20] In Afghanistan, the state has never had either of these critical elements to any serious degree at any point in its history and, with the majority of its population under the age of 30, "the bulk of the Afghan population is relatively unfamiliar with the phenomenon of state power, and some stand to lose if the central state is effectively consolidated."[21] Others have argued that the greatest single weakness of the Afghan state is its utter lack of a fiscal base.[22] Furthermore, Afghanistan's brutal history over recent decades has created a widespread mistrust of motives and agendas related to foreign benefactors and among the various factions of Afghanistan society, making the creation of a functioning civil society all the more difficult.[23] So, by any definition, Afghanistan is a difficult candidate for modern nationhood, and while it is not necessarily impossible to envision Afghanistan meeting these rigorous criteria at some point in the future, it would clearly require an extended, resource-intensive commitment to realize that outcome.

OPERATIONALIZING THE GOALS

The challenges of nation-building and irregular warfare are even more dramatic when these broader goals are operationalized into the specific tasks required to achieve success. To exacerbate the problem, while there is now a wealth of current doctrine related to irregular warfare, COIN, stability operations, and other small wars, there is no commonly accepted definition of the phrase "nation-building," since the U.S.

government has struggled over the last several years to define its various requirements. Without question, however, irregular warfare and nation-building are complex, extensive, expensive, labor-intensive, and risky undertakings. Furthermore, for all of the expense and effort, success or failure is not wholly within our control, and even success may not ultimately yield the political outcome we are aiming for in the first place.

To put the scope and complexity of irregular warfare and nation-building into their proper perspective, former Afghan Minister of Public Finance Ashraf Ghani and Claire Lockhart identify 10 key functions of a state that must be viable for a nation-state to succeed. These include:

1. Implementing the rule of law (most important);
2. Providing security and managing the use of force (an army and police);
3. Providing administrative control (adherence to standards and rules, and eliminating corruption);
4. Managing public finance (budgeting);
5. Developing human capital (education and the workforce);
6. Providing social welfare (equal opportunity);
7. Providing essential services (power, water, communications, and transportation);
8. Managing public assets (buildings, land, and infrastructure);
9. Establishing a commercial market (local and national economy); and,
10. Facilitating public borrowing (a public credit market).[24]

Similarly, the U.S. Government's own relatively recently created Office of the Coordinator for Reconstruction and Stabilization (S/CRS) identifies its own five "technical sector" requirements, analogous to lines of operations and necessary to support a country transitioning from armed conflict to stable society. The sectors are:

1. security;
2. governance and participation;
3. humanitarian assistance and social well-being;
4. economic stabilization and infrastructure; and,
5. justice and reconciliation.[25]

In a sense, these sectors can be viewed as the minimum essential tasks needed for a society to achieve short-term stability, as opposed to the more-robust viable society that Ghani and Lockhart describe. In a major work that fleshes out the specific requirements that correspond to these sectors, S/CRS's *Essential Tasks Matrix* is an exhaustive task-by-task list that stretches to nearly 100 pages of text and includes hundreds of challenging tasks.[26] This matrix represents an incredibly detailed list of nation-building requirements, stunning in its breadth and depth. The huge scope of the matrix also gives a clear sense of how difficult and complex nation-building would be if done comprehensively and correctly.

On the military side of the irregular warfare and nation-building equation, the Army and Marine Corps' *Counterinsurgency Field Manual* sets the bar slightly lower in defining the central task as supporting a government that features "a culturally acceptable level of corruption" while pursuing "legitimacy."[27] Nevertheless, the manual goes on to identify six possible indicators of governmental legitimacy—a primary objective of the COIN effort—including population security; the perception of a "just and fair" selection of political leaders; participative political processes; "regime acceptance;" and social, political, and economic development.[28] As an unintended consequence, these documents also yield a sense of the enormity of the requirements of nation-building, while also exposing the limitations of the various U.S. agencies' existing expertise in the skill areas needed to carry out those requirements. The existing core competencies of the key agencies do not readily translate into the operational- or tactical-level capabilities needed to carry out the demands of nation-building, a topic that is explored in detail in later chapters.

Applying their own perspectives, analysts from outside the Afghan and U.S. Governments largely see the daunting nature of these requirements in the same way. These analysts argue that nation-state development in Afghanistan will require bringing about major normative changes in Afghan culture, even while requiring the simultaneous completion of a truly challenging set of institutional developmental tasks. Among these requirements, these observers note that the "nation-building" effort must achieve:

- National economic integration, since most Afghan economic activity is focused on local markets;
- Employment creation and poverty reduction, requiring both increased investment and increased productivity;
- The elimination of the opium economy, requiring the generation of viable alternatives and the implementation of the rule of law;
- A strengthening of the financial sector, including increasing access to credit markets and basic financial services and protections;
- Investment in basic infrastructure, primarily roads and power generation;

- Investment in human resources and skills development, such as facilities for basic education, literacy programs, and vocational training;
- Securing property rights and land tenure, as the years of war and massive displacement of the Afghan people have left confusion over land titles, property rights, and a variety of competing claims;
- A stable environment for private investment, including tax codes, business procedures, legal protections, enforcement of all codes and procedures;
- Institutions of good governance to overcome security concerns, weak central governing institutions, and a lack of economic infrastructure in finance and public works;
- The creation of a supportive legal environment, including a commitment to eliminate corruption;
- Engagement in international trade and regional economic cooperation;
- Asserting border control while facilitating trade and transportation; and,
- Generating legitimate revenue streams to fund all of these economic development and support activities.[29]

Each of these tasks is complex, broad, and difficult in and of itself, and achieving success in any one of these areas will demand a major and sustained commitment of resources and effort. Putting the magnitude of the costs and labor requirements of nation-building into perspective, the Congressional Budget Office estimates that it currently costs $250,000 to keep a single U.S. soldier in Afghanistan for a year, while a member of the ANSF costs $12,000 to support.[30] Applying contemporary counterinsurgency models, former ISAF Commanding General Stanley McChrystal successfully argued that an appropriately sized COIN in Afghanistan would require a dramatically accelerated development of the ANSF to 240,000 soldiers and 160,000 police.[31] In addition to the 30,000 new U.S. troops that were required to implement the full-blown COIN effort in the near term—bringing the U.S. contingent to about 100,000 troops altogether—he also acknowledged that his population-centric approach would likely result in increased U.S. and coalition casualties.[32] President Obama has recently reaffirmed that this current strategy will stand.

Viewed in the aggregate, and even before considering the increasing costs to the United States needed to meet the expanding requirements of the McChrystal and Petraeus plan, the Obama administration requested $65 billion to fund operations in Afghanistan for fiscal year 2010.[33] Through fiscal year 2009, Iraq and Afghanistan have combined to cost the United States more than $940 billion, with Afghanistan representing $223 billion of that total.[34] The actual U.S. expenditures for FY10 and FY11 will easily top $100 billion.[35] Additionally, there are other less tangible costs that are not captured in these numbers, such as the human costs of civilian casualties, the wear and tear on American troops and their families, the economic drag of deficit spending, and other costs that are often difficult to measure but are just as real and significant to those who absorb them.

OTHER CRITICAL FACTORS

As if the complexity, scope, labor requirements, and cost of nation-building were not difficult enough by themselves, there are also a variety of other factors that have a major impact upon the prospects for success in this endeavor in Afghanistan. Chief among these other factors is the old Army saying that "the enemy gets a vote." That is, these nation-building activities are not taking place in a static environment, but rather in one in which the enemies of a stable, secure, self-sustaining, and democratic Afghanistan are learning and adapting as they actively seek ways to undermine the host-nation government and the coalition's efforts. Furthermore, the war in Afghanistan is asymmetric in nature, meaning that many of the American military's technological and "kinetic" advantages are easily neutralized by the enemy, which aims to attack at points of weakness rather than attacking into U.S. military strengths.[36]

With the rise of globalization and transnationalism, asymmetric warfare is regaining its emphasis, as insurgents, weaker states, and Islamic extremists each seek to challenge the strongest nation-states. Typically, the Afghan mujahedeen of the 1980s would conduct ambushes and raids and avoid direct confrontations with the massed Russian formations.[37] The insurgents today have maintained these same asymmetric tactics, although they also periodically conduct larger coordinated assaults. Even during the mujahedeen's resistance to the Soviet invasion, the fighters tended to operate in small bands without much cross-group coordination or planning.[38] The Soviet intervention in Afghanistan backfired, since their invasion undermined their credibility around the world.[39] More pointedly, the United States was able to expend a few billion dollars in aid to the Afghan resistance, while Soviet Union costs were about $100 billion.[40]

In any event, the asymmetric tactics and the decentralized nature of the organizational structure of the anti-government elements offer both advantages and disadvantages to the insurgents, but they clearly present a major challenge to nation-building. Like the Russian Army of the 1980s, the U.S. Army that entered Afghanistan and Iraq was trained for conventional operations rather than COIN and has had to adapt to these tactics and circumstances. As a significant example of the Taliban's adaptability as a learning organization, the Taliban began to abandon the full-scale frontal assaults that had characterized their attacks early in the war, and by 2006 had implemented suicide attacks as a major tactic, in spite of the Islamic and *Pushtunwali* taboos against suicide.[41] The Taliban have also expanded their use of the Internet and free media as part of their recently more robust and more effective information operations campaign.

Among other key factors, the coalition's objective of winning popular support for the central government is also made more difficult by policy uncertainty in NATO and the United States, and the knowledge that the U.S. forces will leave at some point makes Afghan villagers wary of assisting the coalition.[42] Along these same lines, strategic thinker Colin Gray argues that the American public and the corresponding American military culture are "not friendly to the means and methods necessary for the waging of warfare against irregular enemies." [43] This consideration adds an additional political constraint to the successful prosecution of the allies' irregular warfare objectives — and, by extension, the nation-building goals, as well. He goes on to assert that these operations do not lend themselves to formulaic approaches, with each situation holding its own complexities and nuances; this is another aspect of the challenge that bodes poorly for the coalition, especially given frequent turnover among coalition personnel in the operational theater.[44]

Similarly, theorist Steven Metz argues that in its execution of the war, the United States has failed to distinguish between classic "nationalistic" insurgencies and the complexities of the tribal- and crime-driven scenario in Afghanistan.[45] Among additional challenges that correspond to this scenario, he cites the inherent complexities that result from the enemy's willingness to pursue ad hoc, strategic partnerships and alliances; their ability to move easily across poorly defended or uncontrolled borders; their fluid organization with quick reorganizational capabilities; and their ability to advertise or create name brands with psychological or political themes.[46] Metz also argues that diverse insurgency environments require correspondingly distinct responses, differentiating between scenarios including:

1. A functioning and responsible government with some legitimacy and significant U.S. interests;

2. No functioning or legitimate government but a "broad international and regional consensus" (favoring state-formation and "neo-trusteeship"); and,

3. No functioning or legitimate government and no consensus for "neo-trusteeship" (calling for providing only "safe zones" for humanitarian relief).[47]

Lastly, another critical factor that will affect the coalition's ability to achieve success in nation-building is the less tangible but essential requirement of redefining Afghan political culture to achieve any success that will endure. Afghanistan's long history of violence, conquest, internal conflict, brutality, privation, and hardship is entrenched in Afghan society and its cultural norms. Those features of Afghan society, as well as the influences of *Pushtunwali* and Islam, will each directly and considerably affect the goal of building a stable, secure, self-sustaining, and democratic Afghanistan. Some argue that so far the United States has equated holding elections—however flawed—with democracy, but real democracy and true democratic institutions are far harder to create.[48]

UNDERESTIMATING OR IGNORING THE MAGNITUDE OF THE CHALLENGE

In spite of all of these substantial obstacles to viable Afghan nationhood, there is little evidence from the public record or other indicators that the United States either fully understood or acknowledged the extent of these challenges before committing to the goal of nation-building in Afghanistan. Furthermore, the U.S. Government's heavy reliance on the Department of Defense (DoD) to implement its evolving strategy, along with a basic lack of understanding of Afghan culture, has led to a variety of unintended and adverse consequences that have combined to undermine the Coalition's prospects for success. At the same time, the United States has failed to appreciate the lessons of its own past experiences with regime change and nation-building as it moved forward with operations in Afghanistan, further failing to set conditions for success in the process.

Among other indicators of this strategic and operational shortfall is the low level of resources that the United States committed to the operation. In severely limiting the size of the force initially deployed to Afghanistan, Defense Secretary Donald Rumsfeld sought to validate his vision of a compact, mobile army and the administration's power projection model, described by one observer as "a new model of hegemony defined, above all, by its extreme minimalism."[49] This approach, while possibly appropriate to the early phase of the operation and its focus on counterterrorism, proved wholly inadequate as the mission evolved into nation-building and COIN. Others point to the eventual use of hundreds of thousands of contractors in Afghanistan and Iraq to meet the unanticipated requirements of nation-building as additional evidence of the failure to appreciate the scope of the mission.[50] The effects of these poor choices in Afghanistan were then multiplied by the decision to attempt equally ambitious operations in Iraq.

Describing the U.S. Government's performance as one in which insufficient resources were mixed with "ideological fantasy" regarding the ease of constructing democratic states, Anthony Cordesman of the Center for Strategic and International Studies asserts that the United States was unprepared altogether for the aftermath of the initial military success in Afghanistan.[51] He further argues that the U.S. Government not only failed to distinguish between the military demands of counterterrorism and the much greater requirements of COIN, but that the United States also failed to apply adequate resources to the informational, diplomatic, and economic aspects of the mission.[52] Cordesman notes that from the start, the United States has seemed to lack the political will to commit the resources needed to meet a likely mission timeline of 5 to 15 years.[53]

As a simple measure of this lack of adequate resources and preparation, the U.S. military initiated the operation with only about 1,300 troops in 2001. In spite of the major mission shift to COIN and nation-building by 2004, the United States had only increased its forces to 26,500 troops by May 2007, serving alongside about 28,000 Coalition partners—or far less than what General McChrystal's COIN plan called for in his ultimate request for forces.[54] Operating on a dramatically smaller scale, the State Department typically could not fill even the modest number of positions required for its operations in Kabul, a situation made worse by the agency's internal rules requiring volunteers for overseas postings. The Combined Security Transition Command-Afghanistan (CSTC-A) also reported major shortages in the personnel needed to train the Afghan police, citing a shortfall of 2,300 police trainers and mentors in 2009 that has persisted into 2011, in spite of the surge of military and civilian personnel. Agency by agency then, the resources have fallen far short of the levels needed to meet the demands of a classic COIN, years after the mission had first drifted in that direction.

Along similar lines, the U.S. Government's heavy reliance upon the DoD as the primary vehicle for achieving both military and nonmilitary objectives in Afghanistan brought with it a variety of unintended and adverse consequences. Perhaps most importantly, this military emphasis almost guaranteed from the beginning that the kinetic operations—or the military effort to defeat the Taliban and other anti-government elements—would predominate in U.S. and NATO operations, rather than other nonmilitary objectives. As one significant example of this emphasis, for a long time within CSTC-A, the military headquarters charged with developing the Afghan security forces, even after receiving the police mission, the primary focus remained on the development of the Afghan National Army (ANA) and the Ministry of Defense (MOD), rather than the Afghan National Police (ANP) and the Ministry of the Interior (MOI). It is natural that an army would feel qualified to build another army but not a police force.

In fairness, this natural tendency on the part of the U.S. military to focus on the development of the Afghan Army was reinforced by international policy agreements that initially assigned the police development mission to other countries, agencies, and intergovernmental organizations. These actors were unprepared and poorly equipped to carry out that mission, a dire circumstance given the central importance of those efforts to the COIN and the creation of social order and the rule of law. As another adverse consequence of the U.S. "minimalist" and military-centered approach, NATO and U.S. forces were often forced to rely heavily upon the use of airpower in their operations, resulting in numerous civilian casualties, which served to undermine the credibility and popularity of both the Afghan government and the coalition forces.[55]

As another indicator of inadequate mission preparation, the United States demonstrated a broad lack of understanding of Afghan culture at the start of the operation by making choices then that have since combined to undermine the longer-term prospects for successful nation-building. Perhaps most significantly, one of the main features of the American approach has been the reliance upon Afghan warlords to exert control over the country. This remilitarization of Afghan postwar politics has underemphasized civilian institutional development in favor of military solutions to Afghan problems.[56] Whether this choice was driven by actual operational necessity, inadequate force levels, a lack of Afghan human capital, or mere expediency, the collective effect has been to make achieving the subsequent nation-building objectives that much more difficult, since the United States and then NATO clearly failed to set the conditions for success. The roots of this U.S. (and Karzai) strategy to empower the warlords as a means of controlling the country go all the way back to the 1980s and the aid to the Afghan resistance, when Gulbuddin Hekmatyar — despite being rabidly anti-American — was given the largest portion of U.S. aid in fighting the Soviets.[57]

There are other operational-level examples of this lack of cultural awareness. For example, an American observer recounted an Afghan leader in Kandahar describing his American partners as being "such amateurs." This Afghan leader noted that the Americans "were honest to the point of simplemindedness," taking their designated Afghan intermediaries' claims at face value every time they identified someone as Talib.[58] A U.S. military officer operating in Kandahar early in the military intervention in Afghanistan identified many instances in which American troops demonstrated a clear lack of understanding of Afghan cultural norms — creating animosity among the Afghan population, along with other adverse consequences for the mission.[59]

Another example of this consequential Western misunderstanding of Afghan culture and the state of Afghan governing institutions is that benefactors typically tend to try to support the government by supporting the incumbents in particular offices. However, in Afghanistan, with its absence of checks and balances and its fledgling institutions, this approach too often leads to easy corruption and abuse of authority.[60] Perversely, the U.S. Government's contracting process has had the same unintended effect of strengthening local warlords by enabling them to skim money from contracts as they dole out jobs, pay, and the benefits of the projects to their supporters.[61] So, in a culture that emphasizes superior force and the willingness to use that force, reformers have been easily trumped by manipulative warlords, corrupt officials, and resistant tribesmen, especially given those tribesmen's conservative Muslim cultural norms.

Another telling example of the West's lack of Afghan cultural awareness is that the United States and NATO have professed to be shocked by the rampant corruption that attended the 2009 presidential elections that returned Karzai to office, and in the parliamentary elections of 2010. However, the far more shocking outcome would have been if there had been no widespread fraud or corruption, given the prevailing Afghan political-cultural norms. As another indicator of the inadequacy of the resources committed to nation-building, this corruption was enabled in part by the fact that the coalition lacked sufficient resources to cover most of the hundreds of polling sites spread throughout the country in both sets of elections.

As a final point, the United States has shown an obvious lack of appreciation of its own relevant history of operations aimed at regime changes and nation-building as it has proceeded in Afghanistan. Directly stated, as the mission in Afghanistan evolved into nation-building from its initial emphasis on counterterrorism and the removal of the Taliban, American leaders — much like their Russian counterparts of the late 1970s — overlooked critical factors that have predicted success in past operations of these types.

In particular, permissive security environments and previously existing social, economic, educational, and political structures have served as predictors of the likelihood of success in the past. In a straightforward National Defense University analysis that considered U.S. regime change and reconstruction activities in Germany, Japan, Somalia, Haiti, the Balkans, Iraq, and Afghanistan, scholars Hans Bennendijk and Stuart Johnson find a clear correlation between success in these reconstruction and development operations and low levels of "continuing hostile activities," coupled with the existence of the social, political, and economic infrastructure and human capital needed to serve as the foundation for the reconstructed society.[62] Conversely in Afghanistan, the Afghan government of the 1970s was just as inept and corrupt as it is today, and the country has never had effective social, educational, or governing institutions or even decent standards of literacy.[63] Therefore, Afghanistan's nation-builders are starting from scratch, or are perhaps even worse off than that, given the numerous obstacles that they must overcome to achieve success.

Taken together, these essential considerations were seemingly underestimated or ignored—and Afghan culture and its implications poorly understood—as the United States and NATO undertook this ambitious and difficult mission, much as the Soviets ignored those same adverse circumstances in their rush to prop up a failing Communist regime in the 1980s. So there is little evidence that the U.S. Government fully appreciated the magnitude of the challenge posed by Afghanistan as a candidate for nationhood, just as there is little evidence that the U.S. Government fully acknowledged the scope and challenges of nation-building prior to allowing the Afghan mission to expand in that direction. The evidence also suggests that the United States did not weigh the likely costs or scope of nation-building in Afghanistan prior to embarking on a similar mission in Iraq—even as we recognize that Iraq was a much different situation. In the best of cases, nation-building is extremely challenging, and the U.S. Government failed to grasp both the scope of nation-building in general, as well as the difficulty of Afghanistan in particular, before going forward. The notion of seeing Afghan nationhood through to its fruition remains a daunting, expensive, and lengthy proposition.

ENDNOTES - CHAPTER 2

1. Stephen Tanner, *Afghanistan: A Military History from Alexander the Great to the Fall of the Taliban*, Cambridge, MA: Da Capo Press, 2002, p. 214.

2. *Irregular Warfare: Countering Irregular Threats, Joint Operating Concept Version 2.0*, Washington, DC: Department of Defense, May 17, 2010, p. B-2.

3. *Ibid.*, p. B-1.

4. The President of the United States, *The National Security Strategy of the United States of America*, Washington, DC: U.S. Government Printing Office, March 2006, p. 1.

5. *Ibid.*, pp. 1-2.

6. *Ibid.*, p. 3.

7. *Ibid.*, p. 4.

8. Transcripts of these two speeches of March 27, 2009, and December 1, 2009, are available from *www.whitehouse.gov*.

9. The President of the United States, *The National Security Strategy of the United States of America*, Washington, DC: U.S. Government Printing Office, May 2010, p. 21.

10. U.S. Department of State and U.S. Agency for International Development, *Strategic Plan for Fiscal Years 2007-2012*, Washington, DC: U.S. Government Printing Office, May 7, 2008, pp. 9-42.

11. U.S. Department of State, *Afghanistan and Pakistan Regional Stabilization Strategy*, Washington, DC: State Department, February 2010, Table of Contents.

12. *Report on Progress toward Security and Stability in Afghanistan*, Report to Congress of April 2010, Washington, DC: Department of Defense, pp. 12-13.

13. Victoria Neufeldt, ed., *Webster's New World College Dictionary*, 3rd Ed., New York: MacMillan, 1996, p. 903.

14. Philip L. White and Michael L. White, eds., "What Is A Nationality?" Chap. 1, *Nationality in World History*, 2008, available from *www.nationalityinworldhistory.net*.

15. Neufeldt, p. 1309.

16. White and White.

17. *Ibid.*

18. *Ibid.*

19. William Maley, *Rescuing Afghanistan*, Sydney, Australia: University of New South Wales Press, 2006, p. 15.

20. *Ibid.*

21. *Ibid.*, p. 17.

22. *Ibid.*, p. 16.

23. *Ibid.*, p. 19.

24. Ashraf Ghani and Clare Lockhart, *Fixing Failed States*, Oxford, UK: Oxford University Press, 2008, pp. 124-163.

25. Thomas S. Szayna, Derek Eaton, and Amy Richardson, *Preparing the Army for Stability Operations*, Santa Monica, CA: Rand Corporation, 2007, pp. 16-17.

26. *Ibid.*, pp. 131-226.

27. Department of the Army, *Field Manual (FM) 3-24: Counterinsurgency Field Manual*, Chicago, IL: University of Chicago Press Ed., 2007, p. 38.

28. *Ibid.*

29. Robert I. Rotberg, ed., *Building a New Afghanistan*, Cambridge, MA: World Peace Foundation and Brookings Institution, 2007, pp. 146-152.

30. Rajiv Chandrasekaran, "Sticker Shock," *The Washington Post National Weekly Edition*, October 12-18, 2009, p. 12.

31. Bob Woodward, "The Case for Afghanistan," *The Washington Post National Weekly Edition*, October 4-11, 2009, p. 6.

32. *Ibid.*

33. Karen DeYoung, "A Puzzle for Congress," *The Washington Post National Weekly Edition*, December 7-13, 2009, p. 19.

34. Amy Belasco, *The Cost of Iraq, Afghanistan, and Other GWOT Operations Since 9/11*, Washington, DC: Congressional Research Service, RL33110, May 15, 2009, summary.

35. Joseph J. Collins, *Understanding War in Afghanistan*, Washington, DC: National Defense University Press, 2011, p. 91.

36. Martin Ewans, *Conflict in Afghanistan: Studies in Asymmetric Warfare*, London, UK: Routledge, 2005, p. 1.

37. *Ibid.*, p. 218.

38. *Ibid.*, p. 217.

39. Radek Sikorski, "Mujaheddin Memories," *National Review*, Vol. 56, No. 16, August 23, 2004, p. 43; Review of Steve Coll's *Ghost Wars*, New York: Penguin, 2004.

40. *Ibid.*

41. Brian Glyn Williams, "Mullah Omar's Missiles," *Middle East Policy*, Winter 2008, Vol. 15, No. 4, p. 26.

42. Rajiv Chandrasekaran, "Nobody Wants to Tell Us Anything," *The Washington Post National Weekly Edition*, March 23-29, p. 17.

43. Colin S. Gray, *Irregular Enemies and the Essence of Strategy: Can the American Way of War Adapt?* Carlisle, PA: Strategic Studies Institute, U.S. Army War College, March 2006, p. vi.

44. *Ibid.*, pp. 9-10.

45. Steven Metz, "New Challenges and Old Concepts: Understanding 21st Century Insurgency," *Parameters*, Vol. 37, No. 4, Winter 2007-08, pp. 20-22.

46. *Ibid.*

47. *Ibid.*, pp. 30-31.

48. Matthew J. Morgan, *A Democracy is Born: An Insider's Account of the Battle Against Terrorism in Afghanistan*, Westport, CT: Praeger, 2007, p. 143.

49. Robert D. Crews and Amin Tarzi, eds., *The Taliban and the Crisis of Afghanistan*, Cambridge, MA: Harvard, 2008, p. 316.

50. Zeb B. Bradford, Jr., and Frederic J. Brown, *America's Army: A Model for Interagency Effectiveness*, Westport, CT: Praeger, 2008, p. xiii.

51. Anthony H. Cordesman, "Afghanistan, Iraq, and Self-Inflicted Wounds," unpublished presentation, Washington, DC:

Center for Strategic and International Studies, October 2007, pp. 3-5.

52. *Ibid.*

53. *Ibid.*, p. 12.

54. "New Strategy: 8 Year War," *The Observer-Reporter*, December 1, 2009, p. A2.

55. Crews and Tarzi, pp. 320-321.

56. *Ibid.*, p. 316.

57. Sikorski, p. 44; Review of Coll's *Ghost Wars*.

58. Sarah Chayes, *The Punishment of Virtue: Inside Afghanistan After the Taliban*, New York: Penguin, 2006, p. 77.

59. Morgan, p. 37.

60. Chayes, pp. 168-169.

61. *Ibid.*, pp. 182-183.

62. Hans Bennendijk and Stuart E. Johnson, eds, *Transforming for Stabilization and Reconstruction Operations*, Washington, DC: National Defense University Press, 2004, pp. 4-5.

63. Ewans, p. 219.

CHAPTER 3

EVOLVING U.S. STRATEGIC INTERESTS, OPTIONS, AND RISKS

> Afghanistan is doubtless the most hostile, fanatic country in the world today. There is no pretense of according Christians equal rights with Moslems. There are no banks. . . . (They) detest taxation and military service and welcome chaos and confusion. . . . No foreign lives can be protected and no foreign interests guaranteed.
>
> Congressional testimony of Wallace Murray Smith, Chief of the State Department's Division of Near Eastern Affairs, in 1930[1]

Ignored or shunned by the United States throughout much of history, the region including Afghanistan and Pakistan now commands America's focused strategic attention, encompassing within it a mix of vital, important, and peripheral U.S. national security interests. Among other major issues, these American regional strategic concerns include radical Islamist threats, potential nuclear weapons proliferation, the access to newly developed energy sources, a major flow of illegal narcotics, potential economic opportunities, and the rising challenges of China, Russia, Iran, and other regional powers. Once merely a global afterthought, this region is now one that cannot be safely ignored.

Nevertheless, while the United States unquestionably has clear, compelling, and vital interests in preventing the spread of nuclear weapons and in preventing transnational terrorist elements from staging their attacks from Afghanistan or Pakistan, it is not equally obvious that the United States has an important national security interest in achieving a democratic end-state in Afghanistan. In fact, the pursuit of that peripheral strategic interest is costly enough to potentially undermine the pursuit of other more essential national interests around the globe, without really guaranteeing anything in the long run. This skeptical perspective is reinforced only when one considers the array of nations and transnational actors whose own interests stand in direct opposition to this goal.

Consequently, it is difficult to justify the need for full-blown nation-building and counterinsurgency (COIN) in Afghanistan, as opposed to other strategic options that involve either a minimal presence, such as raiding suspected terrorist bases, or a medium-sized presence in the country that would remain focused primarily on counterterrorism. Both of these alternative strategic options can be framed in ways that protect the vital American national security interests in the region, while also entailing far lower costs and fewer corresponding risks. Likewise, in seeking to create a viable nation-state in Afghanistan, it is not even clear that the United States has framed its Afghan goals correctly, given the decline in the influence of nation-states—especially weak or failing ones—in the face of globalization, growing transnational movements, organized drug crime, and other modern trends. So it is unclear that the nation-state is even the relevant construct, or that the results of nation-building will necessarily be positive and consistent with U.S. interests.

Put more directly, success in nation-building in Afghanistan will not correspond automatically with positive Afghan political relationships in the long run, since there will always be an uncertainty of political outcome even if the United States and the North Atlantic Treaty Organization (NATO) are successful in building some sort of democracy in Afghanistan. That is, it is hard to predict exactly what type of democracy would ultimately emerge in Afghanistan—with potential models ranging from the Western version to the Iranian, Pakistani, or Iraqi types—and that eventual outcome would bring with it different possibilities in terms of a regime that either shares or opposes U.S. interests. Exacerbating these strategic uncertainties, the United States has done a poor job until recently of precisely articulating its interests, leading to a situation in which America's national security strategies and its strategy for Afghanistan and the region have often been unclear, poorly defined, and shifting over recent history.

A THUMBNAIL SKETCH OF PAST U.S. INVOLVEMENT

The history of U.S. involvement in Afghanistan and Pakistan has been characterized by a few key themes, chief among them the fact that the United States has had little interest in the region other than engaging in periodic marriages of convenience when interests dictated them, much like other powers. As another recurring theme, Afghan and Pakistani leaders have shown a keen ability to manipulate those foreign powers and their shifting interests over the years, often to their own personal advantage. These Afghan and Pakistani leaders have shown a consistent willingness to shift allegiances quickly when circumstances favored that choice, and Afghanistan has also shown little inclination to fix its own problems internally over the course of history, since most development has come from external sources. The Pakistani Army and Inter-Services

Intelligence Directorate (ISI) often pursue their own separate interests, aiming to protect their disproportionate influence and privileged positions within Pakistani society.

Throughout the centuries, Afghanistan has been largely viewed as an insignificant backwater territory.[2] In the modern era, the United States had few contacts prior to the 1920s with either the Middle East or South and Central Asia.[3] Among the other major powers, the Germans aimed to achieve some influence in Afghanistan in the 1930s through developmental aid and engineering projects, but met with limited success.[4] U.S. engagement with the Middle East increased prior to World War II, as the American business community succeeded in becoming involved in Middle Eastern oil production, but the United States still had next to no contact with Afghanistan or Pakistan at that point. Upon achieving its independence in 1947, Pakistan reached out to the United States to request economic and military aid, but American policymakers rebuffed the Pakistanis after deciding that the unstable country could offer few real assurances in return.[5]

During this same post-World War II period—a time that featured aggressive American and Russian efforts at building advantageous strategic relationships elsewhere around the globe—the United States held Afghanistan at arm's length, as U.S. policymakers were suspicious of Afghan motives in requesting aid in the late 1940s. The United States believed that the Afghans' overtures were aimed mainly at achieving traction on the Pushtunistan issue, and as a result, the United States gave the Afghan government only a fraction of the aid it had requested.[6] Continuing this ambivalent stance, the United States had little involvement with Afghanistan over those years, including rebuffing Afghan requests for arms and aid as late as the 1950s, during the height of the Cold War. The United States viewed Afghanistan as unstable, and thought that the country would be unlikely to mount any real opposition should the Soviet Union decide to intervene there militarily.[7]

In spite of the fact that the United States was then competing with the Soviet Union for influence in many other places around the world at the time, the United States might have still continued to ignore Pakistani entreaties for aid—and Afghanistan altogether. However, in 1949, India recognized Communist China and, in response, the United States decided to work with India's Muslim enemy.[8] A few years later, in 1954, the United States rebuffed an Afghan request for a mutual security pact, after which the Afghans almost immediately turned to the Soviets for economic and security assistance, which the Russians willingly provided.[9] The Afghans then allowed the Russians to fill this vacuum, but only to a certain extent, as the Afghan leadership saw advantages in playing off one benefactor against the other.[10] In 1955, this Afghan relationship with the Soviet Union was formally approved by a national *loya jirga*, setting the stage for continuing Russian involvement in Afghan affairs in the years ahead.[11]

Reversing course, in the late 1950s the United States decided not to cede control of Afghanistan wholly to the Russians, embarking upon an economic development and cultural exchange program. This program featured educational exchanges, economic aid, and other development assistance, including the construction of an 11,000-foot runway in Kandahar capable of handling high performance aircraft—ironically now serving as the staging area for the major U.S. presence in the southern part of the country.[12] Even so, Afghanistan developed two competing Communist Party factions in the 1960s, and with them came another attempt at social and cultural modernization, reforms which were to be rebuffed once again by the conservative Islamic mullahs and the tribes.[13] The United States continued to provide modest developmental aid into the early 1960s, mostly tied to road construction and infrastructure development, but by the mid-1960s this aid had dwindled to almost nothing in light of the emergence of a significant Communist movement.[14]

As U.S. interest dwindled once again, the Communist movement gained traction through the mid-1970s, and Afghanistan remained relatively calm. In October 1978, the now-Communist government announced major reforms, among them land redistribution, equal rights for women, language rules, and other reforms that antagonized the majority Pashtun and other conservative Muslim elements of society.[15] The Afghan army deserted en masse, the tribes took up arms, and revolts broke out across the country. About 100 Russian military advisers and their families were murdered, some having their severed heads paraded around Kabul and Herat on poles.[16] In retaliation, the Soviets increased their military aid and began attacking rebel positions, committing their own major atrocities as they did so.[17] By December 1979, the Soviets had deployed new forces to support the Communist government and had begun major operations.

Sensing a potential opening, the U.S. Government began to provide small amounts of aid to the rebelling Afghans in the summer of 1979. Having already lost one base of operations with close proximity to the Soviet Union in Iran, the United States perceived an opportunity to gain a foothold in Afghanistan to make up for that strategic loss.[18] Furthermore, during this Afghan resistance to the Soviet invasion, the U.S. Government funneled its arms and aid to the Afghans through the Pakistani government and ISI, reinforcing the Pakistani intelligence services' relationships with the tribal warlords.[19] Throughout the years in which the United States provided support to the mujahedeen, Pakistan's ISI insisted on serving as the middleman in the transfers, and as U.S. aid was funneled through Pakistani warehouses, the ISI came to exert much control over that process.[20] The ISI also conducted the training of the mujahedeen in the new weapons systems that were supplied to them by the United States and others, further cementing their Afghan relationships.[21]

After the eventual Soviet withdrawal and the collapse of the Afghan Communist government, the United States was largely content to walk away from the situation, having achieved its near-term objectives. Even in the period just prior to September 11, 2001 (9/11), the United States in general, and Joint Chiefs of Staff Chairman Hugh Shelton in particular, showed very little interest in seeking any military solutions to the problems posed by al Qaeda and the Taliban in Afghanistan.[22] Reacting to 9/11, and as part of the initial military operations in Afghanistan in 2001, the Central Intelligence Agency (CIA) paid approximately $70 million to warlords and local tribal leaders for support of U.S. operations.[23] This strategic choice, along with the previous reliance upon the ISI for the distribution of aid, ultimately carried with it adverse consequences for the nation-building effort to come, regardless of the merits of the arguments for making the choice in the first place.

U.S. NATIONAL INTERESTS IN AFGHANISTAN AND THE REGION

Among students of American foreign affairs, there are three generally accepted core U.S. national interests: *physical security*, or the protection of the people and property of the United States from attack; *economic prosperity*; and the *promotion of American values*.[24] From these three core strategic interests, strategists derive more specific national interests, interests that ultimately serve as the basis for the generation of strategy, policy, and resource allocation priorities. Applying the U.S. Army War College typology of *intensity*, these specific national interests are typically categorized as being *vital*, *important*, or *peripheral*, depending upon their criticality and the likely impact that their violation would have for the three core U.S. interests. *Vital* interests are that which "will have immediate consequences for core national interests" if unfulfilled, while *important* interests will eventually have adverse consequences. *Peripheral* interests are those that may be desirable but are unlikely to have an effect if remaining unfulfilled.[25]

During the Cold War, primary U.S. interests in the region were in preventing the Soviet Union from achieving dominance over Afghan territory and the associated proximity to the oil fields and warm water ports of Iran and the Middle East.[26] Having achieved those objectives relatively inexpensively with the Soviet withdrawal in 1989, the United States was content to leave Afghanistan alone, much as it had through most of the 20th century. As Afghanistan melted into chaos, the United States had an interest in preventing the Russians and Iranians from gaining control over large portions of the Afghan territory, and so the United States is generally believed to have encouraged the rising Taliban faction to take control of the territory, at least initially.[27] Otherwise, the United States had little interest in Afghanistan and disengaged for the most part from Afghan affairs.

In terms of U.S. current strategic interests in Afghanistan and in South and Central Asia, without question the United States has a vital national interest in disrupting and defeating al Qaeda and in removing the terrorists' Pakistani and Afghan safe havens. Protecting the United States from attacks by other radical Islamist elements operating in the region is another vital U.S. national security interest. The United States also has a similarly vital interest in preventing Afghanistan and Pakistan from becoming exporters of radical Islamic fundamentalism, in addition to ensuring that Pakistan's nuclear weapons are secured and kept out of the hands of terrorists. The United States also has an important national security interest in stemming the flow of opium and heroin from the region. Other important U.S. interests include countering Iran, creating stability in Afghanistan and across the region, and gaining access to the recently discovered Afghan mineral, oil, and gas deposits. Perhaps more peripherally, other U.S. interests include promoting American values throughout the region, realizing an Afghan democracy, and developing the region's potential for creating energy pipelines through Afghanistan and the Central Asian republics. For all of these reasons, Central and South Asia certainly represent a vital front in the global war against terrorism.

Offering a somewhat different take on these interests, strategic thinker Stephen Blank argues that U.S. involvement in the region is primarily strategic in nature, or tied to interactions with other major powers, rather than depending upon access to energy supplies or the goal of democratization, as others have suggested.[28] In particular, he notes that Central Asia's proximity to Russia and China gives those countries a strategic importance as Russia and China rise in economic and military power.[29] These strategic concerns therefore include maintaining access to Central Asian airspace and territory, as well as the development of alternative sources of energy and the access to them. Blank also sees Afghanistan as a place where the United States can blunt rising Iranian influence.[30]

In its own analysis, the Bush administration identified three major U.S. interests in Afghanistan and Central Asia, including security, democracy development, and economic opportunity.[31] The administration perceived a clear and vital national security interest in achieving an "open door" or "equal access" to Central Asian energy markets, as well as preventing a Russian-controlled energy cartel from emerging in the region.[32] Proving this possibility to be no idle threat, then-Russian president Vladimir Putin suggested such a cartel to Iran and the Shanghai Cooperation Organization in 2006.[33] The United States also clearly has a vital interest in the stability of the Pakistani regime, since Pakistan is a nuclear power with radical Islamic elements inside its borders and approximately 60 weapons by most estimates.[34] Illustrating that not all perceive these interests in the same way, Europe is believed to be the source of Pakistan's uranium enrichment technology, while China is believed to have provided the blueprint for Pakistan's nuclear weapons and missile technology.[35] Other analysts have placed the primary emphasis on other U.S. interests in the region, including the promotion of human rights, the equitable treatment of women, stemming the flow of illegal narcotics, retrieving leftover Stinger missiles given to the anti-Soviet forces of the 1980s, and eradicating land mines.[36]

Without question, each of these interests is legitimate. But while they are real, only a few can be characterized as being truly vital to U.S. national security, when compared with the standard of the three core national security interests. So merely identifying legitimate interests is not enough. Simple logic and the realities of resource constraints dictate that the United States cannot pursue any strategic option—however well intentioned—that furthers an important or peripheral national interest, but does so at such a cost that it risks undermining truly vital interests.

COMPETING NATIONAL AND TRANSNATIONAL INTERESTS IN THE REGION

Adding additional layers of complexity to any calculations of strategic interests and their intensity, the United States pursues its national security objectives within a dynamic context of competing national and transnational actors with their own interests. Setting aside for the moment the central challenges presented by the Taliban and other militant factions inside the Afghan borders, many of these national and transnational actors pursue their own competing interests in the region, with some of those competing powers perceiving a stable, secure, self-sustaining, and democratic Afghanistan as antithetical to their own concerns. Examining these competing actors more closely, any serious discussion of competing interests in the region must begin with Pakistan, given that country's close historical, political, and demographic ties with Afghanistan.

Pakistan.

Throughout its brief history, a primary national interest for Pakistan has been the effort to protect its border with India, and this overriding national interest drives most of Pakistan's actions relative to Afghanistan. This relationship is also strained by enduring animosities between Pakistan and Afghanistan over the Pushtunistan issue, dating back to the origins of Pakistani independence in 1947.[37] Pakistan continues to have a clear interest in preventing the creation of Pushtunistan.[38] Pakistan also retains a vital interest in being able to influence events in Afghanistan, the original reason that Pakistan supported the Taliban in their takeover of the government in the 1990s.[39] Pakistan admits to having supported and supplied the Taliban prior to 9/11, and numerous Pakistani government officials—most notably from ISI—have maintained close personal connections to high-ranking Taliban leaders, including Mullah Omar.[40] In the Pakistani view, a weak Afghanistan provides strategic depth in Pakistan's defense against India.

Seeking to reinforce this influence in Afghanistan, Pakistani officials and their agents have been implicated in smuggling weapons and ammunition to the Taliban at least as recently as 2007.[41] The Pakistani government, mainly through ISI, has also maintained a strong relationship with warlord Gulbuddin Hekmatyar, a relationship that predated the rise of the Taliban. From the outset, this relationship had the effect of souring relationships with both Ahmed Shah Masoud of the Northern Alliance and Mullah Mohammed Rabbani, the leader of Afghanistan's pre-Taliban government, and those animosities persist today.[42] Pakistan also has a significant national interest in securing and controlling transit across Afghanistan as a commercial trade route, and the Pakistanis have been more than willing to work with the Taliban to that end in the past.[43] The fact that both Afghanistan and Pakistan are transit countries for the Central Asian drug trade has added further tensions to the already strained Afghan-Pakistani relationship.[44]

As another key element, the massive migration of Afghan refugees to Pakistan has served as a major source of friction between the two countries, with the Afghan refugees of the western Pakistani *madrassas* creating domestic unrest and overloading Pakistani social systems. The number of Afghan refugees in Pakistan as a result of the Soviet invasion was estimated at about 3 million in the 1990s, placing a huge burden on Pakistan's basic social services and creating another major incentive for Pakistan to intervene in Afghan affairs.[45] According to most recent estimates, there are still more than one million Afghan refugees in Pakistan today.[46] Ironically, however, these refugees have also unintentionally provided the Pakistani government with a useful resource in that government's pursuit of the goals of bringing order to unruly Afghanistan and installing an allied government.[47]

In any event, Pakistan has a vital interest in maintaining order and social control in its Federally Administered Tribal Areas (FATA), which, like Afghanistan have a large number of Pashtun tribes and subtribes, among them Mahsuds, Mohmands, Yusafzais, Afridis, Daurs, and Wazirs.[48] As in Afghanistan, the central government wields little control over these tribal groups.[49] Seeking to minimize tensions with this population, the Pakistani government has often treated the various domestic terrorist groups differently, according to their particular targets. For example, Pakistan has habitually attacked al Qaeda terrorists in order to avoid American disfavor, but it has allowed anti-Indian groups to operate in Kashmir while seeking accommodation with Talibanic groups and avoiding direct confrontation until forced to do so by the U.S. Government.[50] Pakistan must also contend with an underlying conflict between Islamic fundamentalist elements and the modernist, secular elements of Pakistani society.[51] Most recently, the Pakistani government has changed its policy toward the Kashmiri militants, resulting in attacks on Pakistani government assets in Kashmir and the rise of the Punjabi Taliban.[52]

Finally, the Pakistani Army also seeks to protect its own privileged position within Pakistani society, and it maintains this position in part due to a patron-client relationship with the Pakistani bureaucracy and a mutually beneficial relationship with several Islamist political parties.[53] Pakistan's military and ISI remain deeply suspicious of long-term U.S. intentions for the region, and they also remain concerned that Pakistan will be left with major turmoil in the FATA and in Afghanistan once the United States departs.[54] The recent massive flooding has only exacerbated these concerns. Like the Afghans, however, the Pakistanis have proven to be quite adept at manipulating their relationships with stronger foreign powers in order to achieve assistance and protection over the years.

Other key players in the region include the Central Asian republics, which also have significant interests in Afghanistan. These interests include the traditional, ethnic, and historical ties that Turkmenistan, Uzbekistan, and Tajikistan have with their ethnic counterparts on the northern side of the Hindu Kush. These countries also have major economic and security interests that are affected directly by the stability, security, and criminality of Afghanistan—concerns heightened further by the Central Asian republics' proximity to Iran, Russia, and China.

Turkmenistan.

As a major oil and natural gas producer, Turkmenistan has an interest in gaining secure access to the energy market in Pakistan, and the Pakistani government sees this possibility as being in its interests as well.[55] Turkmenistan has direct transportation infrastructure linkages to Iran, and that country has also benefited from Afghan instability by signing an energy pipeline agreement that would likely have gone to Afghanistan if the Afghan nation had been stable and secure.[56] In general, Turkmenistan has had closer and more positive ties to Afghanistan than many other countries of the region—relations driven primarily by Turkmenistan's concerns over its ethnic counterparts in Afghanistan and its desire to build a natural gas pipeline across Afghanistan to Pakistan.[57] Turkmenistan is basically liberal in a religious sense, and the country has an interest in preventing the Taliban's radical brand of Islam from making its way into the country, although some *madrassas* have already been established there.[58]

Uzbekistan.

Uzbekistan also has a large ethnic connection to Afghanistan, though the two countries' common border is relatively small and Uzbekistan's transportation infrastructure connections to the country are limited. The Uzbeks have some connection with Afghan warlord Abdul Rashid Dostum, and have openly supported him and his political goals in the past. Along these lines, Uzbekistan has been similar to the other Central Asian republics in seeking to resist Talibanic influence in the country.[59] But while Pakistan supported the Taliban in part as a way of stabilizing its neighbor, the Uzbeks know that much support for the domestic insurgent group, Islamic Movement of Uzbekistan, came from Afghanistan when the Taliban were in control.[60] Uzbekistan also has other economic interests tied to Afghanistan, and the country is like many others in desiring to reduce the drug trafficking that passes through the common border.

Tajikistan.

Like the other Central Asian republics, Tajikistan has a strong ethnic and cultural connection to Afghanistan's Tajik minority, and in fact there are still Tajik refugees in Afghanistan who fled Tajikistan's own civil war.[61] Like its fellow Central Asian republics, Tajikistan has an interest in preventing Talibanic influence from making its way into the country, and has not supported the Taliban, whether in or out of power. Tajikistan has its own problems with domestic radical Islamic fundamentalist groups, evidenced most recently in the ambush and killing of 23 Tajik government troops near the Afghan border. This attack followed on the heels of a series of deadly terrorist bombings and large-scale prison escapes. The country also has economic interests and counterdrug concerns that are affected directly by Afghanistan.

Transnational Drug Criminals.

Transnational crime associated with opium trade directly and significantly affects all the states in the Central Asian region. The opium trade in particular has a significant impact on the Kyrgyzstan and Tajikistan economies and their gross domestic product (GDP).[62] Nine-tenths of the demand for Afghan opium comes from Europe and Russia, giving those actors an incentive to act, as well.[63]

Al Qaeda.

It is worth noting that al Qaeda, as a transnational radical Islamist movement, has its own interests, distinct from the Taliban who formerly hosted them. For example, al Qaeda is less willing to accommodate other actors, as its adherents' primary interests are global rather than regional, and the movement's goals are not tied to any one parcel of territory, unlike those of the Taliban.[64] Before his death, Osama bin Laden was open about his desire to acquire a nuclear weapon, and at least since the 1990s, al Qaeda has been attempting to purchase nuclear materials on the black market.[65] Bin Laden and al Qaeda invested in the government of the Sudan's efforts to produce nerve agents, and clear evidence of the movement's nuclear ambitions was found in Taliban safe houses after the fall of the Taliban in Afghanistan in 2001.[66] As a separate issue, and making this situation even more dangerous for the West, the technology for producing chemical weapons is becoming more readily accessible. And although the technology for producing biological weapons is still problematic for insurgent groups at present, it is expected that advances in other biological research and technology will make this possibility more likely in the years ahead.[67]

Iran.

Iran has long-held animosities toward Afghanistan, going back centuries to the time when Afghanistan's Sunni Muslim army toppled the Persian government. Iran also resents the impact that Afghan drugs and the smuggling of other contraband have had on Iranian society.[68] The Iranians have a historical and cultural aversion to the Taliban, given the movement's Pashtun core and the longtime Pashtun dominance of the Hazaras and other Afghan Shiite factions.[69] Although the evidence pertaining to any direct Iranian support for the Taliban is mixed, Iran clearly aims to expand and consolidate its influence within the country and hopes to influence the outcome of the COIN through an information operations campaign aimed at turning the Afghan people against the U.S. occupation.[70] Various Afghan government sources have also claimed that the Iranians are providing arms and ammunition to other, non-Taliban insurgent factions, but the United States has not confirmed those claims.[71] Other specific Iranian interests include capitalizing economically from their historical and cultural ties to Herat and other parts of western Afghanistan, as well as maintaining access to Central Asia for the purpose of trade.[72]

Some analysts have argued that Iran has a direct interest in keeping Afghanistan unstable in order to make the Iranian trade routes to the sea more secure, leading the Central Asian republics to continue to use Iranian routes in spite of them being longer and less direct.[73] Others argue that these economic interests are trumped by the economic and social burdens imposed on Iran by an estimated one million Afghan refugees who still remain there.[74] The Iranians may also believe that an unstable Afghanistan, one requiring a continued major American presence, will serve to dilute the American hard power that can be aimed at them. But the Iranians also clearly feel the pressure of having American military forces on either side of them in Iraq and Afghanistan.

Russia.

Russia has long had an interest in Afghanistan, dating back at least to the 19th century and the "Great Game" with Britain. Early on, the Russians' primary interest in Afghanistan was in enlarging their perimeter of security, a strategy they pursued by surrounding themselves with Central Asian client states.[75] They were also pursuing this interest, as well as the goal of extending Communism's reach, when they moved to prop up the failing Communist regime in Afghanistan in the late 1970s. Once the Soviet Union broke apart, and with the rise of the Taliban in Afghanistan, the Russians became very concerned about the possibility of the Taliban's radically conservative brand of Islam being exported into those newly independent Muslim republics to their south.[76]

The natural resources and economic markets of the Central Asian countries also remain very important to Russia, so Russia has taken diplomatic, economic, and military steps to help maintain the stability of these republics and Russian access. Russia also has vital domestic interests affected there, including security and energy economics.[77] To this end, they also aim to maintain monopolistic control over energy production in Central Asia, exerted through control of the pipeline networks in the region, enabling the Russians to pay less than market value for natural gas from Turkmenistan, Uzbekistan, and Kazakhstan.[78] The Russians view any move toward an open, competitive market for Central Asian energy as a threat to their vital interests, a stance that is antithetical to U.S. energy interests.[79] Russia also views the continuing U.S. presence in Central Asia as a direct security threat, related to its fear of U.S. airstrikes from Central Asian territory or the Indian Ocean.[80] Since the Russian military considers the United States to be its primary adversary, it has begun to revitalize its air defense systems with a potential U.S. military threat in mind.[81]

China.

The Central Asian countries' close proximity to China has led to Chinese concerns about the possible security threats that these republics represent. As such, China has sought to reduce radical Islamist influence for domestic security reasons, while also seeing an interest in limiting the U.S. influence in the region.[82] For these reasons, along with concerns about the destabilizing nature of the associated transitions, both Russia and China have supported resistance to American efforts at democratizing the Central Asian countries.[83] China also convened the Shanghai Cooperation Group, later the Shanghai Cooperation Organization, with the specific goals of neutralizing Afghanistan's "Islamist proselytizing" and "separatist propaganda."[84] Likewise, China has economic interests in developing trade with Afghanistan and gaining access to Afghan natural resources and raw materials.

Therefore, with all of these interests in mind, both China and Russia have a compelling interest in stability in the region, regardless of the forms or character of the governments that can provide that stability.[85] In this vein, China is well known for setting aside human rights concerns or similar considerations when offering to do business with various regimes. China also views the Central Asian region as representing opportunities for trade that will enhance the Chinese economy and its domestic economic growth.[86] In sum, China clearly values stability over democracy.

India.

India has had a long history of economic and security interaction with Afghanistan that predates the creation of Pakistan.[87] Given India's strained relationship with Pakistan, India sees a potential advantage in poor relations continuing between Pakistan and Afghanistan.[88] To promote this interest, India has on occasion promoted the Pushtunistan issue, with the goal of keeping that source of Pakistani-Afghan contention at the forefront of the relationship between the two countries.[89] Not surprisingly then, India did not support the Taliban in their rise to power, given the Taliban's close connection to Pakistan, and it has no desire to see the Taliban regain control of the country. India's growing economy also demands additional energy sources, so India has another interest in gaining and maintaining access to the energy-producing Central Asian republics. With similar motives in mind, India has typically tried to act in ways that are complementary to Russian interests and policies in the region, since India depends to a fair extent on Russian energy products.[90] As one might expect, given their respective interests, the countries of India, Pakistan, and Iran each offered to rebuild the Afghan army and police, offers the United States managed to deflect for its own reasons.[91] Most directly, India has a clear interest in seeing the confrontation between Afghanistan and Pakistan continue—an interest further served by continuing Afghan instability and a corresponding diversion of Pakistani resources to the Afghan-Pakistan border. In many respects, Indian interests in Afghanistan are antithetical to U.S. interests.

Saudi Arabia.

Saudi Arabia supported the Taliban regime with money and formal recognition during its existence, making it one of only a few countries to do so. Saudi Arabia has also acted to support its regional ally Pakistan, because in the Saudi view, Pakistan serves as a counterweight to its rival in Iran.[92] The Saudis no longer openly support the Taliban, but they still see remaining interests in shaping the Talibanic movement and the region, especially given Osama bin Laden's statements advocating violence against the Saudi government.[93] The Saudis also have a clear interest in limiting the attacks of al Qaeda and other fundamentalist groups on U.S. facilities and interests for reasons related to their own economic interests and physical security.[94]

When these competing interests and influences are viewed in the aggregate, it is particularly noteworthy that the United States actually holds in common a number of vital interests with China, Russia, and other major players in Afghanistan and Central Asia. These common interests are especially clear in shared concerns about regional stability. But while these shared interests could potentially serve as a common ground on which the major powers could engage in multilateral, collective action in pursuit of their common interests, some of these same actors also stand in staunch opposition to the U.S. goal of creating an Afghan democracy. In sum, a peripheral interest may undermine a vital one.

U.S. STRATEGIC OPTIONS AND RISKS

The first and possibly most critical step in crafting strategy is the identification and prioritization of national security interests, since this problem definition should drive the determination of desired objectives, strategic options, and resource allocations. As noted earlier, the United States does in fact have a number of vital national security interests at stake in Afghanistan and the region surrounding it. These vital American national security interests include:
- The disruption and defeat of al Qaeda;
- The denial of terrorist safe havens in Pakistan and Afghanistan;
- The protection of the United States from attacks by other radical Islamist elements operating in the region;
- Preventing Afghanistan and Pakistan from becoming exporters of radical Islamic fundamentalism;
- Stability within the Pakistani regime and the region; and,
- Nuclear safety and security in Pakistan.

Of course, the United States has other important and peripheral interests at stake in Afghanistan and the region, but U.S. national strategy should necessarily be focused first on fulfilling the vital interests, after which important and peripheral interests can be pursued when resources and circumstances permit. In any event, once identified, this list of vital interests serves as the primary basis for the generation of regional strategic objectives, or the *ends* to be pursued using available resources and capabilities, once balanced against the competing but similarly critical requirements driven by other vital American interests in other regions of the world.

So, in this rational crafting of national strategy, the identified vital interests must be linked to potential strategic options—or *ways*—that can be applied to protect or further those interests, constrained by the limits on *means*, or the specific resources and capabilities represented within American instruments of power.[95] These instruments of American power include diplomatic, informational, military, and economic resources and capabilities within the U.S. Government's control. Of course, American decisionmakers intend this process to be as rational as possible, though in reality the process is just as often a political one. In any case, while the strategic *ends* should predominate in the development of national strategy, the *ways* in which those ends will be pursued must necessarily be constrained by the actual *means* available to pursue them.

Noteworthy by its omission from the list of vital interests above is any national interest in a democratic Afghanistan. That is, while a stable, secure, self-sustaining, and democratic Afghanistan might reasonably be expected to help further these vital interests, it is not clear that the creation of a viable, democratic nation-state in Afghanistan is either necessary or sufficient in and of itself to protect those vital interests.

Accordingly, the pursuit of any strategic option centered on the concept of creating a democratic, self-sustaining state must be balanced against the costs, uncertainty, and risks associated with achieving that ambitious and costly strategic objective. This assessment is true of any strategic option. Finally, once these prospective ways and means are identified, the strategic options must be judged against the criteria of *feasibility, suitability,* and *acceptability*.[96] Put another way, the strategic options must be judged against the criteria of available means, legal and ethical suitability, political feasibility, cost, risk, and the likelihood of success; while the ends drive the process, the ways are constrained by resources.

These rational linkages, however, have been conspicuously absent in the numerous debates regarding Afghanistan. That is, throughout the course of the U.S. and NATO intervention, not only has there been little agreement regarding the specific American interests at stake in the region, but there has been even less consensus related to the desirability of any one particular strategic option or any one strategic direction. Instead, a major debate has raged inside and outside the U.S. Government, in its essence focused on the particular ways and strategic methods to be pursued; this debate has basically devolved into a rancorous disagreement over whether American interests are best served by engaging in counterterrorism or COIN as the primary way forward.

Unfortunately, for the most part, this debate has sidestepped any serious analysis or prioritization of interests, or any similarly frank consideration of the existence and availability of the associated agency capabilities and resources required to realize those strategic concepts in the first place. Instead, the debate has devolved into one side arguing for eliminating the terrorists—the primary aim of the U.S. and NATO operations during the Bush years—while others have argued for focusing on classic counterinsurgency techniques and nation-building objectives, among them population protection, the development of social institutions, and other similar tasks.[97] Just as importantly, there has also been little discussion of the second-order implications of these strategic options for U.S. interests, viewed broadly. In this sense, then, American policymakers and their various critics have approached these strategic deliberations almost exactly backwards, arguing about the strategic ways before analyzing the vital interests and the desired ends, and without any serious consideration of the constraints imposed on those ways by the actual means available to operationalize them—let alone the corresponding risks.

Representative of this current debate, strategic thinker Edward Luttwak argues for abandoning nation-building and COIN in favor of raids targeting terrorist operations, citing what he sees as tactical victories that are strategic failures, bringing with them unintended adverse consequences.[98] Other observers, such as former CIA analyst Michael Scheuer and former Afghan public finance minister Ashraf Ghani, offer major criticisms of the mission in Afghanistan, assailing what they see as a lack of strategic direction altogether, while challenging many of the U.S. Government's basic assumptions underlying the mission.[99] The same type of ways-centered debate took place during the Obama administration's strategy review of 2009. This disjointed process was reflected in the eventual outcome, a strategic decision that could be fairly described as falling somewhere in the mushy middle between the two debated options.

Setting aside for the moment relevant questions about the ultimate strategic ends the coalition seeks to achieve, the definition of potential strategic options in Afghanistan encompasses numerous other operational-level variables, as well. Among them are the specific operational objectives, the particular instruments of national power and resources to be employed in the pursuit of those objectives, the costs associated with the options, the risks associated with their commitment, and other essential considerations. Viewed broadly, there are basically four prospective ways forward, if the problem is considered without regard to resource constraints or risks. These four strategic options include the full-blown "COIN and nation-building" option; a "counterterrorist presence" option; a "counterterrorist raiding" option; and the "diplomacy and aid alone" option or in effect walking away from the problem. Of course, recent events and history suggest that this last option is neither feasible nor sustainable now, if it ever was.

Each of the three potentially acceptable strategic options comes with substantial costs. To put these costs into perspective, in fiscal year 2010, the Obama administration requested $65 billion to fund operations in Afghanistan, even before adding the increased costs associated with the McChrystal COIN plan.[100] Through the end of fiscal year 2009, the operations in Afghanistan and Iraq had combined to cost the United States more than $940 billion since their inception in 2001, with the under-resourced mission in Afghanistan representing $223 billion of that total alone.[101] Current costs amount to approximately $2 billion per week for the U.S. operations in the theater. Added to this huge sum are the other less tangible costs of these commitments, as well as the opportunity costs associated with spending these enormous sums of money in sustaining the major force levels required to support the operations. In sum, the missions in Afghanistan and Iraq have added significantly to the burgeoning U.S. national debt, while also increasing the strain on an already overstretched federal budget. This fiscal irresponsibility, made worse by the severe recession, continues to limit U.S. flexibility in fixing its own economic problems at home, while contributing to a crisis of confidence in government.

With all of these effects in mind, strategic thinker Andrew Bacevich argues that the world's remaining superpower lacks the political, military, and economic resources to "support a large-scale, protracted conflict without . . . inflicting severe political and economic damage on itself."[102] The decision to commit massive resources to irregular warfare and nation-building has also severely limited the U.S. ability to apply much-needed military, economic, and diplomatic resources elsewhere around the world, while entailing major strategic and operational risks in the process. Not surprisingly, a 2008 assessment of the U.S. military, widely reported in the press, identified military personnel strained by the long battlefield tours, equipment degradation due to overuse, and threats from countries with weapons of mass destruction (WMD) as major sources of risk, each made worse by the operations in Afghanistan and Iraq. As an even more direct consequence of these strategic choices, Admiral Eric Olson, commander of the U.S. Special Operations Command, acknowledged to the Senate Armed Services Committee recently that the wars in Afghanistan and Iraq had significantly limited the effort to keep WMD out of the hands of terrorists, noting both a "decreased level of training" among the special operating forces as well as a broadly reduced availability of those assets for the mission.[103]

Similarly, the uncertain outcomes of these operations carry with them other sources of potential strategic and operational risk. As an example, we have seen the transnational terrorist elements merely relocate to the FATA when confronted with a U.S. and NATO presence in Afghanistan, since they even now brazenly attack the Pakistani Army. A related risk is the possibility that increasing the numbers, training, and weaponry of the Afghan National Security Forces (ANSF) could, in fact, merely reinforce the network of corruption that already exists in Afghanistan. That is, increasing the ANSF could ultimately connect violence, drug monies, voter manipulation, and the siphoning of funds to corrupt police and public officials, similar to the effects described by Enrique Desmond Arias in his work on "violent democracies" in Latin America.[104] Put another way, a strong Afghan state security apparatus could actually bring with it unintended and adverse consequences, consequences that ultimately prove antithetical to U.S. national security interests in the long run.

Likewise, there are also risks associated with the major assumptions embedded within each of the strategic options, among them the somewhat shaky assumptions that the NATO presence will continue. Another assumption is that the coalition will be successful in building an ANSF of sufficient quantity and quality—and in a timely enough manner—to hand off the battle to the Afghan government within a sustainable timeframe. To date, the effort to build an Afghan Army has been generally successful, but the Afghan police continue to pose major challenges. Other major risks include the continuing impact of these incredibly expensive operations on American national debt, as well as the unanticipated but very real impacts of these missions on America's ability to respond to other emergent crises around the world for the duration of the Afghan mission. There are other similarly serious second-order effects of this major commitment, as well.

Finally, and perhaps most prominently of all the risks embedded within these potential strategic ways, is the major uncertainty of outcome once nation-building is complete — a risk that is clearly most pronounced within the current COIN and nation-building option. That is, the United States, NATO, and other key actors operating in Afghanistan could spend years working to build a viable state and democracy in Afghanistan, only to fail to achieve results consistent with any Western sense of those concepts. At this point, it is neither clear what standard of democracy we aim to achieve, nor what standard of democracy is even feasible in Afghanistan anyway, given the challenges that the country represents. Some scholars argue that a good or better democracy must include a number of basic elements, including: (1) universal, adult suffrage; (2) recurring, free, competitive, and fair elections; (3) more than one serious political party; and, (4) alternative sources of information, as well as the freedom among citizens to organize, debate, and articulate preferences openly.[105] It is hard to imagine this brand of democracy emerging in Afghanistan without a lengthy and costly commitment.

On the other hand, it is not nearly as difficult to imagine the West creating some quasi-democratic Afghan state, only to watch the fledgling democracy fail utterly in its bid to become a self-sustaining society or in its efforts to develop a legitimate economy, while rejecting the narcotics production that currently serves as its only substantial economic activity. As one simple but telling example of this very genuine risk, in a sense it has been democracy that has helped to prevent the country from cleaning up poppy production to date. Although both President Bush and Ambassador Wood publicly supported aerial spraying as a means of eradicating the poppies, Afghan President Karzai did everything he could to avoid the spraying campaign, surmising correctly that serious eradication efforts would likely doom his prospects for reelection. In sum, a quasi-democracy could emerge in Afghanistan that remains a corrupt narco-state, or other alternative outcomes might include an Iranian-style theocratic democracy, the military-dominated Pakistani model, or even the fledgling faction-dominated Iraqi version. The ingrained traditions of warlordism, corruption, political violence, and the conservative Islamic distrust of democracy are also likely to have similar impacts on these prospects.

At the same time, it is not clear that the United States and NATO have even framed the problem correctly in aiming to create a viable nation-state, since the various criminal, terrorist, and demographic challenges are increasingly transnational in nature. In a sense, the effort is reminiscent of hockey great Wayne Gretzky's observation that he had been successful because he skated to where the puck was going, rather than to where the puck had been. In aiming to build a viable nation-state in the face of increasing transnational threats, it is possible that the West is merely skating to where the puck used to be. The United States clearly has an interest in Afghan stability but possibly less so in Afghan democracy, and it is not clear that it will take a viable and democratic Afghan nation to protect the vital American interests in the region. If anything, the United States might be better served by focusing its nation-building effort—using all available instruments of American national power—on Pakistan. There is no question that the United States has a vital national security interest in Pakistan—Afghanistan's far larger, nuclear-armed, and strategically located neighbor to the East—and in Pakistani stability, especially given Pakistan's difficult relationship with India. Furthermore, if done from outside its borders, Pakistani nation-building would come at a fraction of the cost of the Afghan mission.

In closing, the major commitments entailed by these strategic options must be balanced against other major and looming national security challenges that will arise in failed states and the developing world as a result of key demographic trends. These trends and developing concerns include rising population growth, increasing energy demands, global economic interdependency, food scarcity, fresh water scarcity, climate change and associated natural disasters, pandemics, and the increasing sophistication of attacks on global cyber- and space-based infrastructure.[106] At the same time, former Joint Chiefs of Staff Chairman Admiral Michael Mullen has argued that the increasing U.S. national debt represents perhaps the most significant national security threat by itself.[107] Therefore, as American decisionmakers formulate U.S. strategy in response to all of these threats, they need to have an honest and blunt discussion regarding the ends to be achieved and the means available to achieve them, in order to set realistic strategic goals, while selecting feasible, sustainable, and balanced strategic options. As the next section of the book will illustrate, this vision of rational and coherent strategy formulation has not characterized the process that has gotten us to this point in our struggle to build an Afghan nation.

ENDNOTES - CHAPTER 3

1. Quoted in Jeffery J. Roberts, *The Origins of Conflict in Afghanistan*, Westport, CT: Praeger, 2003, p. 161.

2. Stephen Tanner, *Afghanistan: A Military History from Alexander the Great to the Fall of the Taliban*, Cambridge, MA: Da Capo Press, 2002, p. 127.

3. Roberts, p. 133.

4. Martin Ewans, *Afghanistan: A Short History of Its People and Politics*, New York: HarperCollins Press, 2002, p. 142.

5. Roberts, p. 134.

6. Martin Ewans, *Conflict in Afghanistan: Studies in Asymmetric Warfare*, London, UK: Routledge, 2005, pp. 150-151.

7. Tanner, p. 226.

8. Roberts, p. 133.

9. Ewans, *Conflict in Afghanistan*, p. 154.

10. *Ibid.*, pp. 150-151.

11. *Ibid.*, p. 154.

12. *Ibid.*, pp. 156-157.

13. Tanner, p. 229.

14. *Ibid.*, pp. 226-229.

15. *Ibid.*, pp. 231-232.

16. *Ibid.*, p. 232.

17. *Ibid.*

18. *Ibid.*, p. 234.

19. Ewans, *Conflict in Afghanistan*, p. 216.

20. Tanner, p. 255.

21. *Ibid.*, pp. 266-267.

22. *The 9/11 Commission Report, Official Government Edition*, Washington, DC: U.S. Government Printing Office, 2004, p. 208.

23. Tanner, p. 302.

24. J. Boone Bartholomees, Jr., ed., *U.S. Army War College Guide to National Security Policy and Strategy*, 2nd Ed., Carlisle, PA: Strategic Studies Institute, U.S. Army War College, June 2006, p. 388.

25. *Ibid.*, pp. 388-392.

26. Kamal Matinuddin, *The Taliban Phenomenon: Afghanistan 1994-1997*, Cambridge, UK: Oxford, 1999, p. 160.

27. *Ibid.*, p. 161.

28. Stephen Blank, "The Strategic Importance of Central Asia: An American View," *Parameters*, Vol. 38, No. 1, Spring 2008, p. 73.

29. *Ibid.*

30. *Ibid.*

31. *Ibid.*, p. 74.

32. *Ibid.*, p. 76.

33. *Ibid.*, pp. 77-78.

34. Paul Kerr and Mary Beth Nikitin, "Pakistan's Nuclear Weapons: Proliferation and Security Issues," *CRS Report for Congress RL34248*, Washington, DC: U.S. Government Printing Office, January 14, 2008, summary.

35. *Ibid.*, pp. 1-2.

36. Kenneth Katzman, *Afghanistan: Current Issues and U.S. Policy*, Washington, DC: CRS Report for Congress, RL30588, August 27, 2003, pp. 25-30.

37. J. C. Griffiths, *Afghanistan*, New York: Praeger, 1967, p. 90.

38. Ewans, *Conflict in Afghanistan*, p. 146.

39. Seth G. Jones, *Counterinsurgency in Afghanistan*, Santa Monica, CA: Rand Corporation's National Defense Research Institute Press, 2008, pp. 54-55.

40. Antonio Giustozzi, *Koran, Kalashnikov and Laptop: The Neo-Taliban Insurgency in Afghanistan*, London, UK: Hurst, 2007, pp. 22-23.

41. *Ibid.*, pp. 25-26.

42. Matinuddin, p. 125.

43. *Ibid.*, p. 132.

44. Christopher M. Blanchard, *Afghanistan: Narcotics and U.S. Policy*, Washington, DC: Congressional Research Service, CRS 7-5700, August 12, 2009, pp. 34-35.

45. *Ibid.*, p. 125.

46. Larry P. Goodson, *Afghanistan's Endless War*, Seattle, WA: University of Washington Press, 2001, p. 149.

47. *The 9/11 Commission Report, Official Government Edition*, pp. 63-64.

48. Khalid Ashraf, *The Tribal Peoples of West Pakistan*, Peshawar, Pakistan: Peshawar University, 1962, p. 15.

49. *Ibid.*, p. 20.

50. Ashley J. Tellis, "Pakistan—Conflicted Ally in the War on Terror," *Carnegie Endowment for International Peace Policy Brief #56*, December 2007, pp. 1-2.

51. Shuja Nawaz, *Crossed Swords: Pakistan, Its Army, and the Wars Within*, Cambridge, UK: Oxford, 2008, p. xxvii.

52. These insightful points were raised by Colonel Mike McMahon, former CJ-7 of the Combined Security Transition Command – Afghanistan (CSTC-A). See also Raheel Khan's "Untangling the Punjabi Taliban Network" in the Combating Terrorism Center's *CTC Sentinel*, September 3, 2010, available from *www.pashtunforums.com*.

53. *Ibid.*, p. xxviii.

54. Tellis, p. 5.

55. Ewans, *Conflict in Afghanistan*, p. 276.

56. Matinuddin, p. 171.

57. Robert I. Rotberg, ed., *Building a New Afghanistan*, Cambridge, MA: World Peace Foundation (and Brookings Institution), 2007, p. 158.

58. Matinuddin, p. 172.

59. *Ibid.*, pp. 172-173.

60. Rotberg, ed., p. 157.

61. Matinuddin, p. 174.

62. Rotberg, ed., pp. 156-157.

63. *Ibid.*, p. 156.

64. Sarah Chayes, *The Punishment of Virtue: Inside Afghanistan After the Taliban*, New York: Penguin, 2006, p. 35.

65. Daniel Benjamin and Steven Simon, *The Next Attack*, New York: Holt, 2006, pp. 132-133.

66. *Ibid.*

67. *Ibid.*, pp. 133-134.

68. Rotberg, ed., p. 157.

69. Matinuddin, pp. 150-151.

70. Giustozzi, pp. 28-29.

71. *Ibid.*

72. Matinuddin, pp. 147-148.

73. *Ibid.*

74. *Ibid.*, pp. 148.

75. *Ibid.*, p. 175.

76. *Ibid.*

77. Blank, p. 73.

78. *Ibid.*, p. 75.

79. *Ibid.*

80. *Ibid.*, p. 81.

81. *Ibid.*

82. *Ibid.*, p. 83.

83. *Ibid.*, p. 84.

84. Rotberg, ed., p. 158.

85. Blank, p. 82.

86. *Ibid.*, p. 83.

87. Matinuddin, p. 178.

88. *Ibid.*

89. *Ibid.*, p. 179.

90. *Ibid.*, p. 181.

91. James F. Dobbins, *After the Taliban: Nation-Building in Afghanistan*, Washington, DC: Potomac, 2008, p. 123.

92. Goodson, p. 139.

93. Matinuddin, p. 158.

94. *The 9/11 Commission Report, Official Government Edition*, p. 207.

95. Bartholomees, ed., pp. 388-391.

96. *Ibid.*

97. Rajiv Chandrasekaran, "Sticker Shock," *The Washington Post National Weekly Edition*, October 12-18, 2010, p. 12.

98. Edward Luttwak, "Dead End: Counterinsurgency Warfare as Military Malpractice," *Harper's Magazine*, February 2007, available from *www.harpers.org/archive/2007/02/0081384*.

99. Ken Silverstein, "Six Questions for Michael Scheuer on National Security," *Harper's Magazine*, August 23, 2006, available from *harpers.org/archive/2006/08/sb-seven-michael-scheuer-1156277744*; and Ashraf Ghani and Clare Lockhart, *Fixing Failed States: A Framework for Rebuilding a Fractured World*, Cambridge, UK: Oxford University Press, 2008.

100. Karen DeYoung, "A Puzzle for Congress," *The Washington Post National Weekly Edition*, December 7-13, 2009, p. 19.

101. Amy Belasco, *The Cost of Iraq, Afghanistan, and Other GWOT Operations Since 9/11*, Washington, DC: Congressional Research Service, RL33110, May 15, 2009, summary.

102. Andrew J. Bacevich, *The Limits of Power*, New York: Holt and Company, 2008, p. 11.

103. "Wars Hinder Hunt for WMD," *The Pittsburgh Post-Gazette*, August 28, 2010, p. A2.

104. Enrique Desmond Arias and Daniel Goldstein, *Violent Democracy in Latin America: Toward an Interdisciplinary Reconceptualization*, Durham, NC: Duke University Press, 2010.

105. Larry Diamond and Leonardo Morlino, "The Quality of Democracy: An Overview," *Journal of Democracy*, Vol. 15, No. 4, October 2004, p. 20.

106. *The Joint Operating Environment (JOE) 2008*, Norfolk, VA: U.S. Joint Forces Command, November 25, 2008, pp. 10-23.

107. Speech quoted in *ExecutiveGov*, August 27, 2010, available from *www.executivegov.com/2010/08/mullen-national-debt-is-a-security-threat/*.

PART II

DISJOINTED POLICIES AND ORGANIZATIONAL STRUCTURES

In Afghanistan, our focus is building the capacity of Afghan institutions to withstand and diminish the threat posed by extremism, and to deliver high-impact economic assistance. . . . [W]e are also adapting our programs [to] enhance the visibility, effectiveness, and accountability of the institutions that impact the lives of Afghans the most. . . . [W]e must help the Afghan government provide economic opportunities [and] we are encouraging the Afghan government to take strong actions to combat corruption and improve governance . . . while maintaining and expanding on the important democratic reforms and advances in women's rights that have been made since 2001.

> Afghanistan and Pakistan
> Regional Stabilization Strategy,
> February 2010[1]

The Americans may have the watches, but we have the time.

> A common warning from Taliban operatives to Afghan villagers, quoted by Shahid Afsar, Chris Samples, and Thomas Wood in "The Taliban: An Organizational Analysis," Military Review, May-June 2008.

CHAPTER 4

DISJOINTED POLICIES, STRATEGIES, AND OBJECTIVES

> Disjointed = Separated at the joints; Out of joint, dislocated; Lacking order or coherence, disconnected.
>
> The American Heritage Dictionary of the English Language[3]

In its essence, the formulation of strategy is supposed to be a rational and deliberative process, or one that first identifies vital U.S. national security interests and then links them to the ends, ways, and means needed to protect those interests. In this rational, ordered, and coherent process, critical tasks include ensuring that the strategic plans are viable and feasible, and that the chosen strategic methods have a solid probability of success. Just as importantly, strategists must also make certain that the United States has the resources and capabilities needed to carry out those plans. The strategic planners then ensure that the assets earmarked for one region of the world — or the protection of one set of vital interests — are balanced against the competing demands of vital requirements in other parts of the world, all considered within the context of strategic and operational risk. Put most directly, the United States cannot do everything everywhere, so the rational formulation of strategy is supposed to reflect carefully considered tradeoffs between the demands posed by the various threats to U.S. national security and the associated risks of action or inaction, constrained by the specific capabilities and resources available.

In the case of the U.S. involvement in Afghanistan, the strategic reality has consistently fallen far short of this rational standard, whether viewed in terms of process or product. Instead of being characterized by rational deliberation, the evolving U.S. strategy for Afghanistan and the region has most often been disjointed, with the steps in the process of strategy formulation out of order and the strategic products lacking coherence, let alone any methodical linkage of interests, ends, ways, means, and risk. Likewise, the U.S. intervention in Afghanistan has featured shifting mission justifications and objectives over its course, along with overly ambitious ends and ways that have been largely disconnected from any real discussion of the specific means needed to achieve them. As a result, the evolving national-level U.S. and the North Atlantic Treaty Organization (NATO) strategy has consisted of unrealistic, broad-brush goals with little basis in any rational or comprehensive analysis of the challenges posed by Afghanistan, as decisionmakers outside of the operational theater have seemingly misread or ignored the realities of conditions on the ground.

As another aspect of this strategic disjointedness, and perhaps one that is not surprising given how the generation of strategy has unfolded, U.S. strategists have also consistently failed to enforce accountability in the form of specific forcing functions tied to realistic, tangible, achievable, and measurable objectives. Even more disturbing, the evidence suggests that the United States backed into nation-building in Afghanistan for largely political reasons, with little in the way of any serious analysis of the specific U.S. interests at stake. Likewise, the public record yields little evidence of any focused consideration of the relative importance—or *intensity*—of those interests, or the risks associated with the various strategic options available to the planners in the first place. Collectively then, the evidence suggests that in the planning for Afghanistan, strategy formulation occurred almost exactly opposite from what the rational model suggests it should be, with results reflected in correspondingly disjointed strategic products. In the case of Afghanistan, policymakers appear to have settled on the ways first, without any frank discussion of the vital interests at stake, the ends required to protect those interests, or the actual U.S. agency resources and capabilities available to realize them.

STRATEGY: WHAT IT IS SUPPOSED TO BE

The word *strategy* is tossed around often, but the phrase has a specific meaning. Theorist Harry Yarger notes that *strategy* is "the calculation of objectives, concepts, and resources within acceptable bounds of risk to create more favorable outcomes than might otherwise exist by chance or at the hands of others."[4] Yarger further notes that strategy is "a process that seeks to apply a degree of rationality and linearity to circumstances that may or may not be either, accomplishing this by expressing its logic in rational, linear terms—ends, ways, and means."[5] Along the same lines, the Department of Defense (DoD) *Joint Publication 1-02* defines strategy as "the art and science of developing and employing instruments of national power in a synchronized and integrated fashion to achieve theater, national, and/or multinational objectives."[6] *Interests* are desired end-states, linked to specific strategic objectives, or *ends*. *Ways* represent how the end-states will be achieved, and the *means* are the specific resources to be applied through the use of the instruments of national power.

In rational strategy formulation, the analyst also scrutinizes the strategic options under consideration for sources of potential strategic and operational *risk*, challenging the major assumptions inherent within those options. Among other concerns, the strategist asks a variety of risk-related questions: What will the impact be if the major assumptions are wrong? What other internal or external factors could affect the outcome? Is there flexibility or adaptability built into the strategic option, in case other contingencies arise? How will the adversaries and the other regional actors react to the strategic option? Is there likely to be a positive net balance between intended and unintended consequences? And what role might chance or friction play as events unfold?[7]

A CHRONOLOGICAL SKETCH OF THE U.S. STRATEGY AND INVOLVEMENT IN AFGHANISTAN

Although many observers have criticized the U.S. Government for a lack of strategy in Afghanistan, if anything, there have been too many strategies, each disconnected from the resources needed to achieve them. Put another way, the problem for the United States in its approach to Afghanistan has not been a lack of guidance, but rather that the various policy statements and strategic guidance aimed at Afghanistan and other national security threats in recent years have each specified ambitious ends and ways without directly identifying the means to be applied to achieve them. In the case of Afghanistan, U.S. interests were never clearly or conclusively defined until recently. As a result, the justifications and priorities for the mission have shifted often over the course of the intervention.

For the first several years of the mission, the strategic and operational objectives were often poorly defined, and even after they were defined more precisely, those objectives remained unrealistic, given the actual U.S. agency capabilities available to achieve them.

As a chronological sketch of the relevant policies and strategic guidance, in January 2001 — prior to the attacks of September 11, 2001 (9/11) — the Bush administration published *Proliferation: Threat and Response*, a document that identified Osama Bin Laden and his followers as representing a serious threat to gain and use weapons of mass destruction (WMD). This national security document also cited South Asia, and in particular the tensions between Pakistan and India, as representing a key area of concern for proliferation and potential threats.[8] At roughly the same time and as a clear indicator of the Bush administration's pre-war perspective on nation-building, Secretary of Defense Donald Rumsfeld directed that the Peace Keeping and Stability Operations Institute at the U.S. Army War College be shut down, a move he justified on the basis of cost-cutting.[9] In the period since 9/11, the United States has published more than a dozen other national strategies, among them strategies for homeland security, cyberspace security, intelligence, counterintelligence, victory in Iraq, WMD, pandemic influenza, and a host of others.[10] Reflecting the lack of attention to Afghanistan that generally characterized the U.S. effort there for a number of years, only in the past few years has there been a stand-alone national strategy generated for "Afghanistan and Pakistan regional stability."[11] So there clearly has been no shortage of official national-level strategies guiding U.S. agency effort in the years since the attacks of 9/11, and each of these recent strategies has imposed new or expanded responsibilities upon various U.S. agencies without specifying the resources to be made available to meet those requirements.

Regarding Afghanistan specifically, as the United States contemplated a military response to al Qaeda and the Taliban in light of the attacks of 9/11, the early debate surrounded the broad, overarching goals for any potential retaliatory strikes. In October 2001, then-Senator Joe Biden, chairman of the Senate Armed Services Committee, advocated an American-led nation-building effort as a long-term solution to the problem of terrorism in South and Central Asia.[12] The Bush administration and many of its conservative supporters opposed this idea forcefully, variously citing three lines of thinking in their opposition: (1) the goal of avoiding any long-term entanglements in Afghanistan; (2) a desire to validate Rumsfeld's streamlined force theories; and, (3) a basic ideological opposition to nation-building activities in general. Representative of this pre-war line of thinking, General Tommy Franks of U.S. Central Command noted early on that "We don't want to repeat the Soviets' mistakes," and so the United States set remarkably small force levels for the early stages of the Afghan campaign.[13]

Once the military operations commenced, however, the rationale for the Western intervention would ultimately shift during the course of the war, with the war's initial justification of eliminating al Qaeda and the Taliban regime evolving into the idea that Afghanistan merely represented one front on a broader Global War on Terror (GWOT). This shift in perspective would eventually bring with it a commitment to nation-building and democracy promotion.[14] The roots of this expansion of the war toward nation-building can actually be found at the Bonn Conference of December 2001. At that conference, the European Union (EU) contingent emphasized the need for longer-term reconstruction and stabilization efforts aimed at giving the Afghan government control of the Armed and Security Forces in the country.[15] The EU delegation also called for the creation of police services including anti-narcotics units and border police, with the twin goals of enabling the Afghan government to establish law and order and to collect taxes and customs fees as a source of sustaining revenue.[16]

Laying the groundwork for the U.S. Government's own eventual shift toward nation-building, the Bonn Conference also established the framework for an interim Afghan government. The Bonn framework included in it the goals of writing a new Afghan Constitution by October 2003 and holding democratic elections in 2004; these goals were endorsed by the United Nations (UN) Security Council a few days later.[17] In framing these goals, the conference reached back to Afghanistan's last legitimate *loya jirga*, or national representative assembly, of 1964 to establish a basis for the interim government. However, the conferees also established a troubling precedent by accommodating the preferences of warlords such as Ismail Khan of Herat and Abdul Rashid Dostam of northern Afghanistan in their initial governmental appointments.[18]

Further outlining its own broad vision for the future of Afghanistan, the EU called for "the creation of a viable Afghan state based on democracy, rule of law and universal standards of human rights," while also agreeing to "continue active engagement in the build-up of the national institutions related to rule of law and internal and external security," and promising "a significant European contribution to the ISAF [International Security Assistance Force]."[19] Therefore, the roots of the U.S. mission expansion to nation-building can be traced to the Bonn conference, which "set the framework for an ambitious development agenda of economic reconstruction, state building, and democratic governance that made it a test case for international assistance to post-conflict peacebuilding."[20] In sum, the conference established both the practice of accommodating Afghan warlords, as well as European goals for Afghanistan that the United States would have to oblige later in order to secure the Europeans' agreement to shift ISAF mission responsibility from the United States to NATO. In any case, the period from 2001 to 2007 would see the United States gradually abandon Secretary Rumsfeld's "light footprint" approach, an approach originally intended at least in part to avoid the Soviet mistakes of the 1980s.[21]

Complicating the mission further, from the beginning of the U.S. intervention there were competing visions for Afghanistan at work inside the U.S. Government and across its component agencies. As an early example of this persistent lack of coherence in U.S. policy and strategy, White House officials and U.S. Agency for International Development (USAID) leaders differed widely in their prescriptions for Afghan reconstruction priorities in the aftermath of the successful military operations to remove the Taliban, with the White House seeking projects with an immediate impact and USAID preferring longer-term agricultural "capacity building" as the main focus.[22] In the view of Pakistani journalist Ahmed Rashid, from the start USAID director Andrew Natsios tried to focus the agency's efforts on rebuilding Afghanistan's agricultural infrastructure, but he was overruled by Defense Secretary Rumsfeld and Central Intelligence Agency (CIA) director George Tenet, both of whom wanted the focus of U.S. resources to be placed on the hunt for bin Laden and in support of warlords acting favorably toward the United States.[23] So even as the Taliban were still being routed and as many others fled to Pakistan to seek sanctuary there, U.S. officials could not agree upon a common vision for the end-state of the operation. Furthermore, the remarkably low U.S. force levels, as well as the unreliable nature of the Afghan militiamen employed by the CIA to augment those meager forces, allowed the Taliban to melt away into the countryside to fight another day, much as their counterparts from earlier eras in Afghan history had done in the face of superior foreign forces.

In January 2002, Afghanistan's newly appointed interim President, Hamid Karzai, visited Washington, taking full advantage of the opportunity to request a larger international force to "extend his authority beyond Kabul."[24] The following month, Secretary of State Colin Powell formally backed Karzai's request, but President George W. Bush, Vice President Richard Cheney, and Secretary of Defense Rumsfeld all opposed the idea, and it was rejected.[25] A few months later in April, President Bush promised the Afghans a large American-led reconstruction effort "in the best traditions of George Marshall," even as the administration rebuffed USAID's specific budget request for about $150 million in increased Afghan reconstruction aid.[26] Furthermore, in this same year Rumsfeld went public with his disagreements with the State Department regarding NATO's role in ISAF, further demonstrating a lack of message discipline and coherence in the national strategic direction exercised in Afghanistan.[27] Against this backdrop, in June, the Afghans convened a national *loya jirga*, which selected a new government to run Afghanistan, to be headed by Hamid Karzai until a new constitution was approved in October 2003 and national elections were held in June 2004.[28]

Published 1 year after 9/11, the *National Security Strategy of 2002* was squarely focused on counterterrorism and the prevention of the proliferation of WMD. Foreshadowing the invasion of Iraq and espousing a proactive, offensive-minded approach to these challenges, the strategy focused on attacking the terrorists wherever they were, while working to deny them safe havens, financing, and state-sponsored support.[29] In December 2002, the Bush administration also published *The National Strategy to Combat Weapons of Mass Destruction*, a document that outlined the basic goals for counterproliferation, nonproliferation, and consequence management, as well as describing in broad fashion that "U.S. agencies must possess the full range of operational capabilities to counter the threat and use of WMD by states and terrorists against the United States."[30] Typical of each of the recent national strategies, these two documents are long on rhetoric but offer little in the way of specific goals and objectives or any delineation of the resources and agency capabilities earmarked to achieve them.

In December 2002, the U.S. Congress passed the Afghanistan Freedom Support Act, legislation that authorized increased democracy development assistance in the form of economic and military aid to Afghanistan.[31] This act also strongly encouraged the President to designate a coordinator for Afghanistan reconstruction activities in the State Department. This new coordinator would carry out four primary responsibilities: (1) designing an overall reconstruction strategy for Afghanistan; (2) ensuring that interagency coordination occurred; (3) coordinating assistance with other countries and intergovernmental organizations; and, (4) ensuring proper management and oversight of agencies responsible for assistance programs.[32] In response, President Bush declined to act at all on the congressional call for an interagency coordinator for reconstruction. Among other indicators, this choice clearly reflected the Bush Administration's strategic priorities for Afghanistan at that point, as well as the respective levels of influence exercised by the Secretaries of State and Defense during this phase of the operations.

In March 2003, the United States went to war in Iraq, and the impact of the shift in focus and resources from Afghanistan to operations in Iraq cannot be overstated. Under-resourced from the beginning, the campaign in Afghanistan now fell to a distant second place in terms of both military and civilian agency emphasis. For Afghanistan in 2003, the stated focus of the American-led effort at the beginning of the year was toward expanding the influence of the Afghan central government, supporting ISAF, and "setting up regional enclaves to create secure conditions for reconstruction."[33] On May 1, 2003, in an announcement that received far less attention than President Bush's Iraqi-focused counterpart, Defense Secretary Rumsfeld announced that the American and Afghan governments were declaring that major combat operations had ended and that the focus of the U.S. forces would shift to "stabilization."[34] This declaration came only hours before President Bush would make a similar announcement on the aircraft carrier U.S.S. *Abraham Lincoln* regarding Iraq.[35] However, even as the U.S. and Afghan governments declared major hostilities to be over, the spring of 2003 saw growing numbers of Taliban return to southern and eastern Afghanistan from

Pakistan. These returning Taliban first drew attention to themselves by killing soft target international aid workers, with the goals of announcing their presence and impeding reconstruction activities.

At about the same time in 2003, the DoD began to recognize that there was a clear lack of progress in Afghanistan. In response to this recognition, the DoD drafted a political-military strategy for the country, but the DoD plan did not include reconstruction in its design.[36] Reflecting the already strained relations between the major agencies operating in the Afghan theater and the general lack of any effective interagency coordination of effort, the DoD strategy was vetted by the National Security Council and approved by the President in June 2003, even while the State Department and USAID were still working independently on their own plan to expand and expedite Afghan reconstruction.[37] In the end, the competing vision articulated in the State-USAID plan would ultimately serve as the primary basis for the "Accelerating Success in Afghanistan Initiative," announced in September 2003 and aimed at being implemented prior to the Afghan presidential elections scheduled for June 2004.[38]

Soon after the United States announced the end of major combat operations in Afghanistan, Afghan President Karzai threatened to resign, saying that his government was out of money.[39] Shortly thereafter in the summer, the Bush administration approved an increase in forces to oppose the growing new Taliban threat, and in November 2003, Zalmay Khalilzad agreed to serve as ambassador on the condition that he be given access to a major infusion of economic aid, a condition which the Bush administration met.[40] In spite of the announcement that major combat operations had concluded, in 2003, the United States commenced Operations MOUNTAIN VIPER, AVALANCHE, and MOUNTAIN STORM, each aimed at defeating the remnants of al Qaeda and the Taliban leadership, as the U.S. presence remained focused primarily on counterterrorism.[41] At the same time, the United States was working at building an Afghan army, having provided the Afghans with $815 million in aid toward that goal in Fiscal Year (FY) 2002, a figure that would increase to $1.8 billion in FY2003.[42] As 2003 came to a close, some observers also argued that the U.S. decision to invade Iraq in 2003 had brought with it the unintended and adverse consequence of casting the War on Terrorism as a broader struggle of the West against Islam, thus providing the Taliban and other militant factions within Afghanistan with increasing opportunities to gain fighters and other sources of support.[43]

By early 2004, the U.S. presence in Afghanistan had increased to 20,000 troops in support of Operation MOUNTAIN VIPER and the other kinetic operations, an increase that was accompanied by little public comment, although it represented a doubling of U.S. forces in spite of the concurrent demands of Iraq.[44] In January, the Afghan leadership had agreed to a new Constitution, but as the U.S. Government's military and other agency resources became increasingly concentrated on Iraq, the United States sought to shift the primary responsibility for Afghanistan to NATO to free additional resources for the Iraqi operations. ISAF's responsibility was gradually expanded in territory and mission scope beginning in 2004, and as part of this expansion, Provincial Reconstruction Teams (PRTs) were initiated in some parts of the country. As a result of this shift of responsibility to NATO, the mission also took on the added baggage of NATO's solvency and viability. Along these lines, some observers have argued that NATO member countries viewed their acquiescence as an opportunity for those countries to contribute militarily to the U.S. efforts without getting involved in Iraq, but the numerous caveats placed on these commitments have severely limited the practical impact of their contributions anyway.[45]

As the White House ramped up for the President's reelection campaign, the Bush administration hoped to demonstrate progress in the two wars during an election year. Since Iraq was going poorly, some in the administration felt that it would be easier to demonstrate progress in Afghanistan in spite of its deteriorating security situation.[46] At the same time, the international donor community was pushing for state building and development in Afghanistan, and as a result, the Bush administration decided that it could use the upcoming Afghan elections to demonstrate tangible progress "if the mission were recast toward [the] state-building and 'peacebuilding' agendas that much of the international community embraced."[47] Installed as ambassador in the fall of 2003, Zalmay Khalilzad actively promoted this same nation-building agenda, and he was given $1.2 billion in aid to use toward that purpose.[48] To support the Afghan elections in 2004, about 2,000 additional Marines were deployed to Afghanistan, and the elections generally went off without major disruption. However, some analysts have argued that the impact of this expanded U.S. military footprint was itself partly responsible for the growing strength and breadth of the insurgency, which really began to grow in 2005.[49]

Even as the Afghan security situation began to deteriorate further, some observers asserted that the political demands of elections in Afghanistan and the United States were really behind the eventual troop increases. Specifically, it was argued that three political dynamics had contributed directly to the incremental troop increases and the heightened counterterrorism campaign in Afghanistan, among them: (1) a shift in Iraq from the claim of "mission accomplished" to a realization that the war would be lengthy and difficult; (2) the fact that Osama bin Laden remained at large; and, (3) the increasingly effective Democratic criticisms of the Bush administration for its "neglect of the primary front in the war on terror."[50] At this point, however, the main U.S. effort on the ground remained focused on eliminating the al Qaeda terrorists, the Taliban militiamen, and their leaders, rather than on nation-building. In October, President Karzai won the presidential election by a wide margin, and President Bush won his own reelection shortly afterward in November.

As the situation in Iraq became even bleaker, the administration's attention became squarely focused on that theater of operations at the expense of Afghanistan. In June 2005, the talented and experienced Ambassador Khalilzad—a native Afghan—departed Afghanistan at the President's request to become Ambassador to Iraq. Reflecting the lack of attention that Afghan affairs were receiving at the time, the major policy change under consideration was a September debate over whether or not to withdraw 3,000 troops from Afghanistan and divert them to Iraq, a figure representing about 20 percent of the total U.S. force present in Afghanistan at the time.[51] September also saw the Afghan parliamentary elections take place, elections that went off largely without controversy, but also without receiving much attention. This preoccupation with Iraq also took the form of diverting other non-DoD resources from Afghanistan, undermining a reconstruction effort that was already poorly resourced and exacerbating other major challenges in the country.

At the broader national strategic level, in February 2006, the Chairman of the Joint Chiefs of Staff published *The National Military Strategic Plan for the War on Terrorism*, a document that offers a broadly drawn outline of the ends, ways, and means to be applied in the GWOT. Similar to other recent strategies in this sense, there is little in the way of specifics and no suggestion of how the inputs and means of the various agencies would be coordinated and integrated to achieve the strategy's broadly worded ends.[52] Of particular note, the document's *Annex V: Interagency Coordination* consists of only two brief paragraphs, and offers little other than a vague call for "an end to unilateral 'stove piping' of actions within departments, agencies, and staff directorates."[53]

A month later in March, the Bush administration published *The National Security Strategy* (NSS) *of the United States of America of 2006*, a watershed document in the sense that it formally reflected the expansion of the Afghan mission to nation-building. Citing a variety of successes in Afghanistan, including progress in the fight with al Qaeda and two elections having been held without major incident, the strategy makes an extended case in favor of democracy promotion as the way forward for U.S. national security.[54] In the document's prescribed model of democracy, the 2006 NSS delineates between religious and civil society—an approach at odds with the realities of Islamic culture and antithetical to Islamic norms and structures—and offers no specific ways or associated means for achieving those incredibly ambitious and possibly infeasible ends.

Furthermore, the 2006 NSS clearly identifies a Western model as the version of democracy to be promoted—as it includes references to "human rights," "freedom of religion," "submitting to the will of the people," "independent and impartial systems of justice," "limit[ing] the reach of government," protecting "religious communities," and the promotion of "independent business" and "a market economy."[55] That same spring, the new or "neo" Taliban insurgents launched their largest offensive since 2001, while in May, a fatal traffic accident in Kabul caused by a U.S. convoy touched off major riots in the city.[56] Expanding the scope of U.S. effort significantly, early in 2006, President Bush requested $10.6 billion in aid for Afghanistan for FY2007, even as American airstrikes were blamed for civilian casualties that increased tensions with the Afghan population, and as the Taliban expanded their use of suicide attacks and roadside bombings.[57]

Adding to this national strategic mix, in September 2006, the administration published a *National Strategy for Combating Terrorism*, another in a series of strategic documents that offers little in the way of specific means to be applied to the various ends described within it. Like the other strategies, the *Combating Terrorism* document advocates democracy promotion and other physical ways in which terrorism will be combated, but identifies few specific agency capabilities to be used toward those goals.[58] The document is also noteworthy in its clear emphasis on Iraq to the exclusion of Afghanistan, as even the terrorist havens cited in the document make reference to Iraq, with little mention of Afghanistan or Pakistan.[59] During a visit to the

White House by Pakistani President Musharraf that same month, President Bush noted that when Musharraf "looks me in the eye" and says there "won't be a Taliban and there won't be an al Qaeda (in Pakistan), I believe him."[60] Also in September 2006, NATO forces battled hundreds of Taliban near Kandahar, eventually pushing them out of the area. In October, NATO formally assumed responsibility for the security of all of Afghanistan.

Appointed in December 2006, new Defense Secretary Robert Gates initially focused on Iraq, but by the end of 2007, he had presented a new integrated strategy for Afghanistan, aiming to pull together the reconstruction, development, counterterrorism, and counternarcotics activities.[61] This new approach would require increased troop levels, and Secretary Gates also encouraged other key agencies to increase their commitments. Gates also challenged the NATO countries to increase their commitments, but this request was a tough sell for most of them, given their domestic political realities. As the security situation in Afghanistan deteriorated further in 2007, there were publicly aired disagreements over counternarcotics policy, with Ambassador William Wood and President Bush pushing for aerial spraying on one side and Defense Secretary Gates opposing that method, on the other.[62] For his own part, President Karzai opposed aerial spraying or any other serious eradication efforts altogether, out of concerns that any real efforts to undermine poppy production would lead to his defeat in the next presidential election.

As the situation worsened and as the neo-Taliban elements continued to grow in strength and sophistication, the Bush administration began to sour on Pakistani President Musharraf. In July 2007, White House

Homeland Security director Frances Fragos Townsend asserted that Musharraf's anti-terrorism plan hadn't "worked for Pakistan," and she further claimed that al Qaeda had established safe havens inside of Pakistan.[63] That November, the Combined Security Transition Command-Afghanistan (CSTC-A) and ISAF initiated a nation-wide reform of the Afghan National Police, as a means of projecting Afghan governmental authority and reducing the widespread corruption and incompetence in the police force. As the levels of violence in Iraq diminished toward the end of 2007, the administration came under increasing pressure to step up its efforts in Afghanistan, where the security situation was continuing to deteriorate.

In January 2008, U.S. decisionmakers began to consider deploying additional troops to bolster Afghan security, but NATO partner governments were resistant, and President Bush declined to act on troop requests from the theater commanders during the presidential election year. Against this challenging backdrop, it is somewhat ironic that it was in May 2008 that the State Department published the *FY2010 Mission Strategic Plan for Afghanistan, U.S. Mission to Afghanistan*, the authoritative strategic guidance for all civilian U.S. agencies operating in Afghanistan.[64] While this document provides fairly detailed goal descriptions and metrics for measuring the progress toward achieving them, the document remains very vague regarding the specific resources or capabilities to be applied to achieve those objectives. Furthermore, the President had never clearly established State's primacy over the DoD in Afghanistan, and as a result the document could not mandate DoD cooperation.[65] So as President Bush's tenure wound down in 2008, the Afghan effort suffered from shortages in army and police trainers, insufficient forces to enforce security across the countryside, and a wholesale lack of the civilian agency personnel and other specialists needed to carry out both the ambitious and broad goals of the *The National Security Strategy* of 2006, as well as the more specific objectives of 2008's *Mission Strategic Plan for Afghanistan*.

After he took office in 2009, President Barack Obama's first major initiative linked to Afghanistan was his February decision to expand the use of drone aircraft-initiated missile strikes inside of Pakistan, with the goal of attacking the network of militants seeking to bring down the Pakistani government.[66] These attacks represented a significant expansion of the use of force in the region and were aimed at Pakistani militant groups that had "played less of a direct role in attacks on American troops."[67] The second of two attacks at the time targeted a particular militant leader, Baitullah Mehsud, but without success. Soon afterward, in March, President Obama announced a "comprehensive, new strategy for Afghanistan and Pakistan," the result of a policy review led by advisor Bruce Reidel.[68] This new strategy identified a "clear and focused goal" at its center, specifically to "disrupt, dismantle and defeat al Qaeda in Pakistan and Afghanistan, and to prevent their return to either country in the future."[69] In the same address, the President announced the deployment of 17,000 troops who would "take the fight to the Taliban in the south and the east" as part of a long-standing request for forces, a well as a "shift of emphasis" to "training and increasing the size of the Afghan security forces."[70]

While not mentioning particulars, the President also noted that, "This push must be joined by a dramatic increase in our civilian effort," citing widespread corruption, criminality, and the effects of the drug trade.[71] In addition to the new combat forces and army and police trainers, the President's new strategy also included more aid and the deployment of hundreds of civilian experts to Afghanistan. Identifying a compelling national interest in combating the terrorist elements, the President stated that "the safety of the world is at stake," given al Qaeda's continued presence in Afghanistan and Pakistan.[72] With this shift, the President asserted that the strategy would refocus the U.S. efforts on a "clear and focused goal: to disrupt, dismantle and defeat al Qaeda in Pakistan and Afghanistan, and to prevent their return to either country in the future."[73] The civilian surge that was part of the March 27 announcement would roughly double the number of civilian experts deployed to 900.[74]

In May 2009, President Obama and Secretary Gates replaced ISAF commander General David McKiernan with General Stanley McChrystal, as Secretary Gates noted that General McKiernan had asked for more troops but offered no new strategy.[75] In July, National Security Adviser James L. Jones stated that the Obama administration intended to hold troop levels constant in Afghanistan for the time being, but he also noted that the administration wanted to focus effort on the goals of increasing economic development, improving effective governance, and raising the engagement of Afghans in the conflict.[76] The FY2009 supplemental appropriations law had required the administration to develop better metrics to evaluate progress in Afghanistan, among them, "the performance and legitimacy of the Afghan government and its efforts to curb official corruption."[77] Later in August, the White House announced the establishment of about 50 new

Afghanistan benchmarks—measures of progress that were to be more detailed and more specific than the broad-brush approach that had been used without success in Iraq. Most noteworthy for the fact that they were about 8 years in the making, these benchmarks were also intended to look "more broadly, measuring not only what gets done but how well and on what schedule."[78] In another developing trend, the administration began to look to Iraq for lessons learned and techniques that could be applied in Afghanistan, in spite of the dramatic differences between the two situations and the unresolved outcome in Iraq.

Upon taking command of the ISAF forces, General McChrystal had initiated his own broad review of the situation and the strategy in Afghanistan. After completing his internal assessment, he issued a public call for a classic counterinsurgency in his *Initial Assessment* of conditions and strategy for Afghanistan of August 30, 2009.[79] Noting that the situation "defies simple logic or quick fixes," he further asserted, "Our strategy cannot be focused on seizing terrain or destroying insurgent forces; our objective must be the population."[80] As a positive corresponding step, the senior in-country leaders from State and the DoD also jointly published the first *Integrated Civil-Military Campaign Plan* in August of 2009. The document was noteworthy for a variety of reasons, but not the least of which was the fact that it had taken nearly 8 years of operations in Afghanistan for an integrated, interagency document of this type to emerge—and then only because the current incumbents at State and the DoD had agreed to produce it.

Shortly afterward, in September, General McChrystal's confidential assessment of the war in Afghanistan was leaked, in which he contended that without receiving more forces the war "will likely result in failure," according to a copy obtained by *The Washington Post*.[81] An intense debate then began within the administration, with Vice President Joe Biden — ironically the former champion of nation-building — spearheading the White House faction pushing for an increased speed in the development of the Afghan security forces and attacks on Pakistani-based terrorists using drones, with a concurrent de-emphasis of the nation-building objectives. Participants in the deliberations identified Defense Secretary Gates as a primary advocate for General McChrystal's more robust counterinsurgency plan.[82]

For all of the serious internal debate and discussion, however, the U.S. strategy in Afghanistan remained largely unchanged after the Obama administration's 3-month policy review. General McChrystal was given most of what he had advocated publicly, as the modified counterinsurgency and nation-building strategy was approved, with the caveat that the United States would begin a conditions-driven withdrawal in 2011. This caveat once again called into question the coherence of the strategy, given the stated ends and ways. Immediately, however, even that public assertion of a planned withdrawal was called into question as Defense Secretary Gates, Secretary of State Hilary Clinton, and Joint Chiefs of Staff Chairman Admiral Michael Mullen each sought to minimize expectations for the transfer — with Secretary Gates calling the date the "beginning of a process" that would take place "in uncontested areas" and making it dependent upon the development of Afghan security forces.[83] Ultimately, this publicly debated policy evolved into the current plan, which calls for a conditions-based transfer of authority to the Afghan government in 2014 to accompany the initiation of the withdrawal of surge forces, which began in July 2011.

On the heels of this public demonstration of discord within the Obama administration, in February 2010, the State Department's Office of the Special Representative for Afghanistan and Pakistan issued an updated *Afghanistan and Pakistan Regional Stabilization Strategy*. Three months later, in May, the White House issued its own *National Security Strategy of the United States of America* to supersede the Bush-era guidance. In a major speech at West Point just prior to issuing this new guidance, President Obama stated that, "The burdens of this century cannot fall on our Soldiers alone," as he directed that defense and diplomacy must go hand in hand the conduct of U.S. foreign policy.[84] Having completed his internal review at about the same time, ISAF Commanding General McChrystal implemented the full counterinsurgency plan, as he issued the corresponding *ISAF Campaign Strategy* that same May.

The balance of 2010 was most noteworthy for leadership changes and public bickering among a variety of U.S. officials. General David Petraeus succeeded General McChrystal as ISAF commander after McChrystal's impolitic comments surfaced in a *Rolling Stone* article, and other uniformed leaders such as Marine Corps General James Conway offered public second-guessing of President Obama's decision to announce July 2011 as a date for initial troop withdrawals, criticisms echoed by President Karzai. In August, General Petraeus declared the Afghan war strategy to be "fundamentally sound," and in September the President signaled that the strategy would remain intact moving forward.[85]

FIVE KEY STRATEGIC DOCUMENTS

Among the various sources of formal guidance provided to U.S. departments and agencies concerned with national security and the operations in Afghanistan, there are five especially important documents that convey the leadership's strategy and intentions. Unintentionally, these five documents also provide a solid sense of the disjointed nature of American strategic planning, including a lack of true interagency coordination and the comparative advantages in planning capabilities enjoyed by the DoD. Considered in the order of their publication, the first three of these documents include the Bush administration's *National Security Strategy* (NSS) *of the United States* of 2006, the State Department's *FY2010 Mission Strategic Plan for Afghanistan* of 2008, and the *Afghanistan and Pakistan Regional Stabilization Strategy* of 2010. The last two of the five key documents were published about the same time in May 2010, and include the Obama administration's NSS and the *ISAF Campaign Strategy*. A close examination of these five important documents yields a number of key insights into the state of American strategic planning and the causes of our struggles in Afghanistan.

The first of these key documents is the NSS of 2006. National security strategies are public statements that outline a President's vision for national security while setting the strategic priorities for U.S. departments and agencies. Published by the Bush administration, the centerpiece of this vision was "democracy promotion." Whether that ideological choice represented after-the-fact rationalization or forward-thinking guidance when it was written, the 2006 NSS succeeds as inspiring rhetoric and as a statement of ideological preference, but the document fails substantively as a working strategic framework for establishing tangible and feasible ends, ways, and means, or in assessing national security risks. Furthermore, while democracy promotion itself may potentially represent a viable and desirable component of U.S. foreign policy strategy when viewed from a longer-term perspective, the military-heavy application of this approach represented in the 2006 NSS clearly compromised a variety of U.S. national interests in the short run. Put directly, by openly and aggressively adopting democracy promotion as the central feature of our foreign policy, the United States accepted unnecessary risks and costs, simultaneously setting unachievable short-term goals, while predisposing some nations to view American intentions with concern, if not outright distrust.

Expanding on this idea, the heavy-handed, military-centered approach to democracy promotion that was embedded in the 2006 NSS reveals a fundamental misunderstanding of a variety of relevant cultural, political, and economic characteristics of Islam, the South and Central Asian region, and the individual countries within it. At the same time, if democracy promotion is pursued using the right balance of soft power elements of national power and with reasonable expectations, it could eventually realize longer-term advantages that would outweigh its various potential disadvantages. However, as long as that vision remains detached from a serious consideration of the specific resources and capabilities—and duration of commitment—needed to realize it, these goals remain overly ambitious and unrealistic. From a policy standpoint, the 2006 NSS served to formalize the mission creep in Afghanistan from defeating al Qaeda to nation-building, but the document still fell well short of what was needed for it to function as strategy.

In a sense, the NSS represents the macro view of American national strategy, as some administrations use it to outline their vision for strategic intent while others use it to consolidate changes already made or to "create consensus within the executive and to signal changes to Congress and foreign leaders."[86] In either case, the 2006 NSS never once gets into the specific components of strategy in the few places that it mentions the mission in Afghanistan. The document also never offers any policy prescriptions or any real leader emphasis tied to the obvious interagency challenges that were getting in the way of operational success in Afghanistan and in other national security activities. Instead, it stays well "above the fray," offering broad rhetoric such as its celebration of the "extraordinary progress in the expansion of freedom, democracy, and human dignity" since 2002 and its lofty but undefined goals of "ending tyranny" and "advancing freedom."[87] Noteworthy mainly for its primary focus on Iraq and its very limited references to Afghanistan, the document also speaks briefly about consolidating "the successes already won" and the establishment of the Office of the Coordinator for Reconstruction and Stabilization, optimistically noting that the office "draws on all agencies of the government" while integrating "its activities with our military's efforts."[88]

While a broad-brush approach to Afghanistan in the macro 2006 NSS might be understandable to a certain extent, it is much harder to get past the lack of details in the country-specific micro guidance to nonmilitary agencies operating in Afghanistan. The second of these five key strategic documents for Afghanistan is a State Department document known as the *Mission Strategic Plan* (MSP) published in 2008. The MSP is the document that lays out the specific mission guidance to civilian agencies for the execution of their various operations. Accordingly, MSPs are intended to be country-specific action plans that provide the micro view, or a blueprint of the specific objectives, metrics, and priorities for all civilian agencies and operators within that country. Once again, however, the 2008 MSP for Afghanistan falls well short as strategic guidance, since it identifies lofty and ambitious goals without actually linking those goals to existing or projected U.S. agency capabilities or the resources needed to achieve them.

In much the same way, the 2008 Afghanistan MSP also falls short from an interagency perspective. The document optimistically identifies partners among the various U.S. agencies operating in Afghanistan, but it contains no details regarding specific requirements or mechanisms for coordination and specifies no jurisdictional or supporting relationships. Moreover, the document is almost completely devoid of details of the "how to" of its goals, since it makes no mention of the numerous supporting tasks and related objectives required to achieve meaningful, substantive improvements in the goal areas. It is also noteworthy that within the headquarters where I operated in Afghanistan, none of the actors from the Department of State, USAID, or the DoD ever made mention of this document during my time in theater, and to my knowledge, nobody in the military headquarters was aware of the existence of the document or its contents. Even more significantly, there was clearly no common understanding of the specific objectives that each U.S. agency was supposed to be pursuing in support of the MSP goals. As a result, most agencies continued to work in the directions they were used to going in, pursuing goals that they defined for themselves and answering primarily to their higher stateside headquarters.

As another basic indicator of this strategic and interagency disjointedness, Anthony Cordesman of the Center for Strategic and International Studies identified a pervasive lack of meaningful metrics to track progress in Afghanistan and Pakistan in his careful analysis of 2007. Cordesman noted that ISAF and the U.S. Government had been successful in nearly every tactical military engagement, and that the other U.S. agencies commonly cited their own successes by applying their own particular measures of their efforts in Afghanistan. Conversely, however, he also observed that there was no clear and objective sense of the direction the overall effort was heading.[89] Among other measures absent from the discussion, Cordesman's missing metrics included evaluations of overall progress, appraisals of economic performance, assessments of force development, and measures of gains in agency capacity, the rule of law, counternarcotics, and reconstruction.[90] This lack of strategic clarity and coherence, coupled with a concurrent failure to make honest, hard, resource-constrained choices, only combined to undermine the prospects for mission success and the broader protection of U.S. interests.

Published in February 2010 and endorsed formally by Defense Secretary Gates, the State Department's *Afghanistan and Pakistan Regional Stabilization Strategy* offers much more detail in its guidance for the civilian agencies operating in the region. In this strategic guidance, Secretary of State Clinton pointedly asserts that the strategy's programs are "far from an exercise in nation-building," going on to claim that the strategy is instead aimed at achieving "realistic progress in critical areas."[91] Nevertheless, this strategic guid-

ance looks suspiciously like what we would imagine nation-building to be, if there were any generally accepted definition of the term. For example, the document includes major sections on:
- "Rebuilding Afghanistan's Agriculture Sector";
- "Strengthening Afghan Governance";
- "Enhancing Afghan Rule of Law";
- "Supporting Afghan-Led Reintegration";
- "Combating the Afghan Narcotics Trade";
- "Building an Economic Foundation for Afghanistan's Future";
- "Advancing the Rights of Afghan Women and Girls."[92]

So besides reinforcing the notion that we all toss around the term "nation-building" without ever defining it, State's strategic guidance for the civilian agencies operating in Afghanistan clearly aims to create a viable Afghan partner where none existed before.

To this end, the *Afghanistan and Pakistan Regional Stabilization Strategy* clearly represents a major step forward for State in its strategic planning capabilities. For each of the major goals outlined in the document, which includes those listed above and a variety of others for the region, the strategy offers specific budgetary resource requirements, a description of the Key Initiatives recently undertaken in pursuit of those goals, and the Milestones or achievements realized in the recent past. Reflecting the President's effort to reduce expectations, the section on "Strengthening Afghan Governance" severely limits the use of the word "democracy" and instead focuses on enhancing the delivery of basic services. Yet, even after setting the bar lower, the required tasks and the costs associated with the effort are huge and growing, especially considering the realities of Afghanistan's political culture and its demographics, as well as the sunk costs to date. The FY2011 budget request for the function of "Strengthening Governance" in Afghanistan is $1.76 billion all by itself, and this request comes on the heels of actual expenditures of $977 million in FY2009 and $1.72 billion in FY2010.[93] The specific tasks involved in realizing even the scaled-down version of "strong Afghan governance" are monumental ones, among them:

- "Reducing Corruption," which includes creating and administering Afghan anti-corruption tribunals, a major crimes task force, an attorney general's anti-corruption unit, a High Office of Oversight, and a mobile pay and financing capability;
- "Enhancing Sub-National Governance," which includes launching and administering a District Development Plan, local governance and community development activities, an Afghan Social Outreach Program, the Afghan Municipality Support Program, and a Performance-Based Governors Fund;
- "Enhancing Afghan Capacity," which entails "encouraging merit-based appointments," "leveraging our assistance . . . to incentivize improved performance, accountability, and transparency," and "ensuring effective representation . . . in support of Afghan efforts to reform Afghanistan's electoral system and nascent democratic machinery [while] encouraging greater participation by women in Afghan electoral politics."[94]

Of course, these programs and initiatives are not all-inclusive of the U.S. Government or ISAF efforts aimed at strengthening Afghan governance, but instead represent the highest priorities for that sector under State's current strategy. In support of these tough challenges, some of which run directly counter to the entrenched norms of Afghan society, the strategy highlights the "tripling of deployed U.S. civilians that occurred over the past year . . . to nearly 1,000 on the ground today."[95] This level of civilian agency support certainly represents a significant increase in the non-DoD personnel committed to Afghanistan and Pakistan, especially when contrasted with the mere dozens of non-DoD personnel deployed there early in the mission. However, there is still no way those 1,000 experts—however hard they might work—can perform all of the tasks and sub-tasks required to realize the desired end-states for Afghanistan. This small number is even more revealing when it is compared with the approximately 100,000 military personnel who are currently deployed in support of the U.S. Government's security objectives. Lastly, it is noteworthy that Secretary of State Clinton comments that the strategy is "aligned with our security objectives," and that Defense Secretary Gates endorses it.[96]

Otherwise, State's strategic guidance generally side-steps relevant questions about the coordination and integration of civilian agency effort with the DoD effort, and instead only briefly states that an "extensive transformation of U.S. civilian assistance activities" has led to "a more focused and effective assistance effort that is fully integrated across civilian agencies."[97] The implication of these statements is that State and the DoD have derived their strategies independently of one another, although they have aimed to maintain some consistency between them—but only because the Secretaries of State and Defense decided to do so, unlike their counterparts early in the Bush administration. This situation suggests two fundamental questions: First, why isn't there one strategy for Afghanistan that applies equally to all of the agencies and departments operating in the Afghan and Pakistani theater of operations? And secondly, why does the aim of achieving civil-military cooperation toward the same American strategic goals depend upon the willingness of the Secretaries of State and Defense to work together?

A few months after the publication of the revised *Afghanistan and Pakistan Regional Stabilization Strategy*, the Obama administration issued its own *National Security Strategy of the United States of America of 2010*. Although this document backs away from the Bush administration's focused embrace of democratic peace theory and its clear willingness to use the military instrument of national power to achieve those democratic ends, it is remarkably similar to the Bush-era strategic guidance in at least two major respects: First, rather than offering any clear-cut expression of U.S. national security interests tied to feasible ways of protecting or advancing those interests, all coupled to specific governmental capabilities and resources and placed within the context of acceptable risks, the 2010 NSS reads as a laundry list of worthy aspirations. That is, it outlines its vision of interests and ways without couching those noble goals in any real discussion of available resources and capabilities. Secondly, while the document does offer more detail than its 2006 counterpart regarding the specific components of the strategy for Afghanistan and Pakistan, and while it also clearly seeks to de-emphasize the notion of an Afghan democracy, the 2010 NSS reaffirms the U.S. goal of creating a "strong, stable, and prosperous Afghanistan," without making any mention of the associated means, costs, or risks.[98]

Not surprisingly, the DoD strategy for Afghanistan, expressed in the *ISAF Campaign Strategy* of May 2010, reflects both the DoD's extensive experience with strategic and operational planning as well as its access to resources and capabilities far superior to those of other agencies. Having settled upon irregular warfare operations in the form of a classic counterinsurgency campaign as the strategic method, and having acknowledged the need for at least a minimally viable Afghan government to achieve success in those operations, the *ISAF Campaign Strategy* identifies the following strategic and operational objectives:

- "Protect the population."
  - "Prioritize effort in high-density population areas where insurgent groups operate primarily with disaffected Pashtun population."
  - "Reduce civilian casualties."
- "Enable Afghan National Security Forces."
  - "Accelerate and expand indigenous security force capacity and capability."
  - "Partner at every echelon."
- "Neutralize malign influence."
  - "Identify and report corruption."
  - "Forge responsible and accountable governance."
- "Support extension of governance."
  - "Gain active support of the population by empowering legitimate sub-national leaders with effective population security measures."

- "Support socio-economic development."
  - "Gain active support of the population by creating security conditions that provide space for community-based development opportunities."
  - "Connect economic corridors."[99]

The national-level strategic guidance has been further operationalized more recently in an updated *U.S. Government Integrated Civil-Military Campaign Plan for Support to Afghanistan* of February 2011. Like its predecessor, this document represents a well-intentioned and comprehensive effort at integrating the U.S. Government's various instruments of power in Afghanistan. Also like its predecessor, it is worth noting, that this integration is not formally required by statute, but rather has come about as a result of the willingness and desire of the incumbent leaders at State and the DoD—both at the national level and at the operational level in Afghanistan—to see this formal effort at coordination and integration occur. When previous incumbents were not interested in this integration, it did not happen. Furthermore, it is still the case that agency and departmental budgets and programs are managed and funded agency-by-agency, meaning that decisions regarding budgetary priorities and execution are centralized in Washington, just as these budgetary firewalls can make the integration and execution of those budgets unwieldy on the ground. It is also still the case that operators on the ground respond most adroitly to those leaders above them in their agency or departmental supervisory chain, rather than the interagency leadership on the ground.

Finally, for all of the DoD's comparative advantages in strategic and operational planning and resources, two major strategic concerns remain. First, the cost of these operations, both in terms of the funds required to support them as well as the opportunity costs of the long-term commitment of U.S. forces to these strategic ends, is staggering. Specifically, the Obama administration's overall defense budget request for FY2011 was a record $708 billion, with $159 billion of that amount earmarked specifically for the missions in Afghanistan, Iraq, and Pakistan.[100] The costs for Afghanistan alone in fiscal years 2011 and 2012 are expected to amount to well above $100 billion each year. Additionally, while the U.S. military enjoys huge comparative advantages in resources and capabilities when contrasted with the civilian agencies operating in Afghanistan and Pakistan, it is still the case that the existing DoD capabilities are a poor fit with at least two of its strategic objectives—in the areas of governance and socioeconomic development—and likely part of a third, in the form of the police development mission. Lastly, in addition to the major economic and opportunity costs of this lengthy, challenging, and uncertain U.S. military commitment, this strategic choice has brought with it other very real costs in the form of casualties, long-term medical obligations, and the adverse effects of stress and continual deployments on the members of the U.S. military and their families. The long-term consequences of these strategic choices have already begun to emerge in the form of increasing domestic abuse and divorce rates, the prevalence of Post-Traumatic Stress Disorder (PTSD) in the force, and highly elevated rates of suicide in the U.S. military, among other adverse impacts.

DISJOINTED STRATEGY: THE ADVERSE CONSEQUENCES AND IMPLICATIONS

Long on ambition but short on civilian resources and other required capabilities, America's national strategy and the corresponding objectives for Afghanistan and the region have only recently been clearly and consistently defined. Nevertheless, in many respects, this U.S. strategy remains disjointed and disconnected from the specific means needed to realize the U.S. Government and NATO's ambitious vision. While the limits of democratic peace theory have been evident in the outcomes, challenges, and costs of Afghanistan and Iraq, the U.S. Government's strategic guidance has largely failed to set realistic or feasible objectives. The U.S. Government has also failed to take truly substantive actions to overcome the major shortfalls in interagency coordination and integration that have generally characterized the U.S. effort over most of its duration. Moreover, the disjointed strategic guidance has typically included metrics for success that are broad enough that agencies can report "success" on their own terms, without necessarily having to link their agency efforts directly to the overarching goals of the mission.

Without question, these strategic shortfalls carry with them significant and adverse strategic and operational consequences. Not the least of these adverse strategic impacts has come in the form of the incredibly expensive costs of the missions in Afghanistan and Iraq, most recently featuring an additional $33 billion earmarked to pay for the expansion of the Afghan war effort and the 30,000 troops of the Afghan surge. These costs, along with the $159 billion requested for FY2011, come on top of nearly $1 trillion of debt-fueled spending on these missions in prior years. Other related adverse effects have resulted from a strategic and operational disunity of effort, leading to an inefficient and often ineffective use of resources and a basic lack of accountability.

Extending these themes further, the U.S. Government's strategic shortcomings in Afghanistan also represent a recipe for increased strategic and operational risk in other regions of the world, reducing America's strategic flexibility for both "hard" and "soft" power, while severely taxing the U.S. economy during a time of recession and economic instability. The mission's duration and corresponding contributions to the national debt clearly represent major strategic risks of their own. Along the same lines, the U.S. policy in Afghanistan has clearly sacrificed potential opportunities for the multilateral pursuit of common interests, and its generally heavy-handed, military-centered approach—coupled with the decision to invade Iraq—squandered international legitimacy as well as opportunities for cooperation with key potential strategic partners. At the same time, the decentralized and transnational nature of the genuine terrorist threat, along with the portability of WMD and the uncertainty of the eventual outcome in Afghanistan, all represent other risks that call into question the long-range viability and desirability of the U.S. strategic choices. These choices have also contributed to a reliance on the DoD for nonmilitary ends which, when coupled with the military's natural focus on military operations, has resulted in accepting risk in other strategic requirements.

In getting to this point in our history, the United States was quick to specify ambitious ends and vaguely defined and overly optimistic ways, without ever grappling seriously with the questions of the exact means needed or available to achieve those ambitious ends and ways. In this way, the United States "backed" into nation-building without any serious, realistic, or rational discussion of the interests, ends, ways, or means at stake in the expansion of that mission. This strategic shortcoming was subsequently exacerbated, as Afghanistan was basically ignored for several years as a result of the decision to go to war in Iraq. Added to this recipe for serious problems was the fact that Defense Secretary Rumsfeld focused at the outset of the mission on validating his light-footprint theories of modern military power, and the associated under-resourcing of the Afghan mission was only reinforced by the subsequent decision to shift the main strategic effort to Iraq. As such, not only do these strategic choices represent a failure to conduct rational strategy formulation, but they are also indicative of a serious underestimation of the challenges involved in each mission, coupled with an overestimation of available U.S. agency capabilities and resources. In much the same way, this disjointed strategy ignored the broader strategic context, as the United States took on unsustainable costs, while potentially damaging other competing vital interests and sacrificing the strategic flexibility needed to address contingencies and requirements elsewhere in the world.

Contrary to the tenets of rational strategy formulation, U.S. policymakers settled upon their strategic ways first, without any serious discussion of the vital interests at stake, the ends required to protect those interests, or the actual U.S. agency resources and capabilities available to realize that vision. And although the complexity and evolving nature of national security issues will always necessitate modifications to strategic plans as circumstances unfold, in the case of Afghanistan there has been no serious national discussion differentiating between "needs" and "wants." As a result, the United States is now muddling ineffectually through a foreign policy that is too expensive and comes with major uncertainties of outcome and major risks. In the bipolar era of the Cold War, we may have been able to conduct foreign policy this way. However, we no longer have the luxury of saving the hard thinking and hard choices for later, if we ever did. Modern U.S. strategy must consist of more than mere statements of vision and intent.

ENDNOTES - CHAPTER 4

1. Office of the Special Representative for Afghanistan and Pakistan, *Afghanistan and Pakistan Regional Stabilization Strategy*, Washington, DC: U.S. Government Printing Office, February 2010, p. 1.

2. Shahid Afsar, Chris Samples, and Thomas Wood, "The Taliban: An Organizational Analysis," *Military Review*, May-June 2008, p. 64.

3. William Morris, ed., *The American Heritage Dictionary of the English Language, New College Edition*, Boston, MA: Houghton-Mifflin, 1981, p. 378.

4. Harry R. Yarger, *Strategic Theory for the 21st Century: The Little Book on Big Strategy*, Carlisle, PA: Strategic Studies Institute, U.S. Army War College, February 2006, p. 2.

5. *Ibid.*

6. *Ibid.*

7. *Ibid.*, pp. 70-71.

8. Secretary of Defense, *Proliferation: Threat and Response*, Washington: U.S. Government Printing Office, January 2001, summary and chapter on South Asia.

9. Ahmed Rashid, *Descent into Chaos*, New York: Penguin, 2008, p. 173.

10. Richard B. Doyle, "The U.S. National Security Strategy: Policy, Politics, and Problems," *Public Administration Review*, July/August 2007, pp. 624-625.

11. Office of the Special Representative for Afghanistan and Pakistan, *Afghanistan and Pakistan Regional Stabilization Strategy*, Washington, DC: U.S. Government Printing Office, February 2010.

12. Gary Dempsey, "The Folly of Nation-Building in Afghanistan," *CATO Institute*, available from *www.cato.org*.

13. Astri Suhrke, "A Contradictory Mission? NATO from Stabilization to Combat in Afghanistan," *International Peacekeeping*, Vol. 15, No. 2, April 2008, p. 215.

14. *Ibid.*, p. 228.

15. Javier Solana, EU High Representative for the Common Foreign and Security Policy, *Summary of the Intervention*, SO229/02, available from *ue.eu.int/newsroom*, p. 2.

16. *Ibid.*

17. *Afghanistan Reconstruction: Despite Some Progress, Deteriorating Security and Other Obstacles Continue to Threaten Achievement of U.S. Goals*, GAO, GAO-05-742, Washington, DC: U.S. Government Accountability Office, July 2005, p. 8.

18. Kenneth Katzman, *Afghanistan: Current Issues and U.S. Policy*, Washington, DC: CRS Report for Congress, RL30588, August 27, 2003, p. 12.

19. Solana, p. 3.

20. Suhrke, p. 228.

21. *Ibid.*, p. 214.

22. Rajiv Chandrasekaran, "A New Plan for Afghanistan," *The Washington Post Weekly*, June 29, 2009, p. 7.

23. Rashid, pp. 174-175.

24. David Rhode and David E. Sanger, "How the 'Good War' in Afghanistan Went Bad," *The New York Times*, August 12, 2007, pp. A1, 12-13.

25. *Ibid.*

26. *Ibid.*

27. James F. Dobbins, *After the Taliban: Nation-Building in Afghanistan*, Washington, DC: Potomac, 2008, pp. 129-130.

28. Katzman, summary.

29. The President of the United States, *The National Security Strategy of the United States of America*, Washington, DC: U.S. Government, March 2002, p. 1.

30. President George W. Bush, *National Strategy to Combat Weapons of Mass Destruction*, Washington, DC: U.S. Government Printing Office, December 2002, p. 2.

31. *Afghanistan Reconstruction*, p. 8.

32. *Ibid.*, p. 9.

33. Katzman, summary.

34. *Ibid.*

35. Rhode and Sanger, pp. A1, 12-13.

36. *Afghanistan Reconstruction*, p. 10.

37. *Ibid.*

38. *Ibid.*

39. Rhode and Sanger, pp. A1, 12-13.

40. *Ibid.*

41. Suhrke, p. 214.

42. Katzman, summary.

43. Suhrke, p. 220.

44. *Ibid.*, p. 215.

45. *Ibid.*, p. 229.

46. *Ibid.*, p. 218.

47. *Ibid.*, p. 219.

48. *Ibid.*

49. *Ibid.*

50. *Ibid.*, p. 217.

51. Rhode and Sanger, pp. A1, 12-13.

52. Secretary Donald Rumsfeld, *National Military Strategic Plan for the War on Terrorism*, Washington, DC: U.S. Government Printing Office, February 1, 2006.

53. *Ibid.*, p. 33.

54. The President of the United States, *The National Security Strategy of the United States of America*, Washington, DC: U.S. Government, March 2006, p. 1.

55. *Ibid.*, p. 4.

56. Rhode and Sanger, pp. A1, 12-13.

57. Ibid.

58. The President of the United States, *The National Strategy for Combating Terrorism*, Washington, DC: U.S. Government, September 2006, pp. 9-17.

59. *Ibid.*, pp. 12-17.

60. Karen DeYoung and Joby Warrick, "Change Comes to Pakistan," *The Washington Post National Weekly Edition*, August 13-19, 2007, p. 9.

61. Suhrke, p. 227.

62. Jim Hoagland, "Poppies vs. Power in Afghanistan," *The Washington Post Weekly*, January 20, 2008, p. 5.

63. DeYoung and Warrick, p. 9.

64. U.S. Department of State, *FY2010 Mission Strategic Plan, U.S. Mission to Afghanistan*, Washington, DC: U.S. Government Printing Office, May 12, 2008.

65. This observation was offered by Colonel Mike McMahon, former CJ-7 of CSTC-A.

66. Mark Mazzetti and David E. Sanger, "Obama Expands Missile Strikes Inside Pakistan," *The New York Times*, February 21, 2009, available from *www.nytimes.com*.

67. Ibid.

68. "A New Strategy for Afghanistan and Pakistan," *The Briefing Room-The Blog*, blog post on White House public site posted March 27, 2009, available from *www.whitehouse.gov*.

69. Ibid.

70. Ibid.

71. *Ibid.*

72. "Obama: Safety of World at Stake in Afghanistan," *CNN.com* report, available from *www.cnn.com*.

73. "A New Strategy for Afghanistan and Pakistan."

74. Katzman, summary.

75. Fred Kaplan, "The Transformer," *Foreign Policy*, September/October 2010, p. 97.

76. Bob Woodward, "Preventing Another Iraq," *The Washington Post National Weekly Edition*, July 13-19, 2009, p. 19.

77. Katzman, summary.

78. Anne Gearan (Associated Press), *The Washington Times*, available from *www.washingtontimes.com*.

79. Stanley A. McChrystal, *COMISAF'S Initial Assessment*, Kabul, Afghanistan: International Security Force Headquarters, August 30, 2009, p. 1-1.

80. *Ibid.*

81. Bob Woodward, "McChrystal: More Forces or 'Mission Failure'," *The Washington Post*, September 21, 2009, available from *www.washingtonpost.com*.

82. Kaplan, pp. 96-97.

83. William H. McMichael, "Afghanistan Withdrawal in '11 Could Be a Problem, Critics Say," *The Army Times*, December 14, 2009, p. 10.

84. Rod Norland, "Afghan Strategy Shifts to Accent Civilian Projects," *The New York Times*, June 9, 2010, p. A1.

85. Rajiv Chandrasekaran, "General Petraeus Says Afghanistan War Strategy 'Fundamentally Sound,'" *The Washington Post*, August 16, 2010, available from *www.washingtonpost.com*.

86. Doyle, p. 626.

87. *The National Security Strategy of the United States of America*, March 2006, pp. 1-3.

88. *Ibid.*, pp. 12, 16.

89. Anthony H. Cordesman, "The Missing Metrics of 'Progress' in Afghanistan (and Pakistan)," unpublished manuscript from the Center for Strategic and International Studies, Washington, DC, November 29, 2007, pp. 3-6.

90. *Ibid.*, summary.

91. Office of the Special Representative for Afghanistan and Pakistan, *Afghanistan and Pakistan Regional Stabilization Strategy*, Washington, DC: State Department, February, 2010, Message from the Secretary of State.

92. *Ibid.*, Table of Contents.

93. *Ibid.*, p. viii.

94. *Ibid.*, pp. 7-10.

95. *Ibid.*, p. iii.

96. *Ibid.*, Front pages.

97. *Ibid.*, p. 1.

98. The President of the United States, *The National Security Strategy of the United States of America*, Washington, DC: U.S. Government, May 2010, p. 21.

99. Anthony H. Cordesman, "The Afghan War – Part Three: Implementing the New Strategy," Burke Chair in Strategy publication from the Center for Strategic and International Studies, Washington, DC, September 8, 2010, p. 6, available from *csis.org/files/publication/100909_AfghanWarStatus-III_Strategy.pdf*.

100. "Obama Seeks Record $708 Billion in FY11 Defense Budget," *Reuters,* available from *www.reuters.com/article/idUSN01181674201002010.*

CHAPTER 5

A CLASH OF ORGANIZATIONAL CULTURES AND RESOURCES

> We're just very small, and on many occasions I've been asked if the State Department could do things. It's been hard to do. We have roughly 6,500 professionals world-wide. . . . [T]here are twice as many lawyers in the Defense Department as Foreign Service officers.
>
> Secretary of State Condoleezza Rice in testimony before the Senate Foreign Relations Committee, February 13, 2008[1]

While defects in the process of formulating strategy have posed serious obstacles to mission success in Afghanistan, the inadequate policy products that have resulted from that process do not represent the only major barriers to successful nation-building and irregular warfare operations. On the contrary, these efforts have also been hampered by the fact that the institutional means available within the U.S. Government to carry out the complex and extensive tasks associated with nation-building and irregular warfare are inadequate to the demands of these types of missions. While numerous U.S. departments and agencies hold some responsibility for the operations in Afghanistan, the Department of Defense (DoD), the Department of State (State), and the U.S. Agency for International Development (USAID) serve as the "key three" for counterinsurgency and nation-building, with the Central Intelligence Agency (CIA) functioning as a shadowy and essentially independent fourth. For a host of reasons, however, these agencies are not especially well suited for the tasks required of them by these endeavors. In particular, these key agencies are poorly suited for nation-building, due to the realities of their respective organizational cultures, their existing core competencies, conflicting career incentives, and several other factors.

As an added challenge, the adverse effects of these organizational mismatches have been exacerbated by the disproportionate allocation of resources to the DoD that has characterized the mission in Afghanistan over its course. As a consequence of this resource imbalance and the shortfalls in agency capabilities and resources, the U.S. Government has come to rely heavily upon private contractors to perform a wide variety of functions, many of them critical to the overall success of the mission. This reliance on contractors is itself an especially troubling choice, given the contractors' own conflicting incentive structures and the mismatches between their own levels and types of experience and the demands of these complex missions. The relationships among the various agencies and the contractors have also featured muddled lines of authority and ineffective mechanisms for exercising accountability. Viewed in the aggregate, there is evidence of a clear mismatch between the U.S. strategy for Afghanistan and the basic capabilities and resources of the agencies responsible for carrying out that strategy, since the United States has failed to perform the national strategic-level linkage of "troops-to-task"—or capabilities to requirements—needed to set the conditions for mission success.

THE CLASH OF ORGANIZATIONAL CULTURES

The three key U.S. governmental agencies holding the primary responsibilities for the execution of Afghan counterinsurgency and nation-building missions are poorly suited to the demands of these missions, as a result of their prevailing organizational cultures. Organizational culture refers to "a persistent, patterned way of thinking about the central tasks of and human relationships within an organization," an organizational trait sometimes likened to personality in humans.[2] In a more direct sense, organizational culture also refers to an institution's ingrained focus, its interpretation of its core tasks and responsibilities, and the level or levels — strategic, operational, or tactical — at which the members of the organization have the most experience and skill. In the case of State, USAID, and the DoD, these three key agencies' organizational cultures are mismatched with the requirements of nation-building, as their predominant organizational cultural norms, existing core competencies, and comparative levels of resources fall well short of the focus and capabilities needed to succeed in these missions. While these three agencies serve as the focal point for the U.S. Government's efforts in Afghanistan, this same mismatch between organizational capabilities and the demands of the mission exists among the various other U.S. Government agencies operating in Afghanistan as well.

Consequently, a fair portion of the broader disjointedness and lack of coherence that is found across the reach of the U.S. national security apparatus stems from critical differences among the key agencies involved in the interagency process itself. These shortfalls include major organizational cultural disparities, as well as mismatches between the capabilities and expertise required at different strategic levels within those agencies to bring about success in counterinsurgency and nation-building. Furthermore, each of these agencies promotes and rewards certain types of assignments, with the most advantageous assignments in some agencies often being internal to the organizations themselves, rather than in service in an interagency setting or in overseas postings. It is helpful to examine the organizational cultures of each of the "key three" agencies before turning our attention to the ways in which the organizations interact.

The U.S. Department of State.

Over its long history, the Department of State has centered on two primary functions, including representing the interests of the United States and its citizens with foreign countries, and serving as the principal source of advice to the President on foreign affairs.[3] In general, State is known for its organizational culture of talk and diplomacy, and at the theater-strategic level, the department concentrates on the embassy activities within each country. State's expertise in governance resides primarily at the strategic level, and the organization often falters when asked to participate in or shape U.S. governmental actions at the operational or tactical levels. Political scientist and organizational theorist James Q. Wilson notes that State continues to "do what State does," emphasizing its key core competencies of filing reports and crafting official policy communications.[4] Wilson further observes that "Foreign Service officers place a high value on 'the diplomatic approach' that . . . means caution, an aversion to bold language or action, and a desire for consensus."[5]

From an operational perspective, State also has a persistent reputation for being poor at administering embassy security—one of its few and most basic operational responsibilities—and the department views its core tasks as "maintaining relationships and replying to correspondence," or rendering reports that constitute policy when considered in the aggregate.[6] Not surprisingly, then, State's organizational culture focuses upon communication skills, rather than administrative or operational tasks, and the organization has a reputation for inefficiency in the few administrative tasks required of it—promoting and rewarding "effective reporting" and "maintaining relationships"—more than any other qualifications.[7]

Furthermore, these organizational cultural characteristics are deeply entrenched. In viewing the organization from a historical perspective, organizational theorist Donald Warwick's careful study of State and its dominant characteristics shows that the roots of these institutional traits can be traced all the way back to State's origins in 1789 and the ratification of the U.S. Constitution. At that time, the fledgling agency adopted the European model of diplomacy, with its emphasis on "representation, negotiation, and intelligence."[8] These roles were codified formally by Secretary of State Thomas Jefferson, but the American people's native distrust of foreign affairs and foreign entanglements slowed the development of the agency and the American diplomatic service corps for many years—a trend that remained even as late as the end of the 19th century.[9] At the same time, a rivalry developed within the department between the two "career lines" of consular service and diplomacy, leaving State largely unprepared for the demands of World War II.[10] In light of this unpreparedness, as well as the wartime proliferation of 46 other agencies and departments with some overseas roles or functions, it was at this point that State lost its primacy in American foreign affairs and, arguably, has never recovered it.[11]

Conceived mainly by the first Secretary of Defense, James Forrestal, the Secretary of Defense and the Joint Chiefs of Staff were able to consolidate the military's gains in foreign policy influence through the creation of the National Security Council in 1947, a move that further undermined the State Department by giving the military direct access to the President, something it had not had under President Franklin Roosevelt.[12] Describing the internal environment of State over the course of history, Warwick notes that although the agency has modest responsibilities for processing visas, passports, and other miscellaneous services to other government agencies and American travelers, the organization perceives its primary function as producing "foreign policy."[13] With this primary function in mind, the major focus of State activity is on producing written reports that, taken together, constitute foreign policy.[14] As a byproduct of "the vagueness of foreign policy, overlapping of functions, and specialization" within the department, State's organizational culture is one in which constant consultation and discussion are expected before any actions are taken, and the anticipated result of that consultation and discussion is a position on a foreign policy issue, rather than any concrete action plans or the management of operational functions.[15]

Corroborating this perspective, an insider's account of the State Department in the 1920s described the organization as a "small, compact group of men and women, experts in their fields, who were competent to advise the Secretary of State and the President on the conduct of foreign policy."[16] The emphasis then, as now, was clearly on advising decisionmakers, rather than on executing policy. And even as State was subsequently expanded significantly in the post-World War II years, that same insider noted that by the 1950s the agency had become a "bureaucratic empire," one in which leaks of sensitive information and factual errors in State products were common.[17] Citing widespread "overstaffing and inefficiency" across the department in the 1950s, this senior official drew a distinction between the agency's smaller predecessors and their effectiveness in providing "a full and up to date report of what was done by the government in its relations with other governments."[18] Describing an agency full of competing agendas and interests, he cautioned, "Do not make the mistake of thinking of the State Department as the extension of the personality of one man, the Secretary of State, whoever he may be at any particular moment."[19]

In terms of State's modern structures, the organizational configuration at State presents its own challenges, as the subject matter experts are assigned to country and regional desks that are, in turn, juxtaposed against other functional alignments, with each answering to assorted undersecretaries and deputies.[20] Compounding this fragmented and unwieldy organizational structure, State is also often criticized for an organizational culture that tends toward six "faults": (1) a poor quality of staff work and analysis; (2) a slow pace of responses to requests for information or action; (3) a resistance to change and new approaches to problems; (4) an inadequacy in carrying out presidential decisions; (5) a failure to lead on foreign affairs; and, (6) a sense that the State Department leadership does not actually control its subordinate subdepartments.[21]

Regarding State's operations in Afghanistan specifically, a variety of participant accounts corroborate these unflattering perspectives. Among them, Ambassador James Dobbins complained of this same "bureaucratic inertia" within the Department of State in his own account of his efforts to move the mission forward in Afghanistan in 2002.[22] A U.S. military intelligence officer similarly described the embassy compound in Kabul as "the most secure compound I encountered in the country," with a nickname of "Fort Paranoia."[23] Echoing this sentiment, one World Bank official noted that the U.S. Embassy in Kabul was so cut off from the rest of the country that it might as well be in Washington.[24] As a participant in the Country Team's working meetings chaired by then-U.S. Ambassador Zalmay Khalilzad, this officer noted that these meetings had a flavor exactly opposite of the command-centered military meetings he had participated in previously, with the Ambassador providing information to the various agency representatives rather than those agencies bringing information to him.[25] He further describes an atmosphere of bloated bureaucracy and convoluted funding and support arrangements.[26] My own experiences in the embassy and in the interagency environment in Afghanistan matched these observations.

Finally, these dominant norms of the State Department's organizational culture are readily apparent in the department's country-specific products and procedures. Most directly, this general lack of a planning and operator culture is clearly evident in products that are typically long on policy and broadly worded goals, but short on specific action plans and comprehensive metrics for measuring success. With this organizational culture in mind, it has become evident in the theaters in Afghanistan and Iraq that conducting foreign policy does not equal "building foreign governmental capacity." State's lack of operational capability is also evident in the agency's generally unrealistic expectations about what can or cannot be done in a combat theater, along with overly optimistic timelines for the completion of complex operational tasks. Viewed in the aggregate, the members of State are typically thinkers, talkers, diplomats, communicators, and reporters, largely stuck in the embassy and with limited agility when it comes to planning or operating in the field. Recognizing some of these limitations in their own department, State has recently initiated an attempt to change its own organizational culture through the implementation of a "Quadrennial Diplomacy and Development Review" (QDDR), patterned after the DoD's "Quadrennial Defense Review" (QDR).

The U.S. Agency for International Development.

The U.S. Agency for International Development was created by the Kennedy administration in 1961 for the express purpose of administering foreign economic assistance programs and distributing aid. As a product of the Cold War era, USAID was the first agency "whose primary emphasis was on long-range economic and social development assistance efforts . . . freed from the political and military functions that plagued its predecessor organizations."[27] From its inception, USAID has been an action-oriented field organization responsible for carrying out the U.S. Government's routine humanitarian assistance and economic development activities, rather than an agency concerned with the more substantial and comprehensive requirements of "nation-building." As such, the agency's organizational culture centers on its field activities and delivery of aid at the local level of operations.

As a consequence of this tactical-level focus, the agency is much less effective when asked to participate in or shape the U.S. Government's actions at the operational or theater-strategic levels. Representative of this mindset, USAID leaders can typically point to a map and identify hundreds of development projects that are underway or completed, but they are far less adept at coordinating those projects across the theater to achieve broader operational or strategic objectives. Similarly, the agency is not very effective at the task of coordinating all of the components needed for each developmental project, such as linking teachers with schools, judges with courthouses, or jails with police officers. Like State, then, in Afghanistan USAID continues to "do what they do," including subcontracting local development projects, meeting with local officials, and operating mainly in the permissive security environments in the country where their agents and contractors can move about freely. Furthermore, this organizational mindset is not new to the agency, as there were similar criticisms leveled at USAID in Vietnam. During that war, military commanders complained that the USAID operatives tended to cling to the urban centers, rather than remaining in the villages and hamlets where they were most needed.[28]

As another aspect of this organizational dynamic, USAID is nominally subordinate to State in the executive branch's current bureaucratic organizational arrangements. In reality, however, the agency answers to its own hierarchy and pursues its own programs and priorities, consistent with its members' interpretations of the agency's mission and capabilities. Along these lines, while State typically sets goals that are somewhat lofty and broad in their phrasing and scope, USAID typically expresses its achievements in terms of numbers of projects completed and processes implemented, rather than in end-states achieved. Examples of these USAID metrics include immunizations given, miles of roads constructed, government assistance provided, and estimates of "lives saved."[29] Compounding these organizational differences in vision and interpretation of mission, State and USAID have business development, economic assistance, and agricultural programs that cut across different internal organizational boundaries, likely due to the legacy of their past independent operations.[30]

In any event, while USAID is supposed to assist State in a subordinate executive role to help further U.S. foreign policy objectives, the two organizations tend to focus on opposite ends of the national security spectrum. USAID's culture typically focuses on "operators" and the tactical-level, which is clearly at odds with State's "big picture" strategic-level emphasis. Adding to the challenges posed by this juxtaposition of organizational cultures, it was also apparent to me during my own time in Afghanistan that while the U.S. ambassador serves as the senior representative for the President and State on the ground, the USAID leadership in the theater of operations was at least as concerned about the guidance and approval of the senior USAID leaders in Washington as they were with the approval for their activities from the ambassador. It was equally clear that neither the State nor USAID organizational cultures feature the planning and operational mindset that is common within the DoD, a reality that severely limits the effectiveness of both organizations in their execution of the complex requirements of nation-building.

As further evidence of these differences in organizational culture, key documents from each organization and other documents issued jointly by the two institutions provide additional insights into their respective organizational cultural norms. Reflecting the task that led to its creation in 1961, the *USAID Primer: What We Do and How We Do It* interprets the agency's core task as "promoting national security ... by addressing poverty fueled by lack of economic opportunity, one of the root causes of violence today."[31] Surveying its own institutional challenges, the *USAID Failed States Strategy* of 2005 identifies a number of shortcomings that USAID must overcome to be more successful in its reconstruction and nation-building activities. These required changes include increasing the agency's ability to operate within non-permissive environments, and shifting from its current focus on policy reform to institution building when assisting host nations with governance. This document also cites other needed improvements, including a call for a shift in agency emphasis to infrastructure deficits, such as road-building competencies, the development of its rapid response capabilities, and increasing interagency effectiveness.[32]

Along the same lines, State and USAID's jointly issued *Strategic Plan, Fiscal Years 2007-2012* outlines the strategic goals of these two agencies and provides further insights into the dominant norms of their organizational cultures. Defining the organizations' joint mission, the document states:

> Advance freedom for the benefit of the American people and the international community by helping

to build and sustain a more democratic, secure, and prosperous world composed of well-governed states that respond to the needs of their people, reduce widespread poverty, and act responsibly within the international system.[33]

The document further identifies seven broad strategic goals for State and USAID: "1) Achieving peace and security; 2) governing justly and democratically; 3) investing in people; 4) promoting economic growth and prosperity; 5) providing humanitarian assistance; 6) promoting international understanding; and 7) strengthening our consular and management capabilities."[34]

In terms of the processes or means to be used to achieve these lofty ends, the State-USAID strategic plan states that the Assistant Secretary for Resource Management and the senior leaders of the regional bureaus will "hold detailed reviews annually with approximately 30 percent of missions to evaluate recent progress and program changes, including resource and personnel requests."[35] The document also mentions country-specific program evaluations in the form of Country Operational Plans and annual reviews as another process. However, these reviews are focused only on those countries that receive foreign assistance funds, and they are aimed at providing an interagency overview of the execution of that assistance.[36] The State-USAID strategic plan also briefly mentions coordinating with key U.S. agency partners to achieve the seven major goals, though the document offers no details as to how this coordination is to occur—a shortfall that is particularly conspicuous given State's usual responsibilities as the senior U.S. officials in any country in which U.S. agencies operate. In essence, the document is typical of State in that it offers broad rhetoric with few specifics, and in this way it is consistent with the organization's dominant cultural norm of making policy without specifying the ways or means that will be used to achieve the policy's ambitious ends.

Consistent with these national-level documents, the joint State and USAID country-specific products represent an interesting hybrid of the two organizational cultures. These documents reflect a mix of State's broadly worded and ambitious goals that are subsequently reduced to USAID-style metrics focused on individual projects, and thus lack any comprehensive and coordinated measures of success in the process. As noted in the previous chapter, the documents generally fall far short of what is needed to coordinate, integrate, and evaluate the U.S. Government's nation-building performance in Afghanistan. In sum, neither State nor USAID has the norms of planning and operations as central features of their respective organizational cultures. Lacking its own more comprehensive performance measures, State has maintained its own rhetorical style in its articulation of U.S. objectives, while adopting the USAID's project-centered metrics in establishing the benchmarks for measuring success.

The U.S. Department of Defense.

The U.S. Department of Defense is a robust and action-oriented field organization, and one centered on military and security operations. The DoD is highly effective at planning and executing military operations at the theater-strategic, operational, and tactical levels, but to date the organization has been less effective in planning and executing the nonmilitary components of nation-building and counterinsurgency operations. These nontraditional mission elements range from economic and governmental development to the implementation of the rule of law and others. Consistent with its self-identity as an institution that exists to "fight and win our nation's wars," the DoD has at times been resistant to the nonmilitary aspects of counterinsurgency and stability operations. In these settings, the DoD usually interprets "security" as meaning developing and assisting indigenous security forces. As has become clear in Afghanistan and Iraq, however, real security also involves economic development, the creation of a culture that respects the rule of law, and a government with the systems and structures in place to root out corruption and corrupt officials. As an organization, the DoD and its leaders have been somewhat slower to embrace these roles.

While the DoD leadership and the institution have at times resisted the shift to nation-building and other stabilization and reconstruction tasks, for the most part the DoD has worked hard to become a learning organization that increases its capabilities in these areas. Applying its organizational cultural norm of "can-do" to these nontraditional missions, DoD leaders are more likely to request additional resources to avoid mission failure than to give up, as the organization's typical response is to say "yes" to whatever mission it is presented and then do what it takes within the boundaries of the law to get it done. Nevertheless, upon taking command in Afghanistan, General Stanley McChrystal acknowledged in his initial assessment of conditions that nearly a decade into the mission a mismatch still remained between the military's mission requirements and its existing capabilities, noting that "ISAF [International Security Assistance Force] is a conventional force that is poorly configured for [counterinsurgency], inexperienced in local languages and culture, and struggling with challenges inherent to coalition warfare."[37] With these shortfalls in mind, General McChrystal was also adamant in his call for a properly resourced strategy, arguing that "Resourcing coalition forces below this level will leave critical areas of Afghanistan open to insurgent influence while the ANSF [Afghanistan National Security Force] grows."[38] He took similarly aggressive steps to begin to shift the kinetic focus within the U.S. and NATO forces as well.

Lastly, while the key three agencies are the most significant players in these missions, there are many other U.S. agencies playing their own important roles in the nation-building component of the Afghan mission. These other important agencies in Afghanistan include State's Justice Sector Support Program (JSSP) and the International Bureau of Narcotics and Law Enforcement (INL); the Drug Enforcement Administration (DEA); and the CIA. Still others include agencies whose parent organizations are more typically focused on their domestic American activities, such as the U.S. Department of Agriculture (USDA) and its Foreign Agricultural Service (FAS), along with the Department of Justice (DoJ) and its Office of Overseas Prosecutorial Development, Assistance, and Training (OPDAT) and International Criminal Investigative Training Assistance Program (ICITAP).[39] Altogether, these organizations represent an "alphabet soup" of agencies with competing jurisdictions, agendas, interests, capabilities, and visions for the desired end-states in Afghanistan. Unfortunately, what each of them also holds in common is a generally poor organizational fit with the complex and expansive demands of nation-building and counterinsurgency.

As a related adverse consequence of these organizational mismatches, these agencies generally lack a common operating picture and a common understanding of the problem in Afghanistan. Instead, each agency settles upon a different definition of the problem consistent with its own culture, capabilities, and internal operating procedures. Likewise, there are also significant differences between the agencies' respective career incentives for overseas and interagency service, because some organizations require their employees to accept overseas or interagency assignments while others do not. A similar disparity exists in terms of promotion practices, with some agencies and departments placing an emphasis on overseas or interagency postings for the purposes of promotion, while others focus on assignments within the parent organizations in the United States.

Along the same lines, researchers point to these differences in organizational culture and the major disparity in resources as primary causes of interagency coordination challenges and conflicts. In some cases, other sources of organizational friction result from the internal differences between components of the same organization concerned with long-term responses to foreign policy challenges and those concerned with short-term or emergency responses.[40] In sum, these differences in organizational culture present challenges for and between each of the agencies operating in Afghanistan.

THE DISPARITY BETWEEN REQUIRED CAPABILITIES AND RESOURCES

In addition to the challenges posed by these mismatched organizational cultures, the key three U.S. agencies central to nation-building in Afghanistan are also poorly equipped for this mission in terms of core expertise, capabilities, and available resources. There has been no real strategic-level troop-to-task analysis for the nation-building objectives. To put this claim into perspective, one has only to examine the key documents that provide national strategic guidance and agency directives to see evidence of these disconnections. *The National Security Strategy* of 2006 places "democracy promotion" at the center of the U.S. national security effort, "promoting effective democracies" as the primary means of thwarting an "aggressive ideology of hatred and murder."[41] While each document modestly reduces expectations for Afghanistan, the *Afghanistan and Pakistan Regional Stabilization Strategy* and the Obama administration's own *National Security Strategy*, both published in 2010, continue this trend of relatively unconstrained strategic reach.

Examining the country-specific strategy more directly, the published guidance fails to assign responsibilities for the accomplishment of its ambitious goals, and the plans also fail to define clearly the tasks associated with these goals. Likewise, some of the national strategic goals also require capabilities not currently found among the U.S. governmental agencies in question. For example, U.S. Central Command (USCENTCOM) commander Admiral William Fallon stated in his testimony before the Senate Armed Services Committee in May 2007 that U.S. forces were working toward "improving Afghan governance, infrastructure, and the economy," and that the United States was "actively pursuing initiatives in . . . building schools (and) stimulating the growth of small businesses."[42] Admiral Fallon did not offer insights into how the U.S. military was developing the specific expertise needed to carry out these diverse, nonmilitary functions. At about the same time, however, another senior American commander noted that he "could count on the fingers of one or two hands the number of U.S. Government agricultural experts" sent to Afghanistan, in spite of the fact that 80 percent of the Afghan economy is agriculturally based.[43]

As another snapshot of these disconnections, State also published a document that solicits American business investment in Afghanistan, an initiative seemingly wholly out of touch with the realities of the security conditions on the ground.[44] Expressing his own concerns regarding the disconnection of capabilities from requirements, Ambassador John Herbst, State's Coordinator for Reconstruction and Stabilization Operations, identified some of these same gaps in vision and capability in his testimony before the House Armed Services Committee in 2008.[45] Obscuring this broad mismatch between ends, ways, and means, was the fact that it was not until September 2009 that the FY2009 supplemental appropriation required the administration to develop better metrics to evaluate progress in Afghanistan, including "the performance and legitimacy of the Afghan government and its efforts to curb official corruption."[46]

Examining this capabilities gap more specifically, it is unlikely that any agency could achieve success in Afghanistan without a deep understanding of the particular challenges of the country's social, cultural, political, and economic framework, or the constraints posed by them. As a simple but important example of this shortfall, in the early days of the Afghan mission one observer noted that only one member of the State operation in Kabul spoke an Afghan language.[47] Almost 10 years into the mission in Afghanistan, there is still very limited country-specific language capability or Afghan cultural skills within the key U.S. agencies operating in the country.

In this same vein, it has also been difficult for State to fill its embassy postings in Kabul and its positions on Provincial Reconstruction Teams (PRT). At one point, State had to ask the DoD to come up with about 120 personnel to fill 350 new positions created on the PRTs, and the DoD filled the requirement but could do so only on a temporary basis.[48] Part of the reason the DoD had a difficult time filling the 120 positions—in spite of the fact that 2.5 million members serve in the department altogether—was that the PRT positions called for senior personnel who were well-versed in political, military, and economic affairs—unfortunately, personnel with these qualifications where in short supply and needed by the DoD for other assignments as well.[49] State is further challenged by the fact that its overseas postings are filled on a voluntary basis, rather than by mandate. The gap between agency capabilities and mission requirements is even more dramatic when one considers the hundreds of complex tasks and subtasks that nation-building comprises.

These problems are further compounded by the major differences between the DoD and the other-than-DoD agencies, in terms of their respective resources, interests, and jurisdictional authorities. As an oft-cited example, there are more members of Army bands than there are Foreign Service officers, and it is also commonly pointed out that all of State comprises fewer personnel than the sailors who make up one carrier battle group. There are approximately 6,500 Foreign Service officers altogether who are responsible for both the emergency response functions and the longer-term planning at State.[50] Additionally, State's responsibilities increased significantly when the U.S. Government disbanded the United States Information Agency (USIA), and the number of personnel within USAID was also drastically reduced at about the same time USIA was dismantled. Putting a fine point on this imbalance, there are about 2,000 total USAID employees responsible for all of the functions of that agency.[51] Conversely, there are 23,000 people in the Pentagon working on planning and strategy development alone, and the DoD budget now exceeds $700 billion per year.[52] The combined budgets of State and USAID total about $25 billion annually.[53]

In spite of the heightened diplomatic and economic demands of nation-building, this resource disparity is apparent at the operational level of activity as well, with the Commander's Emergency Response Fund serving as another effective example of the major disparity in resources between the agencies. Military commanders are given the funds and authority to pay for local projects that will benefit the indigenous population—funds they can utilize at their own discretion. These projects can cost as much as $50,000 or $100,000, yet the U.S. ambassador to that same country—the senior U.S. official—is limited to disbursing a maximum of $50,000 in the event of an emergency.[54] As a side note, State and USAID also face the distinct political disadvantage of having no natural domestic political constituencies, since their budgets are often targeted specifically for congressional rants about money being "wasted" overseas.

The Department of State.

Examining each organization in turn, the State Department is the agency with statutory responsibility for coordinating all U.S. governmental activity in foreign countries.[55] In spite of increasing U.S. overseas engagement and activity around the globe in recent years, State's budget and operations have steadily decreased over the last few decades, including a 20 percent overall decline in the 1970s and 1980s.[56] These reductions took place as part of Vice President Al Gore's National Performance Review (NPR) of the mid-1990s. This initiative actually reduced the number of overseas posts, and featured other measures aimed at streamlining State around its "core missions" of 1) "building and maintaining alliances"; 2) advancing "the economic interests of the American people"; 3) promoting "democratic values and respect for human rights"; and 4) providing "protection and services to Americans abroad" while controlling "access to the United States."[57] As of 2007, State had only 6,500 Foreign Service officers, and USAID had only about 2,000 around the world.[58]

Having identified seven major strategic goals for itself and USAID in its strategic plan, State is even worse off today than it was in years past in terms of its ability to provide assets in support of those ambitious goals. Perhaps not surprisingly, State is hard pressed to identify its own specific successes, describing its work in Afghanistan by using USAID-driven metrics, such as "provided voter registration," "established ... law library," and "trained over 950 judges," rather than more coherent measures that would capture more specific progress toward the accomplishment of the major national and theater objectives.[59] Furthermore, Foreign Service members who have served on PRTs commonly complain that they have felt like "pins on a map," sent out so State officials in Washington can say they were there.[60] Likewise, an internal report within the Kabul Embassy notes that "Job performance is significantly impeded by very strict security requirements that constrain movements," but lauds the "dedicated, all-volunteer staff."[61]

The United States Agency for International Development.

Like its parent organization, USAID's personnel strength levels peaked during the Vietnam War when the agency had about 15,000 personnel. However, the agency's strength had fallen to fewer than 2,000 personnel by 2002, as USAID had shrunk from its strength of 13,000 personnel at the end of the Vietnam War to about 2,300 prior to September 9, 2001 (9/11).[62] The agency's involvement in Afghanistan in the years leading up to the U.S. intervention consisted mostly of providing funds to the United Nations' (UN) World Food Program, and the agency had few, if any, field officers who knew the country or spoke local languages.[63] This lack of field operatives with Afghan cultural skills caused the agency to rely heavily on private contractors "for the management and oversight of its programs" once U.S. operations began.[64] Caused primarily by the major budget-driven personnel reductions in the agency in the 1980s and 1990s, USAID's shortfall in personnel and its heavy reliance on local contractors has meant that in many, if not most, cases, the U.S. contracts have actually been administered by corrupt or incompetent Afghan agents.[65]

From the start of the operations, the USAID agents operating in Kandahar ran into numerous bureaucratic obstacles that prevented the funding and implementation of their projects, while the U.S. Army's civil affairs teams ran into similar impediments in attempting even the most basic tasks.[66] Participants in the USAID reconstruction process also quickly learned that there was no master plan for Afghan development and reconstruction, so the agency instead emphasized

Projects," or "QUIPs," as they came to be known.[67] USAID's budget doubled to $14 billion after 9/11, but the agency only hired an additional 100 officers, and its operation in Kabul included only 12 personnel, as the agency continued its reliance on contractors for the actual provision of all services and reconstruction projects.[68] Sixteen months after President Bush's "Marshall Plan" speech, USAID still had only seven full-time staffers in Afghanistan, along with 35 full-time contract staffers, who were mostly Afghan.[69]

On the positive side of this equation, USAID has developed a solid understanding of the central tasks of democracy-promotion and capacity-building, requirements that are outlined in the agency's publication of December 2005, *At Freedom's Frontiers: A Democracy and Governance Strategic Framework*. This document identifies critical tasks related to the promotion of the rule of law, human rights, justice, effective governance, freedom, and free political discourse and participation.[70] However, the framework falls short in two key ways. First, there is the fact that it prescribes a Western model of democracy and institutions that may not fit all countries or circumstances. Second, the agency clearly does not have the personnel or funding needed to plan, resource, implement, and monitor the processes outlined in the document.

The Department of Defense.

Against the backdrop of this scarcity of resources at State and USAID, it would seem to be hard to make the case that the DoD is also short of the resources needed to accomplish its missions. However, even within the U.S. military and ISAF's major security assistance effort—arguably the main effort for the NATO forces in Afghanistan—a General Accounting Office (GAO) study in 2008 found that the Afghan National Police lacked police trainers and mentors in more than 75% of the Afghan police districts.[71] Reinforcing this view separately, in October 2008, U.S. commanders said they needed at least 2,300 more military personnel to train the Afghan army and police.[72] And in spite of the many billions of dollars already provided to them, the GAO study found that the Afghan National Army (ANA) lacked 40% of the critical materiel needed for its units, while the Afghan National Police (ANP) suffered widespread shortages in basic equipment such as vehicles, radios, and personal armor.[73] More recently, senior leaders have indicated that the police training effort alone is still short by at least 1,000 trainers.

Furthermore, given the scope of this incredibly complex and broad undertaking, it is clear that success in nation-building requires more than merely establishing security, and the assumption that the other pieces of the puzzle will fall into place once a secure environment is created has been shown to be invalid. In John Nagl's well-known book on counter-insurgency, former Army Chief of Staff General Peter Schoomaker notes that "each follow-on unit learns from the experience of those in contact with the enemy."[74] However, it is impossible to teach the parts of the problem that you do not understand yourself, and the U.S. military is unprepared by its existing core competencies to conduct the majority of the tasks subsumed under nation-building. As a result, the military's conventional tactics in Afghanistan have at times been counterproductive to the longer-term objectives of nation-building, demonstrating the gap between the skills and capabilities needed and the realities of the force's current core competencies.[75] This mismatch has been particularly evident in the extensive use of close air support, a tactic that has resulted in numerous incidents of civilian casualties, including one in which it was alleged that U.S. pilots mistook celebratory gunfire at a wedding for a Taliban attack, resulting in about 50 civilian deaths and an Afghan and international outcry.[76]

Expanding on this theme, in any country it is necessary to understand the linkages and nuances of "tribal loyalties, political motivations, and family relationships," among other factors, and to understand the range of feasible governing and economic systems.[77] In his initial assessment after taking command in 2009, General Stanley McChrystal noted that "ISAF is a conventional force . . . poorly configured for [counterinsurgency], inexperienced in local languages and culture, and struggling with the challenges inherent to coalition warfare."[78] General McChrystal called for "a dramatic change in the way we operate," including a "change in operational culture" that would enable the force to "connect with the people."[79] Not surprisingly, the efforts to develop basic Afghan ministerial capabilities, a legitimate Afghan economy, the elements of the rule of law, and a coherent counternarcotics plan have all lagged well behind the effort to develop the security forces, whether viewed in terms of emphasis, effort, or the resources committed to those purposes. Reinforcing this view, a March 2009, study by the GAO noted that the efforts to create administrative capacity in the Ministry of the Interior continued to suffer both from a lack of military resources as well as a lack of cooperation and effort by the Afghans.[80]

In terms of their own resources, other U.S. agencies operating in Afghanistan are even worse off than the "key three." These agencies suffer from their own distinct challenges in the form of a lack of the particular skills needed for counterinsurgency and "nation-building," and an inadequacy of resources needed to carry out the mission. In the case of some of these other agencies, they are hamstrung further by the fact that they are more typically focused on domestic U.S. matters and have little in the way of deployable personnel capable of carrying out these types of missions. For example, neither the Department of Justice (DoJ) nor the U.S. Department of Agriculture (USDA) has significant nation-building expertise or capabilities. Therefore, in spite of the importance of rule of law development, the counternarcotics effort, and agricultural redevelopment to the overall success of the counterinsurgency, USDA had only about six personnel in Afghanistan in the fall of 2008, while the Drug Enforcement Administration (DEA) had about 20 personnel there at the same time. Though slightly better resourced for its rule of law mission, the DoJ has only a few hundred employees available altogether for missions that require them to deploy to the theaters of operations, and those personnel are limited to deployments of a short duration.[81] The "civilian surge" featured in President Obama's announcement of a new strategy for Afghanistan on March 27, 2009, roughly tripled the total number of civilian experts in Afghanistan to 900.[82]

To place these resource constraints into their proper perspective, in the year that President Bush promised a "Marshall Plan" for Afghanistan, the country actually received less per capita aid than Bosnia, Kosovo, or Haiti.[83] Additionally, other critical resources such as Predator drone aircraft and reconstruction assets were diverted to Iraq, among them "elite CIA teams and Special Forces units involved in the search for terrorists."[84] And while the Obama Administration acknowledges that the counternarcotics programs and other activities in Afghanistan are "under-resourced," its Fiscal Year (FY)2010 budget request did not seek significantly higher funding for any of those programs.[85] The request for FY11 also remained at about the same level.

As a consequence of these disparities between agency resources and program management capability, decisionmakers have come to rely upon the Department of Defense even more heavily than they might have otherwise. This reliance on the DoD has translated into the DoD being provided with even more resources in the process, making the resource imbalance between agencies even greater.[86] These disparities are exacerbated further by the fact that the DoD, with its millions of personnel and assets spread throughout every political jurisdiction, enjoys a natural "constituency" status with the policymakers who allocate resources. State and USAID, on the other hand, have miniscule staffs in comparison and little if any natural domestic political "constituency."[87]

The Advantages and Disadvantages of the DoD's Disproportionate Role.

With all of these considerations in mind, it is important to consider the special capabilities that the DoD brings to the table linked to irregular warfare, even as others question why the military is the primary vehicle for the mission of "nation-building." Among other advantages, the DoD's resources of personnel, organization, and equipment easily dwarf the basic capabilities of the other government agencies, as does the Defense budget, when compared with the resources of the other agencies. Similarly, the DoD is already keenly concerned with counterinsurgency operations as part of its basic national security mandate, unlike some agencies and departments that have resisted the expansion of their own missions in that direction. The DoD also has very well established and more effective hierarchical structures and decision-making processes, when contrasted with the organizational cultures and predominant skill sets of other key agencies and departments. The DoD has well established command and support integration mechanisms already. The Department has also made great institutional strides toward a joint operating culture in the years since implementing the Goldwater-Nichols Act of 1986—the law that required the services to achieve interoperability and a joint services mindset.

Just as significantly, the DoD already has the ability to operate in non-permissive security environments, and the organization brings with it a "Soldier ethos" and "can-do" mission focus. The department has organic sustainment capabilities and logistical support structures, and the DoD organizational culture already features a well-developed norm of responsiveness to civilian political authorities. As an "action-oriented field organization," the DoD is also able to accept casualties in the execution of its mission. In sum, among the "key three" organizations, the DoD has the most well-developed planning and operating culture, and a level of comfort in moving between the different levels of national security activity. These characteristics are unmatched by State's strategic-level "reporting and talking" culture, or USAID's tactical-level and locally focused "field operator" culture. In its ability to bridge these gaps in organizational culture and agency capabilities, the DoD offers distinct advantages in serving as the primary vehicle for nation-building.

At the same time, the overreliance on the DoD in these missions carries with it some distinct disadvantages, as well. For one, the DoD has "generally viewed involvement in stability operations, including humanitarian or development activities, as, at best, a distraction from core warfighting competencies."[88] Along these lines, the Department of Defense is clear in its own perception of its roles and functions, and this self-identity is outlined directly in the *National Defense Strategy* of 2008, a document drafted in support of the broader *National Security Strategy* of 2006. Not surprisingly, and in spite of the dominant theme of democracy promotion prevalent throughout the *National Security Strategy*, there is clearly a conventional military cast to the DoD objectives outlined in support of the NSS, including the primary tasks of defending the homeland, winning "the long war," promoting security, deterring conflict, and "winning our nation's wars."[89]

Reflecting the "can-do" cultural norm that pervades the DoD, the *National Military Strategy* also highlights "soft power" capabilities and the integration of efforts ... but notes that the DoD "has taken on many of these burdens" while stepping "up to the task of long-term reconstruction, development and governance."[90] The document also offers two brief paragraphs that speak generally of continuing "to work to improve understanding and harmonize best practices among interagency partners."[91]

In a 2008 speech that garnered much attention, former Defense Secretary Robert Gates noted that other agencies were more properly suited for the execution of many "soft power" tasks. He called for "greater civilian participation" and for making "better use of our universities and of industry to assist in reconstruction and long-term improvements to economic vitality and good government."[92] The current overreliance on the Department of Defense for nation-building and the disproportionate resourcing of the department has led to DoD dominance in the planning and execution of both missions in Afghanistan—irregular warfare and nation-building—and a concurrent overemphasis on the conventional military or "kinetic" aspects of those operations. As the simplest evidence in support of this assertion, one only has to examine the respective resources, attention, and leader emphasis committed to the development of the ANSF and contrast them with the far lower level of resources and effort applied to improving the Afghan economy, the elements of the rule of law, and effective governance. Even within the effort to design and develop the ANSF, there has been a clear bias in favor of developing the Afghan National Army at the expense of the Afghan National Police. Of course, it is hardly surprising that the DoD would focus on building the Afghan military rather than its police force. As an organization, that is "what we do."

FILLING THE SHORTFALLS: THE ROLES AND RISKS OF CONTRACTORS

In order to overcome the various shortfalls in the agencies and departments charged with nation-building and irregular warfare responsibilities in Afghanistan, the U.S. Government has turned to privately contracted firms on a remarkable scale. There are hundreds of thousands of contractors in Afghanistan and Iraq, a phenomenon that can be attributed directly to the unanticipated requirements of nation-building.[93] During FY2008, for example, there were 265,000 contractors employed by the U.S. Government in Afghanistan and

Iraq, with functions including reconstruction, logistics and base support, advisers, interpreters, bodyguards, and other security personnel.[94] Other skills sought by the DoD in support of the nation-building objectives include drug-sniffing dogs and their handlers, intelligence collection and analysis, and warehousing and logistical distribution services, all intended for areas in and around Kandahar, where some of the most violent fighting has occurred.[95] Contractors have also been hired to overcome shortfalls created by the underfunding and downsizing of USAID, as well as the disbanding of the USIA and the Arms Control and Disarmament Agency (ACDA).[96]

Furthermore, this trend is accelerating. In December 2009, the Congressional Research Service (CRS) projected that the surge of 30,000 additional troops to Afghanistan would need to be accompanied by a corresponding surge of up to 56,000 additional private contractors. In advance of this contractor surge, the DoD's census of late 2009 showed that contractors already outnumbered U.S. forces in Afghanistan, with their numbers rising during all of 2009 to a total of 104,101, compared with 113,731 in Iraq. Most of the contractors, or about 78,000 of them, are local nationals.[97] The CRS study also notes that contractors currently make up approximately 69 per cent of DoD personnel in Afghanistan, representing the highest such percentage of any conflict in U.S. history.[98] In fairness, this use of host-nation contractors clearly realizes some local economic benefits. However, this major dependence on contractors mainly serves as compelling evidence of the broader inadequacy of the U.S. Government's existing resources and capabilities to take on one of these nation-building missions, let alone two at a time.

Viewing the issue from another perspective, the use of contractors also establishes an undesirable situation in which the contracted companies' interest in continuing their lucrative contracts stands in direct opposition to the U.S. Government's desire to finish the mission and go home. Furthermore, these contracted employees are not military personnel and, therefore, the terms of their employment come with numerous caveats, similar in many respects to the national caveats of some allies on the use of combat forces. The net effect of these caveats is that the actual value to the operations of the contracted employees can be significantly limited, depending upon the particular tactical circumstances. At the same time, the U.S. Government — and the contracted agencies, for that matter — has only a very limited pool from which to draw the personnel needed for these highly specialized contracted tasks. As a result, contractor services come at a remarkably expensive cost. Access to contractor salary figures is typically limited by the companies, but it was well known in Afghanistan that many contractors were making two or three times the salaries of comparable U.S. Government employees — including the troops who had to operate "outside the wire," in harm's way — regardless of the tactical situation.

In that same vein, there are also legitimate questions about the value of the output the government has been receiving in exchange for these extremely expensive contracts. For example, in standing up the Afghan National Army and the corresponding Afghan Ministry of Defense, it was common practice for the U.S. contractors — who were mostly ex-U.S. military personnel anyway — to merely "cut and paste" documents from relevant DoD field manuals and other administrative documents. These contractors would then provide the Afghans copies of the cut and pasted documents, or streamlined versions of them, to be used as their own systems and procedures.

Although there were other major factors at work as well, one of the reasons that the effort to develop the Afghan police lagged so far behind the development of the Afghan National Army was the fact that the U.S. military personnel and contractors with the police development mission did not have access to similar baseline institutional documentation to assist in their own efforts. Adding another set of challenges, the U.S. Government's agreements with the contracted firms also typically feature convoluted supervisory relationships and funding arrangements. In many cases, these tangled agreements actually limit the U.S. Government's own supervisors from exercising direct control over the contracted employees' job performance, off-duty behavior, or basic employment parameters. These limits result in major inefficiency and ineffectiveness.

In conclusion, the key three organizations' cultures, existing core expertise, comparative resources, and even some career incentives are at odds with each other and the mission requirements of nation-building and irregular warfare. This situation carries with it a number of adverse consequences, while also increasing the structural constraints that currently thwart interagency success. The use of U.S. agencies in roles for which they are not well suited by mandate, resources, or expertise also distracts those agencies from their traditional roles in the U.S. Government, thus accepting unnecessary strategic and operational risks both at home and abroad. By turning to private contractors to make up for these major shortfalls, the United States has actually increased the risks associated with these missions, while achieving questionable results that have come at an exorbitant cost. Future strategic planning and resource allocation decisions must take into consideration these capability shortfalls, as well as the risks associated with contractor use. In short, strategic planners must do a better job of weighing the costs and the loss of strategic flexibility created by these extremely lengthy and resource-intensive nation-building and irregular warfare commitments.

ENDNOTES - CHAPTER 5

1. Secretary Condoleezza Rice, Opening Remarks before the Senate Foreign Relations Committee Presenting the FY2009 International Affairs Budget Request, Washington, DC, February 13, 2008, available from *www.state.gov/secretary/rm/2008/02/100726.htm*.

2. James Q. Wilson, *Bureaucracy: What Government Agencies Do and Why They Do It*, New York: Basic Books, 1989, p. 91.

3. Amos A. Jordan *et al.*, *American National Security*, 5th Ed., Baltimore, MD: Johns Hopkins University Press, 1999, p. 105.

4. Wilson, pp. 40-42.

5. *Ibid.*, p. 94.

6. *Ibid.*, pp. 90-91, 93.

7. *Ibid.*, pp. 40-42, 93-94.

8. Donald P. Warwick, *A Theory of Public Bureaucracy: Politics, Personality, and Organization in the State Department*, Cambridge, MA: Harvard University Press, 1975, p. 12.

9. *Ibid.*, p. 13.

10. *Ibid.*, pp. 14-15.

11. *Ibid.*, pp. 18-19.

12. *Ibid.*

13. *Ibid.*, p. 85.

14. *Ibid.*, p. 86.

15. *Ibid.*, p. 88.

16. Bryton Barron, *Inside the State Department: A Candid Appraisal of the Bureaucracy*, New York: Comet Press Books, 1956, p. 11.

17. *Ibid.*, pp. 11-29.

18. *Ibid.*, p. 62.

19. *Ibid.*, p. 93.

20. Jordan, *et al.*, pp. 107-108.

21. *Ibid.*, p. 108.

22. James F. Dobbins, *After the Taliban: Nation-Building in Afghanistan*, Washington, DC: Potomac, 2008, p. 139.

23. Matthew J. Morgan, *A Democracy is Born: An Insider's Account of the Battle Against Terrorism in Afghanistan*, Westport, CT: Praeger, 2007, p. 53.

24. Ahmed Rashid, *Descent into Chaos*, New York: Penguin, 2008, p. 194.

25. Morgan, p. 53.

26. *Ibid.*, p. 54.

27. *About USAID: USAID History*, available from *www.usaid.gov/about_usaid/usaidhist.html*.

28. John A. Nagl, *Learning to Eat Soup with a Knife: Counterinsurgency Lessons from Malaya and Vietnam*, Chicago, IL: University of Chicago Press, 2005 Ed., p. 138.

29. *About USAID: A Record of Accomplishment*, available from *www.usaid.gov/about_usaid/accompli.html*.

30. See the online organizational charts for State and USAID on their respective websites.

31. *USAID Primer: What We Do and How We Do It*, available from *www.usaid.gov/about_usaid/primer.html*.

32. USAID, *Fragile States Strategy*, Washington, DC: USAID, January 2005, p. 8.

33. U.S. Department of State and U.S. Agency for International Development, *Strategic Plan, Fiscal Years 2007-2012*, Washington, DC: U.S. State Department, May 7, 2007, cover page.

34. *Ibid.*, p. 5.

35. *Ibid.*, p. 59.

36. *Ibid.*

37. Stanley A. McChrystal, *COMISAF'S Initial Assessment*, Kabul, Afghanistan: International Security Force Headquarters, August 30, 2009, pp. 1-2.

38. *Ibid.*, pp. 2-21.

39. Hans Binnendijk and Stuart E. Johnson, eds., *Transforming for Stabilization and Reconstruction Operations*, Washington, DC: National Defense University Press, 2004, p. 110.

40. Scott R. Feil, "The Failure of Incrementalism: Interagency Coordination Challenges and Responses," Chap. 9 in Joseph R. Cerami and Jay W. Boggs, eds., *The Interagency and Counterinsurgency Warfare: Stability, Security, Transition, and Reconstruction Roles*, Carlisle, PA: Strategic Studies Institute, U.S. Army War College, December 2007, pp. 289-290, available from *www.StrategicStudiesInstitute.army.mil*.

41. The President of the United States, *The National Security Strategy of the United States of America*, Washington, DC: U.S. Government, March 2006.

42. Excerpt from Admiral Fallon's statement before the Senate Armed Services Committee on May 3, 2007, available from *www.centcom.mil*.

43. David Rhode and David E. Sanger, "How the 'Good War' in Afghanistan Went Bad," *The New York Times*, August 12, 2007, pp. A1, 12-13.

44. U.S. Department of State, *Doing Business in Afghanistan: A Country Commercial Guide for U.S. Businesses*, Washington, DC: U.S. Government, 2007.

45. John Herbst, prepared statement for testimony before the House Committee on Armed Services, February 26, 2008.

46. Kenneth Katzman, *Afghanistan: Politics, Elections, and Government Performance*, Washington, DC: Congressional Research Service, CRS Report RS21922, August 28, 2009, summary.

47. Sarah Chayes, *The Punishment of Virtue: Inside Afghanistan After the Taliban*, New York: Penguin, 2006, p. 151.

48. Dennis C. Jett, "Challenges in Support and Stability Operations: Why Each One is Different," Chap. 1 in Cerami and Boggs, p. 14.

49. *Ibid.*

50. Feil, p. 14.

51. *Ibid.*

52. *Ibid.*

53. *Ibid.*

54. *Ibid.*, pp. 296-297.

55. Amos A. Jordan, *et al.*, *American National Security*, 5th Ed., Baltimore, MD: Johns Hopkins University Press, 1999, p. 109.

56. Dana Priest, *The Mission: Waging War and Keeping Peace with America's Military*, New York: Norton and Company, 2004, p. 45.

57. *Fact Sheet: U.S. State Department Structure and Organization*, available from *dosfan.lib.uic.edu/ERC/about/fact_sheets/950526str. html*.

58. Jett, p. 14.

59. Office of the Spokesman, *Fact Sheet*, Kabul, Afghanistan: U.S. Embassy, September 25, 2008, available from *kabul.embassy. gov/press_release_25_09.html*.

60. Jett, p. 14.

61. U.S. Department of State and the Broadcasting Board of Governors Office of Inspector General, *Inspection of Embassy Kabul, Afghanistan*, Washington, DC: State Department, OIG Report ISP-I-06-13A, January 18, 2006, p. 1.

62. Rashid, p. 174.

63. *Ibid.*

64. Stephen J. Flanagan and James A. Schear, eds., *Strategic Challenges: America's Global Security Agenda*, Washington, DC: INSS/National Defense University Press, 2008, p. 143.

65. Rajiv Chandrasekaran, "A New Plan for Afghanistan," *The Washington Post Weekly*, June 29, 2009, pp. 7-8.

66. Chayes, pp. 150-151.

67. *Ibid.*

68. *Ibid.*, p. 174.

69. Rhode and Sanger, pp. A1, 12-13.

70. USAID, *At Freedom's Frontiers: A Democracy and Governance Strategic Framework*, Washington, DC: USAID, December 2005, pp. 10-11.

71. *Report to Congressional Committees: Afghanistan Security*, Washington, DC: Government Accountability Office, June 2008, p. 2.

72. Michelle Tan, "Training Pays," *The Army Times*, October 20, 2008.

73. *Report to Congressional Committees: Afghanistan Security*, p. 2.

74. Nagl, pp. ix-x.

75. Astri Suhrke, "A Contradictory Mission? NATO from Stabilization to Combat in Afghanistan," *International Peacekeeping*, Vol. 15, No. 2, April 2008, p. 222.

76. *Ibid*.

77. Nagl, p. xiii.

78. McChrystal, pp. 1-2.

79. *Ibid*.

80. *Afghanistan Security: U.S. Programs to Further Reform Ministry of Interior and National Police Challenged by Lack of Military Personnel and Afghan Cooperation*, GAO-09-280, Washington, DC: Government Accountability Office, March 2009, summary.

81. Feil, p. 296.

82. Katzman, summary.

83. Rhode and Sanger, pp. A1, 12-13.

84. *Ibid*.

85. Christopher M. Blanchard, *Afghanistan: Narcotics and U.S. Policy*, Washington, DC: Congressional Research Service, CRS 7-5700, August 12, 2009, p. 8.

86. Feil, pp. 290-291.

87. *Ibid.*

88. H. Allen Irish, "A 'Peace Corps with Guns': Can the Military be a Tool of Development?" Chap. 3 in Cerami and Boggs, eds., p. 60.

89. Secretary Robert M. Gates, *National Military Strategy*, Washington, DC: Department of Defense, June 2008, p. 6.

90. *Ibid.*, p. 17.

91. *Ibid.*, p. 18.

92. *Ibid.*, p. 17.

93. Zeb B. Bradford, Jr., and Frederic J. Brown, *America's Army: A Model for Interagency Effectiveness*, Westport, CT: Praeger, 2008, p. xiii.

94. Mark Cancian, "Contractors: The New Element of Military Force Structure," *Parameters*, Vol. 38, No. 3, Autumn 2008, p. 62.

95. Walter Pincus, "Up to 56,000 More Contractors Likely for Afghanistan, Congressional Agency Says," *The Washington Post* online, December 16, 2009, available from www.washingtonpost.com.

96. Bradford and Brown, p. xii.

97. August Cole, "U.S. Adding Contractors at Fast Pace," *The Wall Street Journal* online Ed., December 2, 2009, available from www.wsj.com.

98. Pincus.

CHAPTER 6

DISUNIFIED INTERAGENCY STRUCTURES, PROCESSES, AND EFFORT

> If we're going to win, we have to fight this war differently. We've had a stovepiped approach to combat and to development, too. All that has to change."
>
> U.S. Brigadier General John Nicholson, Deputy Commander of NATO forces in southern Afghanistan, *The Washington Post*, March 14, 2009[1]

As if the mismatch between strategy and agency resources were not challenging enough, the adverse effects of this strategic disjointedness are compounded by the fact that the U.S. Government's systems for interagency integration are inadequate to the task. Specifically, existing interagency mechanisms are failing to coordinate and integrate U.S. Government resources and effort effectively—a major problem that stems primarily from the disjointedness of guidance and authority at the national strategic level—subsequently down to affect the theater-strategic, operational, and tactical levels of activity.[2] When coupled with ineffective organizational structures that make disjointed effort and an incoherence of vision the norm rather than the exception, these interagency failings have prevented any coherent implementation of the "whole of government" approaches needed to overcome the extensive and complex challenges of nation-building and irregular warfare. Instead, the lack of unified authority and fragmented organizational structures make every action a negotiation, as the existing interagency structures and processes are too weak to overcome these numerous impediments.

As a result of the general lack of authority to mandate cooperation or direct the operational allocation of other-agency resources, U.S. agencies have failed to achieve unity of vision, a common understanding of the problem, or an integrated and coordinated effort in their operations in Afghanistan. Adding to the problem, different players control different pots of money, with the definitive authority for resource allocation decisions remaining back in the United States rather than residing near the tip of the spear. And although these failures of the U.S. interagency process are commonly recognized by participants and observers alike, entrenched interests, personal ambitions, and competing agendas within the various agencies combine to stymie the prospects for positive change. Without question, the last few years have seen a marked increase in the emphasis and effectiveness of the interagency effort in Afghanistan, an improvement tied directly to the willingness of the senior agency and departmental leaders to improve the coordination and integration of effort across agency boundaries. However, with human nature being what it is, this coordination and integration of resources and effort is too important to be dependent upon the goodwill or chemistry of any particular set of senior leaders. It is important to review the factors that have combined to prevent the U.S. Government from achieving true unity of effort over most of this mission, since these factors will ultimately need to be addressed directly in order to meet the demands of irregular warfare and nation-building operations in Afghanistan and elsewhere in the future.

NO LACK OF GUIDANCE, BUT NOBODY'S IN CHARGE

Whether viewed at the strategic or operational levels of activity, there is no shortage of directives or coordinating mechanisms pertaining to interagency interaction. That is, neither a lack of guidance nor a scarcity of venues for interagency coordination and integration lies at the root of this problem, because there are more than enough presidential directives and interagency coordinating mechanisms already in place to make the national-level intent clear. In fact, a number of these directives are even focused specifically on the interagency management of reconstruction and stabilization operations, so a lack of guidance or venues in this particular area of national security activity is not the cause of the deficiencies, either. On the contrary, the problem is more one of quality than quantity. Not one of the various documents providing guidance or mechanisms for interagency coordination and integration actually puts any one leader, agency, or department in charge of any other. Therefore, the causes of the U.S. Government's interagency failings are structural and jurisdictional in nature, with a variety of related factors thwarting the pursuit of true unity of effort from the start.

At the national strategic level, the last two decades have seen the publication of numerous directives and guiding documents related to interagency procedures and emphases. In May 1994, the Clinton administration issued *Presidential Decision Directive (PDD)-25: Administration Policy on Reforming Multilateral Peace Operations*. This presidential directive designated the Department of Defense (DoD) as the lead federal agency for the funding and management of all U.S.

agencies participating in United Nations (UN) peace operations, regardless of whether or not U.S. troops were involved.[3] Drafted as a response to the changing security requirements emerging in the post-Cold War era, this document initiated a modern trend in which the DoD was increasingly seen as the lead vehicle for the management and execution of foreign policy. The document acknowledged the increasing number of U.S. interventions involving multiple agencies and departments of the U.S. Government, while proposing a draft framework for deciding when it was in the interests of the United States to participate in peacekeeping operations.

In May 1997, the same administration published *Presidential Decision Directive (PDD)-56: Managing Complex Interagency Operations*, a document that outlined new mechanisms for facilitating interagency coordination in peace and stability operations.[4] PDD-56 was widely viewed as a response to the perceived failures in interagency coordination in Somalia, and codified the Clinton administration's policy for managing complex interagency operations. The document outlined roles and responsibilities, while placing presidential emphasis on interagency coordination and integration.[5] In spite of this focused presidential emphasis, however, PDD-56 only addressed half the problem, since it mandated improved interagency coordination and planning without addressing the underlying shortfalls in the resources needed to facilitate those improvements.[6] In similar fashion, in February of 2000 the administration issued *Presidential Decision Directive (PDD)-71: Strengthening Criminal Justice Systems in Support of Peace Operations*. This guidance assigned roles and responsibilities to federal agencies and departments related to enhancing civilian law enforcement capabilities in peace operations.[7] Once again, the document assigned responsibilities without resources.

On February 13, 2001, only a few weeks after taking office, President George W. Bush issued *National Security Presidential Directive (NSPD)-1: Organization of the National Security Council System*.[8] This document was notable for at least two reasons. First, the NSPD assigned a heightened role to the Vice President in national security affairs. Secondly, the document abolished all of the interagency working groups that had been established by the President's predecessors. After the attacks of September 11, 2001 (9/11), the administration's focus shifted toward crafting specific responses to the newly exposed security challenges. However, another significant change to the interagency landscape occurred in the summer of 2004 with the creation of the Office of Coordinator for Reconstruction and Stabilization, commonly called S/CRS. Housed within the State Department (State) and given specific responsibilities for coordinating reconstruction and stability operations, S/CRS has generally struggled to achieve relevance, compliance, support, and budgetary resources.[9] Of note, S/CRS published the *Post Conflict Reconstruction Essential Tasks Matrix* in April 2005, a remarkable compilation of the hundreds of complex tasks associated with nation-building, reconstruction, and stability operations. It is also worth noting that ultimately the Bush administration reinstated many of the interagency working groups that it had abolished at the start of the President's first term.

As the situation in Iraq continued to deteriorate, the U.S. military was given specific guidance to become more engaged with the reconstruction and stabilization activities in that country. In response, in late November 2005, the DoD published *DoD Directive*

3000.05: Military Support for Stability, Security, Transition, and Reconstruction (SSTR) Operations. In a major shift from past policies and practices, the directive described stability operations as a "core U.S. military mission . . . to be given priority comparable to combat operations and to be explicitly addressed and integrated across all DoD activities."[10] In keeping with the presidential guidance reinforcing the role, this directive also established the U.S. military as the default organization for stability and reconstruction operations, probably the only feasible approach anyway given the lack of capacity among other agencies.[11]

Furthermore, *DoD Directive 3000.05* also stipulated that in stability operations, or "military and civilian activities conducted across the spectrum from peace to conflict to establish or maintain order in States and regions," the U.S. military was now formally assigned a role in helping with a variety of nontraditional development tasks. Among them, the DoD was also now required to help "rebuild indigenous institutions," "revive or build the private sector," and "develop representative government institutions." The directive also asserted that DoD elements must be "prepared to work closely with relevant U.S. Departments and Agencies, foreign governments, and security forces."[12] Nation-building might remain undefined, but requirements that looked a lot like nation-building were rapidly becoming codified in policy. Reflecting DoD ambivalence for these missions, a September 2009 reissuance of *DoD Instruction 3000.05: Stability Operations* places DoD clearly in a supporting role for development tasks.[13]

From an interagency perspective, the original DoD Directive 3000.05 directed that combatant commanders were to "engage relevant U.S. Departments and

Agencies" and other intergovernmental and nongovernmental actors in their "operations planning, training, and exercising, as appropriate."[14] As has generally been the case with recent policy, the directive made no mention of additional personnel, training, equipment, or other resources that might be provided to carry out those expanded responsibilities. On December 1, 2005, United States Joint Forces Command (USJFCOM) and S/CRS jointly issued *The Draft Planning Framework for Reconstruction, Stabilization, and Conflict Transformation*. This framework is aimed at introducing direct input from DoD planners into the development of strategic implementation plans for SSTR operations, with the goal of integrating that input into the planning by other agencies.

Providing its own direct guidance for reconstruction and stability operations, the administration issued *National Security Presidential Directive (NSPD)-44: Management of Interagency Efforts Concerning Reconstruction and Stabilization* in December 2005.[15] A significant document in terms of both scope and emphasis, NSPD-44 established a reconstruction and stability policy coordination committee within the National Security Council (NSC). This NSPD also outlined the goals of promoting peace, democracy, and market economies, foreshadowing the *National Security Strategy* document that would follow just a few months later.[16] In order to achieve those goals, NSPD-44 identified the S/CRS as the "focal point" to "coordinate and strengthen" U.S. agency efforts in support of reconstruction and stabilization operations.[17] The document also assigned S/CRS the responsibility for a wide variety of related activities, including strategy development, policy coordination among departments and agencies, the coordination of interagency processes, the preparation of options for decisionmakers, and the development of a strong civilian response capability, among others.[18]

On the other side of the equation, NSPD-44 directed other executive departments and agencies to coordinate with S/CRS during the budget formulation for reconstruction and stabilization activities, prior to submitting their respective budget requests to the Office of Management and Budget. These key agencies and departments were also directed to provide S/CRS with information regarding their existing capabilities, and to develop further "internal capabilities for planning and for resource and program management that can be mobilized in response to crises."[19] Each agency and department was likewise instructed to develop and provide to S/CRS supporting plans and points-of-contact lists, and to make personnel available "on a non-reimbursable basis" to S/CRS "as appropriate and feasible."[20] Without question, the Bush administration had laid out an extensive and robust plan for enhancing interagency emphasis and effectiveness.

However, while NSPD-44 outlined many requirements and responsibilities that would enable S/CRS to be the focal point for reconstruction and stability operations, the document fell short in several significant ways. First of all, neither NSPD-44 nor any complementary enabling legislation provided S/CRS with any significant funding or other resources to carry out its functions. Nor did NSPD-44 provide S/CRS with actual statutory leverage that it could apply to compel compliance among other agencies or departments. Similarly, NSPD-44 also contained no forcing functions, or mechanisms of accountability that forced other agencies and departments to demonstrate adherence with its requirements. Finally, while NSPD-44 claimed to encompass the full spectrum of reconstruction and stability operations, the document's focus is almost exclusively on stability operations, or security operations designed or established to maintain order in states and regions. In fact, neither DoD Directive 3000.05 nor NSPD-44 included formal definitions for either nation-building or reconstruction operations, thus undermining the prospects for compliance or coherence of effort from the start.[21]

In August 2006, the DoD's Joint Forces Command took this guidance a step further by drafting *The Military Support to SSTR Operations, JOC Version 2.0*. This document expanded the definition of SSTR to include the enhancement of governance, economic development, and the rule of law, but it did so without delving into the details of how those goals were to be achieved.[22] At about the same time, S/CRS began working in conjunction with the NSC to develop an initiative called the "Interagency Management System for Reconstruction and Stabilization," or IMS. IMS operational concepts include three main working groups aimed at facilitating interagency responses to complex contingencies. These organizational structures include the Country Reconstruction and Stabilization Group (CRSG) at the national strategic level, Integration Planning Cells (IPC) for the theater-strategic level, and Advance Civilian Teams (ACT) at the operational and tactical levels.[23] Work on these systems, including securing sufficient funding, personnel, and other-agency "buy-in" for their interagency activities, continues today.

In January of 2009, the three key organizations jointly published the *U.S. Government Counterinsurgency Guide*, with input and contributions from each of the nine U.S. agencies and departments with roles and functions in counterinsurgency and other forms of irregular warfare.[24] The document is consistent with the other directives and guidelines, in that it avoids any serious engagement with the real challenges of interagency integration. For example, the guide notes that while "unity of effort is highly desirable," it is also "not easily achieved, especially in the context of a coalition intervention operation."[25] The document also identifies the U.S. ambassador as the Chief of Mission and as the President's personal representative to the host nation, noting that in having been "appointed by the President and confirmed by the Senate, the Ambassador has extraordinary decision-making authority as the senior U.S. official present."[26] The document also identifies the Country Team as "the central element of interagency coordination and execution in the foreign country."[27] Finally, the guide offers broad-brush guidelines for integrated interagency planning over two and a half pages of text.[28]

The reality, however, is much different. Personnel from the various agencies operating in a particular country generally choose to participate in other-agency plans or not depending on their own agendas and interests, as well as the guidance given them by their parent organizations. And while U.S. ambassadors have great influence over policy matters and wield significant authority related to the fact that they have the ear of the Secretary of State and (often) the President, ambassadors typically control very little in the way of significant budgetary authority. With these organizational realities in mind, the leaders of the various agencies and departments functioning within any major theater of operations are ultimately more concerned about the reactions of the leaders within their own agency hierarchies than they are with ambassadorial approval.

Along similar lines, the *Counterinsurgency Guide* describes the NSC as "the President's principal forum for consultation with senior advisors and cabinet officials on national security and foreign policy matters."[29] The guide also asserts that "The NSC staff provides advice to the President with respect to the integration of . . . policies and manages the processes through which the President's policies are coordinated and implemented."[30] Given the usual turf wars in the NSC over agency roles, jurisdictions, and resources, the discussions at the NSC level are most often focused on broad questions of resources and responsibilities, rather than aiming to resolve questions pertaining to the actual operational implementation of the council's recommendations.

Shortly after the publication of the *Counterinsurgency Guide*, and only a few short weeks after taking office, the Obama administration signaled its intention to order an overhaul of the NSC. President Barack Obama suggested reforms that might include expanding NSC membership, while "increasing its authority to set strategy across a wide spectrum of international and domestic issues."[31] Building on the findings and recommendations of the *Project for National Security Reform*, these changes were first intended to eliminate backchannels to the President. Next, the reforms also aimed to strengthen the position of National Security Adviser, with the goal of enabling that individual to manage the discussions of national security and present consolidated recommendations to the President.[32] After they were announced on February 13, 2009, however, the actual changes to the NSC structures were far less dramatic than had been suggested. The actual changes outlined in the Obama administration's *Presidential Policy Directive (PPD)-1: Organization of the National Security Council System* included placing the Homeland Security Council underneath the NSC, and creating three new NSC directorates. These new directorates included one focused on cybersecurity, another focused on pandemics, and a "Global Engagement Directorate" intended to combine communications, foreign aid, diplomacy, and "domestic engagement and outreach."[33] Otherwise, the document left the Bush-era NSC organization largely in place.

So despite numerous directives emphasizing interagency cooperation, the U.S. departments and agencies have essentially been left to operate as they always have, since a lack of forcing functions in the various presidential directives means that the agencies are typically not held accountable for failing to comply with the interagency guidance. With these bureaucratic realities in mind, it is therefore not surprising at all that different agencies have committed to the NSPD and PDD requirements to varying degrees, with some making meaningful changes in their business practices and others merely paying lip service to change.[34] At the same time, there are still major gaps in doctrine, resources, expertise, capabilities, and the statutory guidance that continue to limit the ability of the various organizations to comply with the NSPD and PDD requirements.

Lastly, since "stability operations are labor-intensive and land power-focused," the DoD—and in particular the Army and Marine Corps—have a keen interest in seeing NSPD-44 and the S/CRS evolve successfully into a strong interagency coordinating framework.[35] On the other hand, the other agencies and departments holding nation-building and irregular warfare responsibilities have far fewer incentives to push for this same integration of effort, along with far fewer resources to make it happen. As a result, these factors combine to undercut the prospects for truly effective interagency cooperation from the start. Likewise, since departmental authorities and appropriations are still managed agency-by-agency at the national level, NSPD-44 has effectively given S/CRS "all of the responsibility but none of the authority," while DoD Directive 3000.05 has done something similar in the DoD. In spite of all of the published guidance to the contrary, at this point the U.S. Government's interagency processes for national security still resemble a coalition of the willing among the various agencies.

INEFFECTIVE STRUCTURES AND PROCESSES FOR INTERAGENCY INTEGRATION

As a direct consequence of these weak interagency directives, the existing institutional procedures and mechanisms for interagency coordination and integration provide opportunities for interagency engagement without requiring any real results. Hampered by a general lack of statutory forcing functions or accountability mechanisms, systemic interagency weaknesses are apparent at both the strategic and operational levels of activity. Numerous venues for interagency coordination exist, but the success or failure of the efforts within these venues usually depends upon the particular force of will or the persuasive skills of the individual agency leader nominally placed in charge. Exacerbating these challenges, the prescribed interagency coordinating processes at the operational level are often convoluted and bottom-driven, rather than streamlined and directive in nature. Too often, these procedures are composed of rigidly bureaucratic rules that yield numerous products containing overwhelming detail, but come at the expense of any clear sense of mission focus or priority.

This problem is much the same at the national strategic level, as well, where the actions within the NSC and in other strategic-level interagency coordination venues are constrained by jurisdictional questions, competing agency agendas, and 1- and 2-year budget cycles. These short-run budget horizons also prevent any coherent planning for nation-building and irregular warfare missions, which typically take much longer. In terms of basic organizational incentives, promotion processes still belong to the parent agencies and departments. Accordingly, it is much easier for the participants in the interagency process to say no to the leaders of other agencies than it is to deny leaders further up the chain in their own parent organizations. Recognizing these fundamental institutional shortcomings, the 9/11 Commission highlighted a lack of interagency coherence as one of the major contributors to the U.S. Government's ineffective performance in the period that led up to the attacks on the United States in 2001.

In Afghanistan specifically, the existing interagency procedures have fallen far short of what is needed to carry out nation-building and irregular warfare operations effectively. Left to exercise their own discretion, the various agencies and departments and their respective leaders disagree about desired end-states, and these organizations then pursue their own visions, because no one agency has sufficient leverage or authority to compel any other agency to follow its lead. As a result of these independent agendas, visions, and operating practices, the overall effort is representative of political scientist John Kingdon's compelling description of American bureaucratic practices in general. That is, the U.S. Government's mission in Afghanistan suffers from a disunity of effort because "nobody leads anybody else."[36]

Corroborating this perspective, Ambassador James Dobbins served as the U.S. representative to the Northern Alliance when the invasion began in October 2001. From the start, Ambassador Dobbins expressed serious concerns about the feasibility of the organization of the U.S. mission, since the arrangement gave State its statutory leading role in the conduct of U.S. affairs but relied upon the DoD for almost all of the assets used to carry out the operations.[37] In his view, the organizational arrangements represented "an abdication of White House responsibility" that would lead to significant problems.[38] Ambassador Dobbins also described his single most frustrating experience in Afghanistan as his inability to get a basic interagency agreement on how the United States should compensate innocent Afghans who were victims of American firepower.[39]

Strategic-Level Interagency Structures.

At the strategic level of national security affairs, the formal organizational structure for conducting the interagency coordination and integration of foreign policy in the executive branch is the NSC, created by the National Security Act of 1947. By statute, the NSC literally refers to the President, the Vice President, the Secretary of Defense, the Secretary of State, and a few other Cabinet-level officials, with the Director of the Central Intelligence Agency (CIA) and the Chairman, Joint Chiefs of Staff, serving as advisors.[40] With this senior membership in mind, it is a bit of a stretch to claim that the NSC truly integrates anything, as the actual process of working out the details of interagency coordination ordinarily happens at levels well below the Principals Committee (PC). Ironically, the modern stovepiping of effort and information that plagues the U.S. Government today was created in part by that same National Security Act of 1947. This act intentionally established a strong Secretary of Defense position, as a move aimed at overcoming the numerous weaknesses within the coordination and integration of the various branches of the U.S. military.

Since its inception, however, the structures and influence of the NSC have shifted with each successive presidency since Truman, depending upon the particular President's personal intentions. While there are decisionmaking processes that correspond to particular routine or recurring decisions, in general the decisionmaking process for any one issue can be ad hoc and highly particularized.[41] Intended originally to be an honest broker among the national security agencies represented within it, the NSC has instead evolved into a policymaking and policy executing body that operationalizes the President's policy choices.[42] In this role, the NSC—especially the National Security Advisor and the 225 members of the NSC staff—serves as an institutional guardian for the national security strategies, as well as other strategic national security products.[43]

As a snapshot of the processes and products that characterize the organizational procedures of the NSC, administrations generally use the national security strategy and other NSC products, both to express broad national intent and to give specific guidance to the various agencies of the government. The drafts of the national security strategy and other similar NSC documents are typically produced by Policy Coordination Committees (PCC) within the NSC itself.[44] At times de-emphasized during the Bush administration, these policy coordination committees are interagency working groups. Some of them are organized by geographic region, while others are established by functional area. Each committee includes senior agency officials and subject matter experts in those particular regions or functional areas.[45]

In the particular case of the national security strategy, the products of the various policy coordination committees are then combined into the NSS draft, representing the consensus of those committees. The draft is then submitted to the Deputies Committee, which is an assembly of senior department deputies that serves as the "senior sub-Cabinet interagency forum."[46] In the Deputies Committee, these senior agency officials review the draft strategy to ensure that agency concerns are met. Once the draft NSS passes this review, it is then forwarded to the Principals Committee for final review and ratification, with the modern PC consisting of the Cabinet-level leaders from State, the DoD, Treasury, the National Security Agency, the Director of National Intelligence, and the Chairman, Joint Chiefs of Staff.[47]

As noted, while the NSC serves as the honest broker for the interagency process and for strategy formulation, there are no specific rules telling the NSC how to perform this interagency adjudication function.[48] Accordingly, the roles and functions of the NSC vary significantly from administration to administration. This lack of clarity in NSC operating practices often exacerbates the already formidable challenges of dealing with different organizational cultures, organizational interpretations of presidential guidance, and jurisdictional and resource parochialism.[49] With the ad hoc nature of the organization in mind, the NSC's performance can be viewed as uneven at best; its organizational culture and structures remain tied mostly to the role and resources assigned to it by the sitting President.

For example, during the Truman administration, the NSC was staffed by career civil servants. In stark contrast, President Dwight Eisenhower equipped the NSC with systems and processes adapted from his experience in military organizations, staffing the council with mainly military professionals and participating in weekly information and decision meetings. The Eisenhower model also featured a Planning Board and an Operations Control Board (OCB), with the first for planning and the second to oversee operations.[50] Upon succeeding Eisenhower, President John Kennedy reduced both the size of the NSC staff and its level of influence, staffing it with political appointees, while preferring to manage national security affairs within his inner circle.

Subsequent administrations saw President Richard Nixon use a strong NSC model, with Henry Kissinger in the lead as both the National Security Adviser and as Secretary of State. President Ronald Reagan also employed a strong NSC model, but one staffed to enable operations to be controlled from the White House. The first President George Bush chose to use the NSC primarily to formulate policy.[51] From an interagency perspective, the most significant changes made by President Bush in his NSPD-1 were the centralizing of decisionmaking authority higher in the NSC chain, increasing the role of the Vice President in national security affairs, and dissolving the existing Interagency Working Groups (IWG). The Bush-era guidance specifically called for dismantling the IWGs, as well as "all other existing NSC interagency groups, ad hoc bodies, and executive committees."[52] Partly in response to 9/11 and the demands of Afghanistan and Iraq, however, eventually the administration reinstituted most of the IWGs.

In addition to the NSC, there are a number of other national-level interagency coordinating activities. In recognition of the obvious national-level interagency shortfalls exposed by a number of recent national security events, other major initiatives have been undertaken in the past decade. As a primary example, the creation of S/CRS in State in 2004 assigned this office a variety of tasks of an interagency flavor. Among other roles, S/CRS is responsible for conducting interagency planning for reconstruction and stabilization missions, coordinating with relevant agencies to develop interagency contingency plans, monitoring political instability worldwide, and taking steps to ensure that training and education of civilian personnel is adequate and carried out.[53] A few years later, the Civilian Stabilization Initiative was approved as part of the FY2008 supplemental appropriation. This initiative includes the Civilian Response Corps, with separate Active and Standby components aimed at creating an interagency pool of reconstruction and stabilization experts.[54]

Other recent initiatives have included the creation of seven new reconstruction and stabilization training courses being offered to military and civilians at the Foreign Service Institute, along with the creation of the *U.S. Government Planning Framework for R&S and Conflict Transformation* and the *Interagency Conflict Assessment Framework*, each approved in July 2008.[55] S/CRS and the Civilian Response Corps (CRC) were authorized funds under the FY2009 National Defense Authorization Act, thus reinforcing the assignment of S/CRS as the lead office for coordinating interagency responses to reconstruction and stabilization missions. As a complementary step, the Interagency Management System for Reconstruction and Stabilization was approved in March 2007, creating a three-tiered system to manage interagency planning and operations.[56]

Expanding on the description of these major initiatives, IMS is a three-tiered planning and operations system aimed at facilitating "whole of government" responses to national security crises. It includes the Washington-based Country Reconstruction and Stabilization Group (CRSG), intended as a resource to assist in planning and operations functions at the national level. In turn, the Integration Planning Cell (IPC) represents a set of interagency experts who can deploy to a theater-level headquarters and assist in synchronizing civil-military planning and operations. Finally, Advance Civilian Teams (ACT) aid a particular country's ambassador with integration, coordination, planning, resource allocation, operations, knowledge management, and strategic communications.[57]

The CRC consists of 250 generalists who are available for rapid response and can be deployed to assist in reconstruction and development operations within 48 hours of notification. The plan for the CRC also calls for the augmentation of this core group by 2,000 additional civilian agency experts, who will be deployable within 30 days. Ultimately, the CRC will also have available another 2,000 reserve members from outside U.S. governmental agencies. These reserve members are projected to be deployable within 60 days, with each having some specific area of reconstruction and development expertise.[58] At present, the CRC initiative is funded for 250 personnel in its Active Component and 600 personnel in the Standby Reserve.

Although these initiatives are promising in many ways, they also have a number of shortfalls. Among these shortfalls is the fact that there is still no unified operating system for the U.S. Government and, given the scope of the theater requirements, these resources are still quite limited. Likewise, these initiatives still feature very limited civilian capacity, a lack of specialized training, no common repository for capturing and applying lessons as they are learned, and very limited funding to support rapid response deployment.[59] Additionally, other shortfalls of these measures include a lack of operator-level personnel to build actual capacity and to mentor the host nation personnel, since these personnel are intended to serve as higher-level planners. Another challenge to the viability of the initiative comes in the volunteer and reserve nature of these professionals. That is, any reserve force comes with distinct challenges in terms of the ability to predict and coordinate the availability of the individual personnel—a decided disadvantage when compared with an established, standing development corps. Finally, the congressional support for this initiative to date has been comparatively limited, with the "bridge fund" for Fiscal Year (FY)2010 set at $40 million. This sum is inadequate to the tasks required and the needs of the mission in Afghanistan, let alone any other contingencies.

Theater- and Operational-Level Interagency Guidance and Structures.

The DoD has keen institutional interests in the success of these missions, and the Department also enjoys a major advantage in terms of its planning capabilities, with more than 20,000 well-trained planners working in the Pentagon alone. When this human capital is contrasted with the several hundred planners working altogether among the other organizations, it should come as no surprise that the DoD has published far more guidance related to theater-strategic and operational-level interagency structures and procedures than the other U.S. departments and agencies combined. As representative samples of this published guidance, the U.S. Government's comprehensive *Counterinsurgency Manual* encourages interagency cooperation but provides no rigorous means for achieving it. For its own part, State has emphasized publishing operational-level documents such as its *Doing Business in Afghanistan: A Country Commercial Guide for U.S. Companies*, and other similar pamphlets and guides. These documents are consistent with State's culture and its perception of its own mission in Afghanistan, but are neither integrated into the broader U.S. nation-building effort nor realistic in light of conditions on the ground.[60]

For its own part, the DoD has produced a wide variety of publications and field manuals, which address the interagency challenges at the theater-strategic and operational levels of activity. As the core document that establishes the baseline for U.S. military forces, *Joint Publication 1-0: Doctrine for the Armed Forces of the United States* claims to provide a bridge between policy and doctrine by outlining the goals and principles that inform the employment of our nation's armed forces.[61] This doctrine identifies unified action as a key enabler for achieving the jointness that underpins the pursuit of specific U.S. strategic objectives, as well as broader applications of U.S. foreign policy. As defined by the publication, "unified action" refers to the goal of achieving a unity of vision and effort among a wide variety of governmental and nongovernmental actors, with each having their own agendas, interests, and resources that they bring to situations relevant to U.S. national interests.[62]

Extending these themes to the operational level, the DoD's *Joint Publication 3-0: Joint Operations*, elaborates upon the JP 1-0 discussion of "unified action" and identifies "unity of effort" as the result of effective unified action.[63] The publication also introduces the concept of the "lead federal agency" (LFA) and likewise speaks generally to the requirements for coordination and integration amid the challenges associated with those operations. The Army's corresponding *Field Manual 3-0: Operations*, addresses peace operations, including peacekeeping, peacemaking, peace enforcement, peace building, and conflict prevention, as varieties of joint military operations short of conventional warfare.[64] The manual also provides examples of irregular warfare operations, including foreign internal defense, support to insurgency, counterinsurgency, combating terrorism, and unconventional warfare.[65] Although this publication gives little in the way of detail related to interagency operations, the field manual does link stability tasks directly to State's post-conflict reconstruction and stabilization technical sectors.[66] DoD *Joint Publication 5-0: Joint Operation Planning* is equally vague, devoting all of three-and-a-half pages to interagency planning considerations.[67] In fact, the publication highlights the joint force commander's (JFC) likely lack of leverage, noting that "In the absence of a formal command structure, JFCs may be required to build consensus to achieve unity of effort."[68] JP 5-0 also introduces the concepts of the State-provided political adviser (POLAD), a brief annex for Interagency Coordination, and the Joint Interagency Coordination Group (JIACG), a theater-strategic level venue for interagency coordination.[69]

Along the same lines, there are various supporting joint publications and field manuals that elaborate upon the mechanisms available to commanders at the theater-strategic level and below to facilitate interagency coordination. These manuals include *FM 3-07: Stability Operations* (2008); *JP 3-08: Interagency, Intergovernmental Organization, and Nongovernmental Organization Coordination during Joint Operations, I* and *II* (2006); *JP 3-33: Joint Task Force Headquarters* (2007); *JP 3-57: Civil-Military Operations* (2008); and the *Commander's Handbook for the Joint Interagency Coordination Group* (2007). In sum, there is no lack of doctrinal guidance or structures for the interagency process on the military side of the equation, and each of these publications makes some reference to interagency coordination and integration.

Reflecting the fact that the military has no statutory leverage to compel compliance or even cooperation from the other agencies in question, however, each manual also has in common the fact that they are each long on the "what" of interagency coordination and very short on the "how." That is, in each case the commander is largely left to rely upon hope or goodwill to bring about interagency coordination, since there is nothing in the way of command authority or any other real leverage available to compel that cooperation. Even the well regarded *FM 3-24: Counterinsurgency Field Manual*, for all of its merits, suffers from the same authority gap and thus glosses over the problem by optimistically highlighting Civil-Military Operations Centers and other operational and tactical-level interagency venues as offering opportunities for integration.[70]

The period since the passage of the Goldwater-Nichols Act of 1986 has seen the military make dramatic strides toward jointness, or an interoperability and commonality of effort in the execution of security operations. But while the military's own doctrine charges the DoD with embracing the goal of unified action as a major principle of its mission execution, this same doctrine falls far short in actually operationalizing that goal across U.S. agencies. That is, it intuitively makes sense for the military professional to extend the idea of jointness across agency boundaries when confronted with missions that focus on other nonmilitary instruments of national power, but joint doctrine cannot provide specific guidance as to how that interagency reach should occur.

The Special Case of the Provincial Reconstruction Team.

Created as an operational-level organization aimed at overcoming the interagency obstacles to success in nation-building and irregular warfare, the Provincial Reconstruction Team (PRT) deserves special attention. PRTs are ad hoc interagency organizations with a focus on local economic and governmental development. A typical American team is led by a military officer and has about 80 personnel assigned to it altogether. The American teams usually include representatives from State, the U.S. Department of Agriculture (USDA), the U.S. Agency for International Development (USAID), Afghan government officials, and Afghan police, though in many cases the personnel from the other-than-DoD agencies are contractors.[71] The PRTs were created with three goals in mind, including providing a safe environment in which U.S. agencies and international development organizations could operate, "strengthening the Afghan central government's reach," and facilitating reconstruction in Afghanistan.[72] From the beginning, the American-led PRTs in Afghanistan have been largely left to themselves to organize and operate, receiving little monitoring, guidance, or accountability from the nominal International Security Assistance Force (ISAF) supervisory chain.[73]

As a nondoctrinal concept, the PRTs were not part of the military's original plan going into the mission in Afghanistan, and so were not actually initiated for more than a year after the initial stages of the operations. The first PRT began operation in February 2003 in Gardez. By October 2005, however, there were 22 PRTs operating across Afghanistan, with 12 of them led by American personnel and the others by coalition partners.[74] It was not until 2006 that NATO pledged to place PRTs in each of Afghanistan's 34 provinces. Even as those additional PRTs were formed, however, the national caveats placed on the other-than-American PRTs by their home governments were severe enough to limit their range and effectiveness substantially.[75]

While much of the literature on the PRTs to date has focused on their positive contributions to regional stability and development, the operation of the PRTs has also revealed a number of obstacles to effective interagency cooperation embedded within their structure and organization. Among other issues, a first-order challenge for the PRTs has been "the lack of clear guidelines and goals for key PRT personnel."[76] While the PRTs do provide a venue for interagency coordination at the operational and tactical levels, in truth the PRTs have varied widely in their levels of effectiveness, cohesion, and coherence. For example, a very senior member of ISAF indicated that he did not believe that he or other ISAF leaders could push the PRTs' efforts in a direction consistent with ISAF's specific lines of operations, in spite of ISAF's nominal command authority. Instead, he felt that the PRT members' ultimate loyalties resided with their parent U.S. agencies or their home governments.[77] In line with this assertion, State and USAID personnel assigned to the American-led PRTs "reported directly to the U.S. embassy in Kabul on the local government's suitability and capacity for development projects."[78]

Reinforcing this point, my own experience showed it was clear to all participants in the interagency process that any agreements reached in those venues would ultimately have to be approved by the parent organizations, whether they were U.S. Central Command (USCENTCOM) and the DoD, the State Department headquarters in Washington, or other agency leaders far from the tip of the spear. Furthermore, these jurisdictional challenges were exacerbated by the heavy concentration of civilian contractors employed in these operational activities, since the supervisors from the contractors' company headquarters and various contracting provisions added another convoluted layer of bureaucracy to the mix. These leaders and the limits of the company contracts must be accommodated before operational plans and decisions can be finalized.

Corroborating this mixed assessment of PRT effectiveness, a comprehensive Rand study in 2008 found that the quality of performance among the PRTs varied widely, depending upon the makeup of the team and the approach used to facilitate reconstruction and development. The study contrasted a British-led PRT in Mazar-e-Sharif that was very effective in mediating intertribal conflicts and in completing construction projects, with a German-led team in Konduz that rarely left its secure forward operating base.[79] The study also noted that these same variations were found among American-led and NATO-led teams, and that a common shortcoming of the teams was that most "were dominated by soldiers, many of whom had little or no development experience."[80] The study also cited a number of other problems that commonly hampered PRT performance. Among these were the unwillingness of civilian agency personnel to serve in non-permissive areas, the typically short duration of civilians' tours of duty, and a widespread lack of knowledge of Afghan culture and the dynamic of the local areas in which the teams operated.[81] The study finally noted that while the North Atlantic Treaty Organization (NATO) had been able to place PRTs in most major Afghan cities, the rural areas—the real center of mass of the Afghan challenge—remained almost wholly uncovered.[82]

Viewing these problems from inside the teams, the other-than-DoD agency personnel who participated in the PRTs identified their own set of obstacles standing in the way of effective interagency coordination. Echoing the concern of others about the lack of guidance and a common set of goals, the PRT members noted that the civilian agency personnel had "little understanding of the specific role they were expected to fulfill."[83] The members also cited the "rigid military-oriented structure of the teams" as a further hindrance to PRT effectiveness.[84] Regarding the last point, by agreement State and USAID personnel are supposed to lead the PRT on political and reconstruction issues, with the military leader taking charge of security activities. However, the State and USAID report asserted that the "PRT culture, people, and resources are predominantly military."[85] The State and USAID personnel also reported other obstacles to effective interagency coordination on the PRTs, among them, "poor tour synchronization and team deployment policies," "considerable personnel gaps," "poorly established team member relationships," and "periods of relative disjointedness."[86]

Based on its personnel's experience gleaned from service on the PRTs, USAID published *Provincial Reconstruction Teams in Afghanistan: An Interagency Assessment*, in June 2006. In the report, the agency summarized the substantive issues that would have to be addressed to make the PRTs more effective. Echoing some of the same challenges that undermine the interagency process at the national level, these issues included:

- a need for "guidance that clearly outlines the mission, roles, responsibilities, and authority of each participating department or agency";
- a need for "the U.S. Embassy and [U.S. military] to reinvigorate an in-country interagency coordinating body that articulates how national programs and PRT efforts fit into broader U.S. foreign policy objectives";
- a need for DoD-centered guidance that would "direct U.S. PRT commanders to incorporate non-DoD representatives into PRT strategy development and decisionmaking";
- a need to strengthen "U.S. PRT management and information systems";
- a call to improve "PRT access to funds and capabilities"; and,
- a need for non-DoD agencies to receive dedicated funding and training.[87]

Noting that the PRT concept is "most appropriate where there is a mid-range of violence (that is) not so acute that combat operations predominate," the report asserts that "PRT assets and funding must be tailored to specific cultural and security contexts [and feature] specialized skills other than those held by many military and civilian officers."[88] The study then described three other major obstacles to the PRTs' potential for success. These obstacles include a common lack of understanding of respective agency cultures, missions, and capabilities; a lack of language and cultural training appropriate to the PRTs' specific areas of operations; and "inadequate staffing and resources provided by the civilian agencies."[89] With this analysis in mind, it is clear that there is yet much room for growth in the PRT concept. These other-than-DoD perspectives also demonstrate that the use of the DoD as a proxy for genuine "whole of government" approaches to reconstruction and nation-building brings with it both advantages and consequential disadvantages. In a sense, these ad hoc organizations represent a microcosm of the broader interagency challenges that remain.

Recognizing these shortcomings, leaders in Afghanistan have recently set in motion a variety of other operational-level initiatives aimed at improving interagency coordination. These initiatives have included the establishment of a new military command to bring all U.S. military forces under the authority of one commander to achieve unity of command. This command element is called U.S. Forces-Afghanistan (USFOR-A).[90] In November 2007, a police reform initiative called "Focused District Development" was begun, eventually becoming a vehicle for synchronizing economic development, rule of law development, reconstruction, and police reform in targeted police districts, with a goal of completing all districts as soon as possible. Along the same lines, NATO's Regional Command-South has created a Civil-Military Planning Cell to facilitate a comprehensive regional approach to operations and development that "promotes the primacy of governance and development in all planning and operations."[91] In November 2008, the U.S. Embassy Kabul established an Integrated Civil-Military Action Group that works for the Executive Working Group and consists of all the major deputies of the various agencies at work in Afghanistan.[92] Likewise, ISAF initiated the "Action District Program" to increase Afghan, USFOR-A, and United Nations Assistance Mission in Afghanistan (UNAMA) coordination, with pilot districts identified and operations beginning in the summer of 2009.[93]

In spite of all of these promising developments, however, some serious national-level impediments to interagency effectiveness obviously remain in place. As one simple indicator, the DoD functional and geographic combatant commands do not align with State's geographic and functional organizational structures. Furthermore, the various agencies and departments have taken no steps to synchronize their overseas tour assignment practices, so rapid personnel turnover continues to run counter to the Afghan cultural norms of relationships and trust. This lack of continuity also means that agencies are continually relearning the same lessons, while revisiting the same decisions and redoing the same tasks. The same conflicting career incentives remain in place, and the lack of any true forcing functions that mandate the integration of effort still allows the agencies to continue to use their own disjointed, internal metrics of success.

As a result, the U.S. Government is still struggling to get its arms around these interagency challenges. There is still no common agency-to-agency language, no shared understanding of the problem, no universal metrics for measuring progress, nor any clearly understood set of statutory guidelines that delineates specific responsibilities among the various U.S. actors at work within Afghanistan. As one indicator of these remaining shortfalls, in June 2009, the U.S. Government Accountability Office (GAO) issued a report that recommended to Congress that it make any additional funding for the Afghan mission contingent upon the "completion of a coordinated, detailed plan for the ANSF [Afghan National Security Force], including a sustainment strategy."[94] This recommendation was based on the GAO's assessment that State and the DoD had failed to comply with the agency's exact same findings and recommendations in 2005, meaning that about 4 years had passed without the creation of "a coordinated, detailed Defense and State plan with near- and long-term resource requirements."[95] For all of the years of hard work that had gone into improving interagency coordination—and Afghanistan—the underlying causes of interagency dysfunction remain in place, rooted in human nature, misaligned bureaucratic incentives, convoluted jurisdictions, and mismatched resources. There is still much work to do.

THE RESULTS: DISUNITY OF EFFORT

The disunity of effort that stems from the fragmented authority and ineffective interagency processes is demonstrated in many ways. Projects are undertaken where they are needed the least, as the other-than-DoD agencies and departments cannot operate in non-permissive security environments. Often ignoring the regions that need their attention the most, these agencies frequently complete projects that are only partially resourced, such as constructing schools without providing the teachers needed to staff them, building courthouses or jails where no trained judges or prosecutors exist, or undertaking other similarly short-sighted projects that make sense only if one's metric for success is counting how many "projects have been completed."

Consistent with its own capabilities and culture, the DoD likewise is often guilty of focusing disproportionately upon security-centered metrics. This narrow perspective then limits the development of the elements of the rule of law; the creation of institutions of national and local governance; the growth of a legitimate economy; and the crushing impact of widespread illiteracy; among others. Needless to say, all of these tasks are of central importance to the nation-building and counterinsurgency that sit at the heart of the mission in Afghanistan today. It is not all that surprising that these critical aspects are overshadowed when the military's main metric for success to date has been "trained army and police units fielded." Of course, the ISAF Campaign Strategy reflects a focused effort to work at these nonmilitary tasks in parallel to the security effort. At the same time, even the objectives that correspond to the ISAF lines of operations are expressed mainly in terms of population security and ANSF development. It is what we do.

In any event, rather than pulling together, U.S. agencies are still essentially free to opt out when they dislike a decision or disagree with another agency's end-state vision or interpretation of guidance. As specific examples of this disunity of effort, a participant in the interagency and nongovernmental operations in Afghanistan noted a "devastating rift between the Defense Department and State Department" early on in the mission that saw the senior leaders of both organizations in Afghanistan rarely interacting with one another at all.[96] This same observer described the U.S. military and CIA working at cross-purposes to one another in Kandahar as the Taliban fell, issuing orders that contradicted one another while executing apparently conflicting policies.[97] Others noted that the CIA operated on its own much of the time, and that the agency was even given control over the processes of awarding aid and reconstruction contracts.[98] As a particularly telling example of this lack of coherence, President Karzai strongly advocated the rebuilding of the ring road highway as a means of enhancing the Afghan economy in support of the emerging Afghan government, but USAID countered with its own desire to undertake other more "local" projects.[99]

Taking a more comprehensive view, the evidence is not much better. Applying its customary metrics of "projects completed" and "aid delivered," USAID claims that its programs have been effective in Afghanistan, citing the construction of 1,600 miles of road, the reconstruction or construction of more than 650 schools, and the training of thousands of civil servants as evidence of their success.[100] However, from a broader view, it is far less clear that these projects have been integrated effectively into the overarching U.S. national security objectives for the country. For example, in 2004, USAID awarded a $135 million contract to Chemonics International to rehabilitate the agriculture industry in the poppy-producing Helmand province, but the project was abandoned when there were no U.S. Soldiers available to protect the workers.[101] In 2005, a canal cleaning project was similarly abandoned when the Taliban killed five workers. That same year, USAID and the British aid ministry were able to spend only $4 million out of $119 million set aside for development—and all of that for salaries—due to security concerns and contracting difficulties.[102] In 2006, after being spurred by presidential interest and only after Dole Foods decided the project was not feasible, USAID wasted several million dollars in reconstruction aid on a commercial farm project near Mazar-e-Sharif before realizing that the land was too dry and salty to support agriculture. This fact was already well known to the local Afghans.[103]

Upon becoming the Obama administration's lead action officer for Afghanistan, and as a USAID veteran of the Vietnam War-era himself, Richard C. Holbrooke ordered a complete overhaul of the USAID effort in Afghanistan. In fact, after surveying USAID's efforts to that point, he cited an urgent need to revamp what he saw as a poorly coordinated program that "wasn't just a waste of money [but] was actually a benefit to the enemy."[104] Identifying a variety of similar challenges within the military upon taking command of the operations in 2009, General Stanley McChrystal reorganized the ISAF organizational structure, noting that "ISAF's subordinate headquarters must stop fighting separate campaigns."[105] As recently as February 2010, Senate Armed Services Committee Chairman Carl Levin travelled to Afghanistan, describing as "inexcusable" his finding that there was still a major shortage of instructors to train the Afghan security forces, in spite of the administration having put ANSF training at the forefront of its Afghan strategy.[106] This shortage in trainers remains today.

CONCLUSIONS AND IMPLICATIONS

The disunity of effort that results from ineffective coordinating mechanisms and the underlying disjointedness of U.S. strategy represents just one more way in which U.S. Government means are disconnected from its strategic interests, ends, and ways. As a direct consequence of this disjointedness at the operational level, various host-nation leaders and members of the international community are able to "exploit the seams" exposed by these fragmented organizational structures, taking advantage of this situation by going from agency to agency until they get the decision or the resources they want. As important as our allies' contributions have been to the effort in Afghanistan, the truth is that the United States has dwarfed the other nations in terms of commitments of manpower and funding. So with this reality in mind, it is vitally important that the U.S. agencies and departments act coherently if the United States is to provide the vehicle for the international community's collective efforts to improve the situation.

In sum, the U.S. Government cannot realize true success in nation-building or irregular warfare operations without achieving unified action. The world's ongoing transition from an international system to a global one with significant nonstate and transnational actors will only magnify the complexity of the security challenges that our nation will face in the years to come. Furthermore, this disunity of effort and ineffective interagency coordination is not limited to Afghanistan, just as it is also not limited to nation-building and irregular warfare operations. One only has to look at the U.S. Government's uneven response to Hurricane Katrina, its ongoing reorganization of the intelligence community, or the faltering reorganization of the Department of Homeland Security, to find other examples.[107] Our nation has many incentives to take action.

Nevertheless, from an interagency perspective, little of real substance has changed since the attacks of 9/11, at least from the standpoint of jurisdictional reorganization, any serious rebalancing of resources, or the addition of agency and departmental capabilities. The findings of the 9/11 Commission and the hard lessons of almost a decade of warfare in Afghanistan and Iraq suggest that incremental changes will not be enough, given the structural nature of these strategic and interagency challenges. Instead, improvements in coordinating structures, updated jurisdictional arrangements, and a review of agency and departmental capabilities must come at all levels if the interagency process is to become more effective. A failure to implement meaningful changes that redirect resources, provide for the operational control of other-agency resources, and establish binding mechanisms of accountability will only ensure that the existing presidential directives and other interagency guidelines will continue to have little real impact on how business is actually done. If we fail to act decisively, the outcomes will continue to reflect this disunity of effort.

ENDNOTES - CHAPTER 6

1. Rajiv Chandrasekaran, "Nobody Wants to Tell Us Anything," *The Washington Post National Weekly Edition*, March 23-29, 2009, p. 17.

2. Portions of this chapter originally appeared in the author's "Filling Irregular Warfare's Interagency Gaps," *Parameters*, Vol. 39, No. 3, Autumn 2009, pp. 65-80. The author is grateful to *Parameters* for the permission to reprint portions of his arguments here.

3. U.S. Joint Forces Command, *Commander's Handbook for the Joint Interagency Coordination Group*, Norfolk, VA: Joint Warfighting Center, March 1, 2007, p. II-3.

4. Thomas S. Szayna, Derek Eaton, and Amy Richardson, *Preparing the Army for Stability Operations*, Santa Monica, CA: Rand Corporation, 2007, p. 9.

5. John F. Troxell, "Presidential Decision Directive-56: A Glass Half Full," Chap. 2 in Joseph R. Cerami and Jay W. Boggs, eds., *The Interagency and Counterinsurgency Warfare: Stability, Security, Transition, and Reconstruction Roles*, Carlisle, PA: Strategic Studies Institute, U.S. Army War College, December 2007, pp. 25-26, available from *www.StrategicStudiesInstitute.army.mil*.

6. *Ibid.*

7. Szayna, Eaton, and Richardson, p. 9.

8. *National Security Presidential Directive-1: Organization of the National Security Council System*, Washington, DC: The White House, February 13, 2001, pp. 1-2.

9. Szayna, Eaton, and Richardson, p. 9.

10. *Department of Defense (DoD) Directive 3000.05: Military Support for Stability, Security, Transition, and Reconstruction (SSTR) Operations*, Washington, DC: Department of Defense, November 28, 2005, p. 2.

11. Zeb B. Bradford, Jr., and Frederic J. Brown, *America's Army: A Model for Interagency Effectiveness*, Westport, CT: Praeger, 2008, p. 29.

12. DoD Directive 3000.05, 2005, pp. 2-3.

13. *Department of Defense (DoD) Instruction 3000.05: Stability Operations*, Washington, DC: Department of Defense, September 2009.

14. DoD Directive 3000.5, 2005, p. 9.

15. Szayna, Eaton, and Richardson, p. xiv.

16. *National Security Presidential Directive (NSPD)-44: Management of Interagency Efforts Concerning Reconstruction and Stabilization*, Washington, DC: The White House, December 7, 2005, pp. 1-2.

17. *Ibid.*, p. 2.

18. *Ibid.*, pp. 3-4.

19. *Ibid.*, pp. 4-5.

20. *Ibid.*

21. Troxell, pp. 27-28.

22. Szayna, Eaton, and Richardson, p. 9.

23. *Ibid.*, p. xv.

24. *U.S. Government Counterinsurgency Guide*, Washington, DC: U.S. Government Interagency Counterinsurgency Initiative, January 2009, acknowledgements.

25. *Ibid.*, p. 15.

26. *Ibid.*, p. 30.

27. *Ibid.*, p. 31.

28. *Ibid.*, pp. 45-47.

29. *Ibid.*, p. 51.

30. *Ibid.*

31. Karen DeYoung, "A More Nimble Approach," *The Washington Post National Weekly Edition*, February 16-22, 2009, p. 33.

32. *Ibid.*

33. Peter Feaver, "Has Change Come to the National Security Council?" *Foreign Policy* online, May 27, 2009, available from *shadow.foreignpolicy.com*.

34. Szayna, Eaton, and Richardson, p. xiv.

35. *Ibid.*, p. xvii.

36. John W. Kingdon, *Agendas, Alternatives, and Public Policies*, 2nd Ed., New York: Pearson, 1997, pp. 71-89.

37. James F. Dobbins, *After the Taliban: Nation-Building in Afghanistan*, Washington, DC: Potomac, 2008, p. 118.

38. *Ibid.*

39. *Ibid.*, p. 140.

40. Amos A. Jordan *et al.*, *American National Security*, 5th Ed., Baltimore, MD: Johns Hopkins University Press, 1999, pp. 100-101.

41. *Ibid.*, pp. 218-219.

42. *Ibid.*, p. 219.

43. Richard B. Doyle, "The U.S. National Security Strategy: Policy, Politics, and Problems," *Public Administration Review*, July/August 2007, p. 625.

44. *Ibid.*, p. 626.

45. *Ibid.*

46. *Ibid.*

47. *Ibid.*

48. *Ibid.*

49. *Ibid.*

50. Scott R. Feil, "The Failure of Incrementalism: Interagency Coordination Challenges and Responses," Chap. 9 in Cerami and Boggs, pp. 296-299.

51. *Ibid.*

52. National Security Presidential Directive-1, 2001.

53. Office of the Coordinator for Reconstruction and Stabilization, "Preventing and Responding to Conflict: A New Approach," April 2009 presentation, p. 3, available from *www.CivilianResponseCorps.gov*.

54. *Ibid.*, p. 5.

55. *Ibid.*

56. *Ibid.*

57. *Ibid.*, p. 10.

58. *Ibid.*, p. 14.

59. *Ibid.*, p. 6.

60. *Doing Business in Afghanistan: A Country Commercial Guide for U.S. Companies*, Washington, DC: Department of State, 2008.

61. Chairman, Joint Chiefs of Staff, *Joint Publication (JP) 1-0: Doctrine for the Armed Forces of the United States*, Washington, DC: May 14, 2007, Chap. 1, p. I-1.

62. *Ibid.*, Chap. 2, p. II-2.

63. *Joint Publication (JP) 3-0: Joint Operations*, Washington, DC: Department of Defense, September 17, 2006, with Change 1 as of February 13, 2008, pp. II-1 to II-3.

64. *Field Manual (FM) 3-0: Operations*, Washington, DC: Department of the Army, February 2008, pp. 2-3 to2-5.

65. *Ibid.*, p. 2-4.

66. *Ibid.*, pp. 3-15 to 3-16.

67. *Joint Publication (JP) 5-0: Joint Operation Planning*, Washington, DC: Department of Defense; December 26, 2006, pp. II-6 to II-9.

68. *Ibid.*, p. II-9.

69. *Ibid.*, pp. II-7 to II-8.

70. *Field Manual (FM) 3-24: Counterinsurgency Field Manual*, Chicago, IL: University of Chicago Press edition, 2007, Chap. 2.

71. Carlos Hernandorena, "U.S. Provincial Reconstruction Teams in Afghanistan, 2003-2006: Obstacles to Interagency Cooperation," Chap. 5 in Cerami and Boggs, eds., p.130.

72. *Ibid.*, pp. 128-129.

73. Ahmed Rashid, *Descent into Chaos*, New York: Penguin, 2008, p. 198.

74. Hernandorena, p. 128.

75. Rashid, pp. 200-201.

76. Hernandorena, p. 134.

77. Personal interview with the author in Afghanistan in December 2007.

78. Hernandorena, p. 132.

79. Seth G. Jones, *Counterinsurgency in Afghanistan*, Santa Monica, CA: Rand Corporation's National Defense Research Institute Press, 2008, p. 107.

80. *Ibid.*

81. *Ibid.*

82. *Ibid.*

83. Hernandorena, p. 136.

84. *Ibid.*

85. *Ibid.*

86. *Ibid.*, p. 138.

87. *Provincial Reconstruction Teams in Afghanistan: An Interagency Assessment*, Washington, DC: U.S. Agency for International Development (USAID), June 2006, pp. 5-6.

88. *Ibid.*, p. 6.

89. Hernandorena, p. 143.

90. *Progress toward Security and Stability in Afghanistan: June 2009 Report to Congress in accordance with the 2008 National Defense Authorization Act*, Washington, DC: Department of Defense, June 2009, p. 17.

91. *Ibid.*

92. *Ibid.*

93. *Ibid.*, p. 18.

94. *Report to Congressional Committees: Afghanistan Security*, Washington, DC: U.S. Government Accountability Office, June 2008, p. 2.

95. *Ibid.*

96. Sarah Chayes, *The Punishment of Virtue: Inside Afghanistan After the Taliban*, New York: Penguin, 2006, p. 277.

97. *Ibid.*, p. 52.

98. Rashid, p. 185.

99. *Ibid.*, pp. 185-186.

100. Chandrasekaran, p. 6.

101. Rashid, p. 323.

102. *Ibid.*

103. Chandrasekaran, p. 6.

104. *Ibid.*, p. 7.

105. Stanley A. McChrystal, *COMISAF'S Initial Assessment*, Kabul, Afghanistan: International Security Force Headquarters, August 30, 2009, pp. 2-14.

106. Rob Norland, "With Raw Recruits, Afghan Police Build-up Falters," *The New York Times* online edition, February 2, 2010, available from *www.nytimes.com*.

107. Bradford and Brown, p. x.

CHAPTER 7

THE UNSURPRISING AND UNEVEN RESULTS

> The guerilla can win simply by not losing, whereas the counterinsurgent power can lose by not winning.
>
> Jeffrey Record[1]

In light of the various factors that have combined to undermine the Coalition's prospects for success in Afghanistan, it is not at all surprising that progress has been messy and slow. Key causes at the core of these difficulties include the particularly challenging case that Afghanistan represents as a candidate for viable nationhood, along with the enormously broad and complex scope of nation-building and irregular warfare missions in the best of circumstances. Added to this mix is the disjointedness of U.S. strategy, as well as a mismatch between the demands of the mission and existing governmental capabilities and resources. This substantial mismatch between intended ways and available means is aggravated further by inefficient and ineffective mechanisms for integrating resources and agency efforts. Even worse, these strategic and operational shortcomings have contributed directly to distress for many average Afghan citizens. The United States, our allies, and the host nation have all absorbed major costs in the form of blood and treasure.

Perhaps inevitably, the results on the ground have reflected these inherent problems. Writing in 2008 before the modified strategy and surge were implemented, and identifying a progressive loss of momentum in Afghanistan since 2006, analysts from the Institute for

National Strategic Studies attributed the trend at the time to several primary obstacles, among them, "the inherent weakness of state institutions, the dearth of human capital, inadequate international resources, and a lack of visible progress at the local level to give Afghans hope."[2] These analysts went on to cite poor development practices, the drug trade, violence, and corruption as factors that had contributed to a continuing short Afghan life expectancy of 43.8 years and a meager 28.1 percent literacy rate, as well as other indicators of a dismal quality of life for the average Afghan.[3] Writing about the same time, former Afghan Interior Minister Ali Jalali noted, "Afghanistan faces the distinct possibility of sliding back into instability and chaos [given a] record rise in drug production, deterioration of the rule of law, and [a] weakening national government in the regions outside the major cities."[4]

In his own insightful pre-surge report of the conditions on the ground in 2008, General Barry McCaffrey lauded the quality of the military's kinetic operational efforts, but he then went on to describe an Afghanistan that was in misery. General McCaffrey cited a constant state of warfare, short life expectancy, high infant and pregnancy death rates, and wholesale dysfunction and governmental corruption within Afghan society as some of the major causes of Afghan suffering.[5] After revisiting the country in November 2009, General McCaffrey noted that illiteracy continued at the same rate, and he also found that 87 percent of Afghan women complained of violence against them, half of it sexual in nature.[6] Additionally, he discovered that drug abuse, tuberculosis, and other diseases and maladies were still widespread.[7] More recent measures in 2010 confirmed that the Afghan average life expectancy is slightly improved but still short at 44.4 years, while the literacy rate has remained at 28.1 percent.[8] Without question, progress toward improving the quality of life of the average Afghan has been slow, in spite of massive aid and the focused efforts of the international community.

On a brighter note, General McCaffrey observed that about eight million Afghans now have phones, and that there are 650 active print publications, 15 television networks, and 55 private radio stations.[9] He also identified the Afghan National Army (ANA) as a success story, with 82 of its 132 authorized battalions fielded by November 2009.[10] General McCaffrey was also pleased to find that the approval rate for U.S. and North Atlantic Treaty Organization (NATO) forces in the country was over 60 percent.[11] Measured more recently, however, approval rates for NATO forces have fallen off significantly since his last visit, as 68 percent of Afghans surveyed answered "no" in a 2010 poll when asked whether NATO forces "protect the local population."[12] Other recent adverse indicators include 70 percent of the respondents stating that NATO and Afghan military operations are "bad" (rather than "good") for their local areas, and 75 percent responding that foreigners "disrespect" their "religion and tradition."[13]

On a more positive and recent note, however, the effects of the 2010 surge of U.S. and coalition forces, augmented with additional civilian agency personnel and heightened resources, have in fact resulted in significant progress on the security front. This progress is measured by the number of key districts with a substantial security presence and by the increased pressure on the Taliban.[14] Disapproval of the Taliban among the Afghan population also increased to

75 percent from 68 percent at the end of the last reporting period. Additionally, the measures of Afghan National Security Force (ANSF) generation and effectiveness also increased significantly over the period.[15] At the same time, progress in improving governance has continued to lag the security gains, and casualties among the civilian population remained at significant though decreased levels, with the Taliban and other anti-government elements responsible for the great majority of those casualties.[16] When considered as a whole, the results in Afghanistan have been uneven—and unsurprising.

THE ANSF AND POPULATION SECURITY: PRE-SURGE AND POST-SURGE

While General McCaffrey was correct in identifying the rapid development of the ANA and its effective performance as the coalition's major success story in 2008, other measures of Afghanistan's security posture provided cause for concern. These trends were especially troubling, given that the Coalition's security-related efforts—including developing the ANSF and their administrative institutions and protecting the Afghan people—had been at the forefront of the military's endeavors in Afghanistan since the beginning of the intervention. Without question, population security and ANSF development have received the lion's share of the coalition's attention, resources, and effort in the period since the transition to a more robust counterinsurgency and the introduction of the surge forces.

Analyzing these security trends in detail, a 2008 Rand study concluded that the quality of the Afghan security forces remained poor, with the police in particular being characterized as "corrupt and often unable to perform basic patrolling (much less) conduct counterinsurgency operations, protect reconstruction projects, prevent border incursions, and conduct counternarcotics operations."[17] This Rand study found "deep-seated corruption" in the Ministry of the Interior, the agency with responsibility for administering the police forces.[18] In general, the Rand study corroborated General McCaffrey's perspectives on the ANA, concluding that it had developed into a credible force that featured "tenacious fighters" who were "effective in gathering intelligence," largely as a result of the "critical factor" of receiving effective training from U.S. and Coalition forces.[19] Of course, these respective ANSF outcomes are not all that surprising, given that the U.S. military certainly has more experience in building an army than it does a police force. In fairness, it should also be noted that the United States did not originally have the police development mission, which initially belonged to the German government.

At about the same time the Rand study was underway, the U.S. Government Accountability Office (GAO) conducted its own study of the Afghan army and police development mission. GAO found that in spite of the more than $10 billion already spent on the Afghan security forces by 2008, there still was no coordinated, detailed, or comprehensive Department of State (State) and Department of Defense (DoD) plan for ANSF development. Like the Rand study, the GAO assessment found major problems within the ANSF in terms of force capabilities, administrative capacity, reenlistment and retention rates, equipment fielding, and other measures.[20] The GAO study also questioned why the $6 billion investment in the Afghan National Police (ANP) to that point had resulted in no fully trained police districts out of the 365 across the country.[21] Only 12 of the 433 police units were judged to be capable of conducting operations, even with significant Coalition support. GAO also found other persistent and major shortfalls in the supporting elements of the judicial sector, as well as problems with police pay systems, widespread corruption, and injuries and deaths due to insurgent attacks.[22] The police mission also continued to struggle with a persistent shortage of mentors for the district police and the offices of the Ministry of the Interior. Even worse, these same problems had been previously identified in a similar GAO study of 2005.[23]

Projecting forward, the GAO study pointed to the lack of a sustainable model for the police; as such, the agency suggested that the U.S. commitment might have to remain in place indefinitely, given the Afghans' inability to sustain themselves. More recently, in 2010, U.S. officials have in fact acknowledged that the United States expects to subsidize the training and support of the ANSF at the rate of about $6 billion per year, even after the United States begins withdrawing troops from the country in 2011.[24] In spite of the massive U.S. investment so far, the GAO also found that the police continued to lack basic equipment, including shortages in everything from vehicles to radios to body armor.[25] GAO observers found more to like in the development of the ANA, but the agency questioned why over the 6 years from 2002 to 2008, only two of 105 Afghan army units had been assessed as fully capable.[26] In the GAO's view, this slow production rate called into question the viability of the ambitious plans to increase the end-strength of the ANSF significantly and rapidly in the coming years. Finally, in another GAO study about 6 months later, GAO reported that the agency had major concerns about the lack of tracking and accountability mechanisms for the weapons and other sensitive items, such as night vision goggles, that had been provided to the ANSF.[27]

In June 2009, the Department of Defense (DoD) submitted its own mandatory report to Congress on the state of the mission in Afghanistan. The DoD thumbnail sketch of the situation resembled both the McCaffrey and GAO reports in many respects, because the document painted a dreary picture in terms of population security and the development of the ANSF. At the same time, the document offered more positive measures related to the provision of basic services to the Afghan people. In the DoD summary, the report noted that "the security situation continued to deteriorate in much of Afghanistan," while "insurgent-initiated attacks were 60% higher than the preceding year."[28] Reflecting in part on the Coalition's efforts to take the fight to the enemy in areas they had not previously been able to reach, the report noted that U.S. casualties had increased by 24 percent from the previous year. Overall military deaths, including those within the ANSF and among the allies, had increased by 48 percent.[29] On a brighter note, DoD reported in 2009 that civilian casualties had decreased by 9 percent from the previous year. Furthermore, the civilian population's willingness to cooperate with the Coalition in ways, such as turning in improvised explosive devices (IEDs), had actually increased.[30] As another measure of population security, a companion report from the Congressional Research Service published a few months after the 2009 DoD report observed that despite success in enrolling Afghan children in schools, the educational initiative had suffered numerous setbacks due to Taliban attacks.[31]

Following up on its assessments from earlier in the year, GAO conducted another study in September 2009, this time focusing upon the interagency process. The study reported:

> Most U.S. initiatives we reviewed, such as the efforts to build capable Afghan security forces, needed improved planning, including the development of coordinated interagency plans that include measurable goals, specific time frames, and cost estimates. . . . The Departments of Defense and State lacked a coordinated, detailed interagency plan for training and equipping the Afghan National Security Forces.[32]

While acknowledging the incredibly difficult working conditions confronting U.S. personnel, the GAO report also identified a number of other recurring problems. These persistent problems included the continuing high costs of the mission, the limited success in reforming the Afghan army and police, a lack of accountability over "billions in U.S. assistance to Afghanistan and Pakistan," and shortfalls in managing and overseeing contractors, road construction, other development activities, and counternarcotics.[33]

Commenting on the state of population security and the irregular warfare operations, General McCaffrey's follow-on report of November 2009 described a resurgent Taliban with a "serious presence in 160 of 364 districts," up from 30 such districts in 2003.[34] He also reported that in July 2009 alone, the Taliban had employed 828 IED attacks against Coalition forces. The Taliban had also mounted two large-scale, battalion-sized, complex, and coordinated attacks on Coalition forces earlier in the year.[35] As an additional measure of the deteriorating security posture, the casualties among the ANP had also increased dramatically.[36]

For its own part, the DoD's 2010 report to Congress provides additional evidence of the major security challenges still confronting the Coalition. The annual DoD report notes that, "The insurgents perceive 2009 as their most successful year."[37] The report further acknowledges that "the insurgents' strategy has proven effective in slowing the spread of governance and development."[38] More positively, the DoD report of 2010 asserts that "the insurgency has been under unprecedented pressure," and that "52% of Afghans believe insurgents are the greatest source of insecurity, while only 1% believes the National Army/Police are primarily to blame."[39] At the same time, these positive developments are offset by the fact that the insurgents are now active in more areas than they had been in the previous year, with their levels of activity increasing in 2009 and then again in 2010. The level of IED attacks in 2010 in Afghanistan increased by 236 percent over the prior year.[40]

In its internal assessments of the development of the Afghan forces, the 2009 DoD report asserted that ANSF capability had continued to improve, but the report also admitted that the effort was still slowed by shortages of police and army trainers. Specifically, in 2009 NATO only had 1,665 of the 3,313 personnel needed for the Afghan Army's Embedded Training Teams (ETTs) and comparable shortfalls for the ANP Police Mentor Teams (PMTs).[41] The DoD's 2010 report indicates that these significant shortages of trainers continue, even as the Afghan government's request to expand the ANSF end-strength goals to 171,600 in the Afghan Army and 134,000 in the police were approved.[42] The 2009 report also notes that ANA development continues to proceed at an accelerated pace, but expresses concerns about the lagging development of Afghan ministerial capacity and the quality of the Afghan police personnel once they graduate from training.[43] Other major concerns in 2010 with ANSF development include high attrition rates within the highly trained Afghan National Civil Order Police (ANCOP), lagging leader development among Army officers, shortages of officer and noncommissioned officers, and continuing poor literacy rates.[44]

Reflecting the impact of the surge of trainers and other enablers in 2010, the April 2011 DoD report paints a more positive picture in terms of the quantity and quality of ANSF production. The report notes that in the period since the 2009 report, 92,000 additional Afghan army and police personnel had been brought onto the rolls and trained, a rate that actually exceeded the targeted rates of development.[45] The report also cites gains in ANSF literacy training, the development of enabling and sustaining forces, and the initiation of efforts to develop an internal Afghan training capability, all aimed at achieving the goal of moving "Afghanistan closer to a professional, sustainable ANSF that is subject to civilian control and is capable of independently providing security to the Afghan people."[46] Toward this effort, the report also lists 292 Coalition trainers as working in the Ministry of the Interior alone to facilitate the Afghan police development and the creation of the institutional capabilities needed to administer the police programs, as a measure of the magnitude of resources required to achieve these challenging goals. Despite the surge, the police training effort lacks 740 of the 2,778 trainers required.[47]

Moreover, the lack of police trainers and the question of the sustainability of the ANSF are not the only red flags to emerge from the latest assessments. In a report to Congress in January 2011, GAO analysts cite a similar shortfall of trainers for the Afghan army development effort, in addition to noting that the long-term costs of ANSF development and sustainment have not been seriously considered in the push to rapidly expand the size of those forces in advance of the planned 2014 transfer of authority.[48] Additionally, while recent initiatives to tighten contracting procedures and oversight have been implemented to positive effect, the congressionally appointed Commission on Wartime Contracting estimated in its final report of August 2011, that approximately $60 billion in U.S. war funds had been wasted across civilian and military programs in Afghanistan, fueling fraud and corruption while undermining the efforts on behalf of the Afghans.[49]

Finally, in terms of population security, counterinsurgency and counterterrorism, the Coalition has realized significant recent successes, including the high-profile terminations of al Qaeda leaders Osama Bin Laden and Atiyah Abd al-Rahman, both in Pakistan. Describing security progress as significant, yet "fragile and reversible," the 2011 DoD report also cites increased insurgent use of asymmetric tactics in light of significant losses due to direct engagement with the increased ISAF forces.[50] As a result of the increased ISAF pressure and significant Taliban losses, the total number of suicide attacks actually fell from 51 to 45 over the report period, although the enemy's heightened use of asymmetric tactics, such as IEDs, infiltration of the ANSF, assassinations, and other techniques have also resulted in higher civilian casualty levels.[51] The coalition also reported steady progress with improving ANSF reach and the security posture of identified "Key Terrain Districts" (KTDs) during the report period.[52]

THE STATE OF AFGHAN GOVERNANCE AND CORRUPTION

In his 2007 analysis of the declining conditions in Afghanistan and his prescriptions for improvement, former Afghan Interior Minister Ali Jalali asserted that the "political consensus of 2001 has been lost to disruptive factionalism."[53] As a further indicator of the poor state of Afghan governance, he also highlighted the fact that several years later, the Coalition and Afghan government had failed to create constitutionally required provincial and local governing institutions, pointing out that the "subnational institutions mandated by the national constitution are only partially established."[54] Offering a grim assessment of the state of Afghan political affairs, Jalali asserted, "The structural legitimacy of the current Afghan government suffers from a lack of capacity, particularly at the subnational level, where the vacuum is filled by insurgents, militia commanders, combined with local criminal gangs."[55] He further noted, "The introduction of district, village, and municipal councils has been delayed indefinitely. ... Provincial councils are in place but are fraught with confusion regarding their roles and responsibility."[56]

In support of Jalali's bleak analysis, Afghan government capacity remained so poor in 2005 that the government could only spend 44 percent of the aid it received for development, lacking the basic capacity to award and monitor contracts.[57] Adding further evidence of the widespread Afghan governmental dysfunction, the June 2009 DoD report confirmed this gloomy assessment, noting that, "The [Afghan government] is, and will for the foreseeable future continue to be hampered by lack of capacity, resources, and interagency planning and coordination." The report further asserted that government corruption remained a major problem that "saps the credibility of the institutions of governance and undermines Afghan and international efforts to build these institutions."[58] Even in the few cases in which ministerial leadership had been strengthened, the national-level governing institutions remained remarkably thin, as evidenced by the DoD report, which cited significant weakness in the second- and third-tier leadership.[59] In an incident that showed just how far the Afghans have to go before they can approach any Western standards of democratic governance, in March 2009, after international outcry and some domestic protest, President Karzai finally suspended the enforcement of the Shi'a Personal Status Law, a law that would have required Shi'a women "to have their husband's permission to leave the house and would have legalized marital rape."[60]

In August 2009, the presidential elections were disturbing on several levels, with allegations of widespread fraud among all of the candidates, and NATO appearing feeble, given its inability to administer the various polling sites. The United Nations (UN) Elections Complaints Commission (ECC) determined by October that about one million Karzai votes, as well as another 200,000 Abdullah votes, were fraudulent and therefore deducted from the candidates' totals.[61] Initially resistant to the notion that any fraud had occurred at all, President Karzai eventually relented once the ECC had rendered its report, and he acknowledged the need for a run-off election. However, on November 1, the challenger, Abdullah, withdrew from the projected run-off, stating that there was no way he could possibly get a fair election.

In another troubling trend, the Afghan government had grown in size, but it also had narrowed ethnically, becoming progressively dominated by ethnic Pashtuns.[62] While the parliament has done better in terms of its ethnic diversity, it is still sometimes criticized for its large contingent of former mujahedeen. As a broader measure of Afghan governmental reach, U.S. analysts estimate that the Karzai government controlled about 30 percent of the country in 2009, while the Taliban controlled about 4 percent and had a significant influence in another 30 percent.[63] Other observers have gone so far as to assert that the Afghan national governing institutions are far less effective than the ad hoc shadow institutions that the Taliban have constructed, and that the current legitimate government of Afghanistan even compares poorly with the leftist and monarchical governments of Afghanistan's past.[64]

The pattern of fraudulent elections has continued, as demonstrated by the 2010 elections, which resulted in thousands of allegations of fraud and the widespread practice of ballot-box stuffing. Also in 2010, a top Afghan prosecutor was forced into retirement by the Karzai administration after repeatedly complaining that top Afghan officials were thwarting corruption investigations against themselves. The two government officials in question, Interior Minister Hanif Atmar and intelligence director Amrullah Saleh, both had strong ties to the American and British governments.[65] After another senior Afghan official was forced out by Karzai under similar circumstances, analysts began to question Karzai's mental fitness for office, his motives, and his potentially shifting interests. Not surprisingly, the Afghan president also voiced his staunch opposition to the U.S. plan to begin withdrawing forces from Afghanistan in 2011, with the clear implication being that the Afghan government was nowhere close to being able to govern for itself without the continuation of major U.S. and NATO assistance.

In the first major assessment in the post-surge period, the April 2011 DoD report finds that the perception of the Afghan government has clearly improved in some respects. Afghans reported more optimism about their government's prospects, along with increases in the belief that their government had more influence than the Taliban, and increasing levels of perceived safety in traveling about the country.[66] At the same time, actual progress in the provision of services, ministerial capacity, and the achievement of benchmarks agreed upon in the Kabul Conference of 2010 remained slow. Along the same lines, then-Chairman of the Joint Chiefs of Staff Michael Mullen testified before Congress that "improvements in subnational and reconstruction have not kept pace with progress in improving security," a result that "has impeded our ability to hold, build, and transfer." Likewise, a special task force convened by General David Petraeus in 2010 and 2011 estimated that approximately $360 million in U.S. tax dollars had made their way to the Taliban and various criminal elements as a result of corruption in the Afghan government and lax oversight mechanisms in the contracting processes.[67]

RECONSTRUCTION, ECONOMIC DEVELOPMENT, AND THE DRUG TRADE

The news on the economic side of the Afghan equation is mixed, whether viewed from the perspective of U.S. agency and departmental performance or in consideration of actual Afghan economic results. Among other factors, the impacts of the deteriorating security situation and the disjointed commitment of resources to reconstruction and development are clearly evident in the marginal economic progress that the mission has made to date. These challenges were first identified systematically in a GAO study of July 2005. This study noted that the U.S. Agency for International Development (USAID) had intended to build or rehabilitate 286 schools by the end of 2004, but had only completed eight.[68] That same report noted that USAID also could not provide complete financial data to show where its economic assistance funds had been committed, which was also the case in 2002 and 2003; the GAO report further stated that the agency "lacked a comprehensive strategy to direct its efforts."[69]

Drilling down further, GAO found that USAID had also failed to "consistently require contractors to fulfill contract provisions," and the agency "did not systematically collect information needed to assess the progress of its major projects." This shortfall was exacerbated by the fact that "measures provided by the embassy to decisionmakers in Washington did not comprehensively portray progress in each sector or the overall U.S. program."[70] The GAO report then identified problems with the coordination and integration of agency, host-nation, and donor efforts, including "confusion" between the ad hoc "Afghanistan Reconstruction Group" and the USAID contractors.[71] In a carefully documented analysis in 2008, a military participant in the Khost PRT questioned whether or not these ad hoc interagency groups were really as effective as they were claimed to be, citing some of the same challenges as the GAO.[72]

Reporting in June 2009, the DoD identified to Congress some areas of progress in the broader economic and developmental efforts, including the completion of 78 percent of the ring road and the fact that 82 percent of the population now had access to the Ministry of Public Health's "Basic Package of Health Care Services."[73] The report gave credit to the increased public health measures for the fact that 40,000 more infants were surviving each year than had been previously.[74] Also, despite the fact that heightened Taliban attacks continued to limit actual attendance, access to education had increased, with more than seven million children being enrolled in school on the opening day in March 2009, another positive indicator of success.[75]

At the same time, the 2009 DoD report also noted that uneven taxing practices and a lack of security had diminished the potential benefits of the highway which, while low on the list of USAID priorities, was absolutely vital to any sustained and legitimate Afghan economy. The production and distribution of electricity also remained problematic; in spite of some progress, the going was slow. USAID had set a goal of reaching 65 percent of the urban population with electricity and 25 percent in the rural areas by the end of 2010.[76] Perhaps the most promising indicator of all, Afghanistan doubled its legitimate agricultural output over the past 5 years, although much of this growth depended upon the continued infusion of aid.[77] So, in 2009, the massive infusion of aid from the United States and the international community was clearly having an impact on the provision of the most basic social services. However, the need remained overwhelming, and sustainable economic growth for Afghanistan remained elusive.

More recently, the 2010 DoD report to Congress illustrates that these economic difficulties remain, with progress coming in small increments, when it comes at all. Only a handful of Afghanistan's key districts are realizing sustainable or even dependent economic growth, since most regions of the country are characterized as having "minimal" or "stalled" growth levels—or had their "population at risk" or were "not assessed."[78] Although government revenues grew significantly as a result of the institution of improved tax collection techniques and anti-corruption measures, a concurrent increase in spending has led to a huge Afghan budget deficit. Actual Afghan revenues generated by legitimate domestic economic activity accounted for only 30 percent of the 2010 Afghan government budget, and this model is clearly unsustainable—a lesson the United States must also learn. The 2011 DoD report notes that much like the Afghan public's perception of governance, public optimism regarding the country's economic prospects has increased, though the actual pace of reconstruction and development remains slow.[79]

Viewing these challenges more broadly, former Afghan Interior Minister Jalali pointed to the wholesale lack of security and rule of law, as well as the prospering drug trade, as being major hurdles to economic progress in Afghanistan and to the counterinsurgency.[80] For example, in 2004, for the first time ever, poppy was farmed in all 34 Afghan provinces and the actual illegal drug production rate increased greatly, as over 80 percent of the poppy was refined into heroin in the country, a far greater amount than in previous years.[81] A 2005 GAO study also noted that the deteriorating security in the country not only severely limited economic development, but that the increased opium production also served to undermine the legitimate economic activity.[82] In terms of the scope of this effect, UN and U.S. estimates placed the drug activity at approximately 50 to 60 percent of Afghanistan's gross domestic product in the years between 2002 and 2004.[83] Partly related to the drug trade, terrorist violence in Afghanistan also increased more than 20 percent between 2006 and the second half of 2007.[84] As another negative aspect of the enforcement of the rule of law, the nation's 34 provincial prisons and its 203 detention centers remain in terrible condition, and prisoner abuse among the Afghan guards remains widespread.[85]

Measuring these impacts more recently, DoD's June 2009 report to Congress stated that opium cultivation decreased by 20 percent compared against the previous year, a trend largely attributed to changes in ISAF rules of engagement that allowed ISAF personnel to target drug facilities and traffickers. Overall, total poppy eradication was double the rate in 2008, but still less than in 2007, largely due to weaker performance by Provincial Governor-led Eradication. At the same time, a positive trend saw nearly 20,000 farmers agree to grow alternative crops to poppy.[86] Conversely, the 2010 DoD report admits that ISAF and the international community also learned that President Karzai was right on one point, as "large scale eradication targeted toward Afghan poppy farmers was counterproductive and drove farmers to the insurgency."[87] Accordingly, the National Security Council (NSC) subsequently approved a new U.S. counternarcotics strategy aimed at overcoming these unintended consequences that had actually reinforced the insurgents' prospects.

OTHER SUMMARY MEASURES OF MISSION PROGRESS

As a broader measure of the security climate in Afghanistan and the impact of the violence on the Afghan people in recent years, a poll of Afghan citizens undertaken by Western media in late 2007 revealed that 24 percent of the respondents claimed that civilians in their areas had been killed or seriously injured by Western forces in the past year, while 27 percent indicated that civilians in their areas had been killed or seriously injured by the Taliban.[88] At the end of 2007, an NSC assessment noted that it was possible that the United States and NATO could lose the war altogether based on the deteriorating security situation and the lack of progress.[89] A 2008 Rand study identified major continuing failures in the development of indigenous security forces, local governance, and the denial of insurgent sanctuaries in Pakistan, among other critical shortcomings in the Afghan mission.[90] At about the same time, a World Bank study identified the "absence of a clear policy framework regarding a desired institutional structure and a strategy to implement it" as the most pressing shortcoming of the effort in Afghanistan.[91]

In its own assessment of mission progress in 2009, the DoD report reflected a move on the part of the Obama administration to ratchet back the expectations for gains in governance and economic development. Noting a need for realistic and achievable objectives, the report backed away from the goal of a democratic Afghanistan, instead defining the objective as, "Promoting a more capable, accountable, and effective government in Afghanistan" and "civilian control and stable constitutional government in Pakistan."[92] The document also mentions building a stronger democracy in Pakistan, but offers a more limited call for a self-reliant government in Afghanistan, although the document does mention a continuing effort to "bolster the legitimacy of the Afghan government by helping to ensure free and fair elections for Afghan leaders."[93] Coming just 2 months after the release of the DoD report, the actual elections would prove to be anything but free and fair.

Regardless, these diminished expectations still come with a major price tag. In constant 2009 dollars, Afghanistan and Iraq were costing about $377 million per day in that year, compared with $622 million per day for World War II, and the cost for Afghanistan alone was more than $9 billion per month in Fiscal Year 2010 (FY10).[94] The baseline budgetary request for operations in Afghanistan FY10 was $65 billion, even before the costs of the Afghan surge were added into the actual total.[95] Through the end of fiscal year 2009, operations in Afghanistan and Iraq had already combined to cost the United States more than $940 billion since 2001, with Afghanistan amounting to $223 billion of that total.[96] As noted previously, the administration's combined Fiscal Year 2011 (FY11) budget request for Afghanistan, Pakistan, and Iraq is $159 billion, and anticipated costs for Afghanistan in FY10 and FY11 are expected to exceed $100 billion in each year. Clearly, nation-building and irregular warfare are not only uncertain undertakings, but they are also extremely expensive ones. The results in Afghanistan also confirm the less-than-optimal nature of the interagency effort, coming after almost 10 years of operations, many billions of dollars of U.S. aid, and the major concurrent effort by the international community and NATO.

Perhaps most disturbingly, it is not clear at all that the Afghans really appreciate the magnitude of this effort, or even wish it to continue. In opinion polling conducted in September 2010, 55 percent of the Afghans surveyed said they were not willing to "work with a Westerner in the same place."[97] A clear majority of 74 percent think it is "wrong" to work with foreign forces.[98] If asked to choose between two options, 72 percent would choose an elected government—but 24 percent of the others would reinstate the Taliban government.[99] Given more of a choice, a plurality of the respondents (45 percent) continue to prefer an Islamic state, and there are more Afghans who prefer a "strong leader" who "rules for life" (30 percent) than want democracy (23 percent).[100] A large majority of 74 percent favor negotiating with the Taliban, though 75 percent of those favoring that option would require the Taliban to stop fighting first.[101] As far as how the counterinsurgency was perceived in 2010, 55 percent of those surveyed believed that NATO and the Afghan government held the upper hand, while 39 percent saw the Taliban succeeding, and another 6 percent could not or would not answer.[102] While there were a number of recent positive trends represented in the Afghans' views of their government, 83 percent of the respondents asserted that government corruption affects their daily lives.[103] There is clearly a long way to go.

Finally, and as perhaps the measure of the opinions that will ultimately have the greatest impact on the U.S. mission in Afghanistan, support among the American people for continuing the war in Afghanistan lags considerably. In 2009, General McCaffrey cited polling that indicated that 66 percent of the respondents felt that the war was not worth fighting.[104] In

2010, 60 percent of the Americans surveyed described Afghanistan as a "lost cause."[105] More recently, 58 percent of Americans responded in one poll that "the U.S. should not be involved in Afghanistan now," while in another, a full 75 percent supported the President's decision to remove the surge forces from Afghanistan, while still others supported further withdrawals.[106] The Taliban clearly understand that insurgents win by not losing, while counterinsurgents lose by not winning. We cannot afford to remain disjointed in our strategy or disunified in our methods.

ENDNOTES - CHAPTER 7

1. Jeffrey Record, "Why the Strong Lose," *Parameters*, Winter 2005-2006, p. 19.

2. Stephen J. Flanagan and James A. Schear, eds., *Strategic Challenges: America's Global Security Agenda*, Washington, DC: Institute of National Security Studies (INSS)/National Defense University Press, 2008, pp. 134-135.

3. *Ibid.*, p. 136.

4. Ali A. Jalali, "Afghanistan: Regaining Momentum," *Parameters*, Vol. 37, No. 4, Winter 2007-08, p. 5.

5. General Barry R. McCaffrey, "After Action Report: Visit NATO SHAPE HQ and Afghanistan, 21-26 July 2008," unpublished memorandum, New York: Department of Social Sciences, U.S. Military Academy, July 30, 2008, p. 3.

6. *Ibid.*, p. 7.

7. *Ibid.*

8. *CIA World Fact Book-Afghanistan*, available from *https://www.cia.gov/library/publications/the-world-factbook/geos/af.html*.

9. *Ibid.*, p. 9.

10. *Ibid.*, p. 6.

11. *Ibid.*

12. Anthony H. Cordesman, "The Afghan War - Part Three: Implementing the New Strategy," Washington, DC: Center for Strategic and International Studies, Burke Chair in Strategy Publication, September 8, 2010, p. 16, available from *csis.org/files/publication/100909_AfghanWarStatus-III_Strategy.pdf.*

13. *Ibid.*

14. *Report on Progress Toward Security and Stability in Afghanistan and United States Plan for Sustaining the Afghanistan National Security Forces,* Washington, DC: Department of Defense, April 2011, p. 1.

15. *Ibid.*, pp. 1-3.

16. *Ibid.*, pp. 4-5.

17. Seth G. Jones, *Counterinsurgency in Afghanistan,* Santa Monica, CA: Rand Corporation, National Defense Research Institute Press, 2008, p. 69.

18. *Ibid.*

19. *Ibid.*, pp. 74-75.

20. *Report to Congressional Committees: Afghanistan Security,* Washington, DC: U.S. Government Accountability Office, June 2008, pp. 2-15.

21. *Ibid.*, p. 2.

22. Congressional testimony of Charles Michael Johnson, GAO, on "Afghanistan Security: U.S. Efforts to Develop Capable Afghan Police Forces Face Challenges and Need a Coordinated, Detailed Plan to Help Ensure Accountability," June 18, 2008, *GAO Report GAO-08-883T,* Washington, DC: GAO, 2008, Summary.

23. *Ibid.*

24. Desmond Butler, "U.S. to Subsidize Afghan Training for Years," *The Pittsburgh Post-Gazette*, September 7, 2010, p. A-3.

25. *Ibid.*, p. 2.

26. *Report to Congressional Committees: Afghanistan Security*, GAO, p. 2.

27. *Afghanistan Security: Lack of Systematic Tracking Raises Significant Accountability Concerns about Weapons Provided to Afghan National Security Forces*, GAO-09-267, Washington, DC: GAO, January 2009, pp. 3-5.

28. *Report on Progress Toward Security and Stability in Afghanistan: June 2009 Report to Congress in Accordance with the 2008 National Defense Authorization Act*, Washington, DC: Department of Defense, June 2009, Executive Summary.

29. *Ibid.*

30. *Ibid.*

31. Kenneth Katzman, *Afghanistan: Post-Taliban Governance, Security, and U.S. Policy*, Congressional Research Service (CRS) Report RL30588, Washington, DC: CRS, November 10, 2009, p. 59.

32. Congressional testimony of Jacquelyn Williams-Bridgets, GAO, on "Afghanistan and Pakistan: Oversight of U.S. Interagency Efforts," September 9, 2009, *GAO Report GAO-09-1015T*, Washington, DC: GAO, 2009, p. 2.

33. *Ibid.*

34. General Barry R. McCaffrey, "After Action Report: Visit to Kuwait and Afghanistan, 10-18 November 2009," unpublished memorandum, West Point, NY: Department of Social Sciences, U.S. Military Academy, December 5, 2009, pp. 5-6.

35. *Ibid.*

36. *Ibid.*, p. 6.

37. *Report on Progress Toward Security and Stability in Afghanistan: April 2010 Report to Congress in Accordance with the 2008 National Defense Authorization Act*, Washington, DC: Department of Defense, April 2010, p. 23.

38. *Ibid.*, p. 24.

39. *Ibid.*, pp. 23-24.

40. *Ibid.*, p. 23.

41. *Report on Progress Toward Security and Stability in Afghanistan: June 2009 Report to Congress in Accordance with the 2008 National Defense Authorization Act*, Washington, DC: Department of Defense, June 2009, Executive Summary.

42. *Report on Progress Toward Security and Stability in Afghanistan: April 2010 Report to Congress in Accordance with the 2008 National Defense Authorization Act*, Washington, DC: Department of Defense, April 2010, p. 87.

43. *Ibid.*, pp. 87-89.

44. Cordesman, p. 16.

45. *Report on Progress Toward Security and Stability in Afghanistan and United States Plan for Sustaining the Afghanistan National Security Forces*, Washington, DC: Department of Defense, April 2011, p. 14.

46. *Ibid.*

47. *Ibid.*, pp. 19-20.

48. *Afghanistan Security: Afghan Army Growing, but Additional Trainers Needed; Long-Term Costs Not Determined*, GAO-11-66, Washington, DC: GAO, January 2011, pp. 1-3.

49. "AP Exclusive: Up to $60B in War Funds Said to Be Wasted," *The Observer-Reporter*, August 31, 2011, p. B5.

50. *Report on Progress Toward Security and Stability in Afghanistan and United States Plan for Sustaining the Afghanistan National Security Forces*, Washington, DC: Department of Defense, April 2011, pp. 53-55.

51. *Ibid.*, p. 54.

52. *Ibid.*, pp. 56-57.

53. Ali A. Jalali, "Afghanistan: Regaining Momentum," *Parameters*, Vol. 37, No. 4, Winter 2007-08, p. 5.

54. *Ibid.*, p. 9.

55. *Ibid.*, p. 8.

56. *Ibid.*, p. 9.

57. Ahmed Rashid, *Descent into Chaos*, New York: Penguin, 2008, p. 194.

58. *Report on Progress Toward Security and Stability in Afghanistan: June 2009 Report to Congress in Accordance with the 2008 National Defense Authorization Act*, Washington, DC: Department of Defense, June 2009, Executive Summary.

59. *Ibid.*

60. *Ibid.*

61. Katzman, pp. 11-12.

62. *Ibid.*, p. 13.

63. *Ibid.*, p. 14.

64. Antonio Giustozzi, *Koran, Kalashnikov and Laptop: The Neo-Taliban Insurgency in Afghanistan*, London, UK: Hurst, 2007, p. 18.

65. Alissa J. Rubin, "Karzai's Increasing Isolation Worries Both Afghans and the West," *The New York Times*, June 8, 2010, p. A12.

66. *Report on Progress Toward Security and Stability in Afghanistan and United States Plan for Sustaining the Afghanistan National Security Forces*, Washington, DC: Department of Defense, April 2011, p. 71.

67. Richard Lardner and Deb Reichmann, "Afghan Corruption Costing U.S.," *The Pittsburgh Post-Gazette*, August 17, 2011, p. A4.

68. *Afghanistan Reconstruction: Despite Some Progress, Deteriorating Security and Other Obstacles Continue to Threaten Achievement of U.S. Goals*, GAO-05-742, Washington, DC: GAO, July 2005, Summary.

69. Ibid.

70. Ibid.

71. Ibid., p. 4.

72. Robert J. Bebber, "The Role of Provincial Reconstruction Teams in Counterinsurgency Operations," *Small Wars Journal*, November 10, 2008, available from *smallwarsjournal.com*.

73. *Report on Progress Toward Security and Stability in Afghanistan: June 2009 Report to Congress in Accordance with the 2008 National Defense Authorization Act*, Washington, DC: Department of Defense, June 2009, Executive Summary.

74. Ibid.

75. Ibid.

76. Katzman, p. 60.

77. Ibid.

78. *Report on Progress Toward Security and Stability in Afghanistan: April 2010 Report to Congress in Accordance with the 2008 National Defense Authorization Act*, Washington, DC: Department of Defense, April 2010, p. 60.

79. *Report on Progress Toward Security and Stability in Afghanistan and United States Plan for Sustaining the Afghanistan National Security Forces*, Washington, DC: Department of Defense, April 2011, p. 83-84.

80. Ali A. Jalali, "Afghanistan: Regaining Momentum," *Parameters*, Vol. 37, No. 4, Winter 2007-08, pp. 9-12.

81. Rashid, p. 325.

82. *Afghanistan Reconstruction*, Summary.

83. *Ibid.*, p. 5.

84. Astri Suhrke, "A Contradictory Mission? NATO from Stabilization to Combat in Afghanistan," *International Peacekeeping*, Vol. 15, No. 2, April 2008, p. 227.

85. McCaffrey, "After Action Report: Visit to Kuwait and Afghanistan, 10-18 November 2009," p. 7.

86. *Report on Progress Toward Security and Stability in Afghanistan: June 2009 Report to Congress in Accordance with the 2008 National Defense Authorization Act*, Washington, DC: Department of Defense, June 2009, Executive Summary.

87. *Report on Progress Toward Security and Stability in Afghanistan: April 2010 Report to Congress in Accordance with the 2008 National Defense Authorization Act*, Washington, DC: Department of Defense, April 2010, p. 73.

88. Suhrke, p. 227.

89. *Ibid.*, p. 228.

90. Jones, *Counterinsurgency in Afghanistan*, pp. xii-xiii.

91. Quoted in Ali A. Jalali, "Afghanistan: Regaining Momentum," *Parameters*, Vol. 37, No. 4, Winter 2007-08, p. 9.

92. *Report on Progress Toward Security and Stability in Afghanistan: June 2009 Report to Congress in Accordance with the 2008 National Defense Authorization Act*, Washington, DC: Department of Defense, June 2009, p. 11.

93. *Ibid.*, p. 12.

94. McCaffrey, "After Action Report: Visit to Kuwait and Afghanistan, 10-18 November 2009," p. 7.

95. Karen DeYoung, "A Puzzle for Congress," *The Washington Post National Weekly Edition*, December 7-13, 2009, p. 19.

96. Amy Belasco, *The Cost of Iraq, Afghanistan, and Other GWOT Operations Since 9/11*, Washington, DC: Congressional Research Service, RL33110, May 15, 2009, Summary.

97. Cordesman, p. 16.

98. *Ibid.*, p. 18.

99. *Ibid.*

100. *Ibid.*

101. *Ibid.*, p. 17.

102. *Ibid.*

103. *Ibid.*, p. 22.

104. McCaffrey, "After Action Report: Visit to Kuwait and Afghanistan, 10-18 November 2009," p. 4.

105. A Bloomberg National Poll of 721 likely voters nationwide, conducted from October 7-10, 2010, with a margin of error of +/- 3 percent, available from *www.pollingreport.com/afghan.htm*. Of the respondents, 31 percent felt "the U.S. can win."

106. Quinnipiac University polls of June, July, and August 2011, each with statistically significant sample sizes, available from *www.pollingreport.com/afghan.htm*.

PART III

POTENTIAL SOLUTIONS

As presently configured, the national security institutions of the U.S. government are still the institutions constructed to win the Cold War.

The 9/11 Commission Report, 2004[1]

The history of the United States shows that in spite of the varying trend of the foreign policy of succeeding administrations, the Government has interposed or intervened in the affairs of other states with remarkable regularity."

Small Wars Manual of 1940[2]
The U.S. Marine Corps

CHAPTER 8:

COMMONLY PROPOSED SOLUTIONS AND FAULTY ASSUMPTIONS

> USG [United States Government] agencies may have different organizational cultures and . . . conflicting goals, policies, procedures, and decision-making techniques and processes. . . . Typically, USG agencies will coordinate among and between agencies and organizations if they share mutual interests, not because of some formalized C2 (command and control) system.
>
> U.S. Joint Forces Command,
> *Commander's Handbook for the Joint Interagency Coordination Group,*
> March 2007[3]

Far from going unnoticed, the disjointed strategic guidance and disunified effort that have most often characterized the mission in Afghanistan are commonly recognized by most participants and observers alike. Moreover, these problems have not been limited to the Afghan theater of operations alone, as the U.S. Government's major strategic and interagency shortcomings have also been readily apparent in other major endeavors of recent years. Among other examples, similar deficiencies have manifested themselves in Operation IRAQI FREEDOM, in the U.S. Government's response to Hurricane Katrina, and in the reorganization of the U.S. intelligence community. Perhaps most famously, the U.S. Government's poor interagency performance before and after the attacks of September 11, 2001 (9/11), was well documented by the 9/11 Commission in its careful report of 2004.[4] In light of these and other serious shortfalls, numerous national security reform initiatives have been set in motion, and other potential solutions proposed, each aimed at addressing one or more aspects of these broader strategic and interagency challenges. In some cases, these implemented corrective measures and the proposed reforms have focused upon enhancing strategic-level structures and systems, while in other cases the reforms are intended to achieve operational-level or broader institutional effects. In any case, there has been no shortage of ideas or initiatives aimed at solving these major problems.

Unfortunately, however, each of these implemented or proposed measures falls short of what is actually needed to solve the fundamental structural and systemic issues. Specifically, the most commonly proposed solutions to the U.S. Government's strategic and interagency problems fall short mainly because each fails to confront the underlying root causes of the problems directly. While these major challenges are recognized by almost everyone involved in the American national security community, the most commonly proposed solutions to the U.S. Government's problems are likely to fail to overcome the structural and organizational deficiencies inherent in the existing processes. These proposed and ongoing reform measures generally fall into one of four categories, but they share in common the characteristic that they are all largely incremental in scope and substance. Furthermore, these proposed solutions also rest upon a set of faulty assumptions that combine to undermine their ultimate prospects for success.

COMMONLY RECOGNIZED PROBLEMS

In its landmark study published in 2004, the 9/11 Commission emphasized the inappropriateness of fit between institutional structures built in 1947 for the post-World War II era and the more agile structures needed to deal with the emerging security threats of the 21st century. Highlighting a general lack of cooperation and integration among U.S. agencies and departments, before and after the attacks of 9/11, the Commission suggested that a major overhaul of the U.S. intelligence community and a concurrent reorganization of our nation's homeland defense activities were warranted. The Commission also identified a need to reorganize and reinvigorate congressional oversight in the realm of national security.[5] The 9/11 Commission's report also offered a series of other major organizational recommendations, among them calls for unifying strategic intelligence and operational planning in a National Terrorism Center, unifying the intelligence community with a new National Intelligence Director, and creating a network-based information-sharing system. The Commission also recommended reinforcing the Federal Bureau of Investigation (FBI) and other homeland defenders to enable them to deal with the new emerging threats.[6]

In 2006, two other high-profile internal assessments drew many of the same conclusions. The reports of both the *Quadrennial Defense Review* (QDR) and the "Katrina Lessons Learned" commission identified significant problems with interagency coordination and agency performance. As part of its broad review of the U.S. national security posture, the 2006 QDR specifically supported the creation of a National Security Officer corps intended "to effectively integrate and orchestrate the contributions of individual government agencies on behalf of larger national security interests."[7] Reinforcing this view more recently, the Center for the Study of the Presidency & Congress's "Project on National Security Reform" (PNSR), identified a variety of major and persistent systemic national security problems in its July 2008 preliminary findings. Each of these identified problems continues to contribute directly to the U.S. Government's strategic disjointedness and its operational disunity of effort today.

Among other concerns, the PNSR identified the lack of a robust national security strategy, the lack of a "common U.S. Government framework for delineating regional areas of responsibility," and disjointed resource allocation processes as fundamental causes of recent national security shortfalls. The report also highlighted shortcomings in agency and interagency cultures, poor human resource development practices, and a wide variety of other major concerns that have combined to undermine the effectiveness of the U.S. national security apparatus and American strategic responses.[8] Of particular note, the PNSR also found that while the Policy Coordinating Committees, the Principals Committee, and the Deputies Committees of the National Security Council are supposed to conduct the major portion of coordinating agency and departmental effort, their formal work is typically "fueled by the briefing papers and issue papers generated by individual agencies and interagency working groups."[9] In its essence, the PNSR identified five core problems in its assessment of the U.S. Government's organization for national security. These major problems include:

- A grossly imbalanced system that features strong departmental capabilities at the expense of interagency coordination and integration;

- Resource allocation decisions that are driven by agency and department core missions instead of broader or integrated national security requirements;
- A reliance on presidential intervention to compensate for the system's inability to compel coordination and integration among agencies and departments;
- An overburdened White House staff that is unable to manage national security concerns, especially during presidential transitional periods; and,
- The fact that the legislative branch conducts its resource allocation and oversight functions in ways that reinforce these problems.[10]

Likewise, the PNSR also cited the inability of the President to delegate national security authority, the failure of the "lead federal agency" model, and the failure of the "czar" model as other key causes of these national security shortfalls.[11] In the group's follow-up recommendations of September 2009, the PNSR focused on reforms it claimed were "synergistic, practical, doable, and necessary."[12] Specifically, the group called for revisions in the form and substance of the national security strategies, an overhaul of the National Security Council (NSC) and its staff with emphasis on the body's interagency role, and the linking of strategy to resources, among other reform recommendations.[13] Adding to this strategic and interagency mix, still other observers have noted that there is no consensus just yet regarding the new boundaries of national security concerns in the 21st century's global context.[14] Accordingly, the United States must build agility and flexibility into its national security structures, rather than retaining structures and mandates that are stovepiped and unwieldy, having been designed originally as responses to the bipolar world of the Cold War era.

FOUR CATEGORIES OF COMMONLY PROPOSED SOLUTIONS

Within the national security community, there are numerous initiatives underway aimed at improving the disjointed aspects of our national security systems, with many other potential reforms being seriously debated within policy circles, as well. Typically, each of these commonly proposed solutions falls into one of four categories.

Increasing Technical and Bureaucratic Synchronization.

One category of commonly proposed solutions to the U.S. Government's strategic and interagency problems emphasizes the goal of increasing departmental and agency synchronization. These technocratic approaches typically advocate the creation and adoption of new interagency checklists, common terminologies, and the realignment of operating procedures to bring departments and agencies more closely into alignment with one another. As an example of this approach, the State Department's Office of Coordinator for Reconstruction and Stabilization (S/CRS) issued *The Post Conflict Reconstruction Essential Tasks Matrix* in 2005, a compilation of the hundreds of different tasks that represent the actions and end-states required for a major nation-building mission.[15] While certainly stunning in its breadth and depth, the matrix is also noteworthy for the fact that many of its required tasks do not correspond to any existing departmental or agency capabilities within the U.S. Government.

In this same category, others have suggested realigning the Department of State (State) and the Department of Defense (DoD) regional operational boundaries—or redrawing the theater-strategic and operational maps—to help facilitate common operating practices and unity of effort among those departments.[16] Similar proposals have called for official interagency languages and terminologies, and still others have focused on the creation of standard operating checklists for the Joint Interagency Coordination Groups (JIACG) and other theater-strategic and operational-level interagency coordinating venues. The assumption that underlies these proposed solutions is that a lack of common understanding serves as a primary limitation on effective interagency coordination.

With this idea in mind, S/CRS has been designated as the lead proponent for "The Whole of Government Lessons Learned Hub." This knowledge center is intended to coordinate and facilitate the collection, dissemination, and sharing of reconstruction and stabilization best practices across the U.S. Government.[17] Some observers have suggested that this approach might be unnecessarily limiting, since reconstruction and stabilization missions typically do not occur in isolation. Instead, these missions usually take place within the context of other operations, and so the thinking goes that this knowledge center might unintentionally narrow the perspective of these practitioners, rather than expand.[18]

Along similar lines, S/CRS was instrumental in the creation of another initiative called the *U.S. Government Planning Framework for Reconstruction, Stabili-*

zation, and Conflict Transformation. This approach uses the *Interagency Conflict Assessment Framework* (ICAF) and other assessment methods to analyze the operating environment. In many respects — and probably not coincidentally — the ICAF is very similar to the military's decisionmaking process (MDMP) and its techniques for articulating policy options and assigning resources.[19] In its essence, the ICAF is a broad-brush analytical framework that draws details regarding the scope of work from the S/CRS *Essential Tasks Matrix.* Other similar proposals in this category have included the Hart-Rudman Commission's 2001 call for the creation of an interagency cadre called the National Security Service Corps (NSSC), with an emphasis on developing leaders "skilled at producing integrative solutions to U.S. national security problems."[20] More recently, the Center for Strategic and International Studies in its "Beyond Goldwater-Nichols" project expanded this call to include the creation of an interagency advisory group that would ensure that promotion rates for the NSSC were comparable to those within the parent organizations.[21]

In response to these calls, in 2007, the Bush administration initiated an interagency cadre program called the National Security Professional Development (NSPD) program. The program has not gotten much attention or interest since its inception.[22] Two particular features have held the program back. First, is the fact that personnel from DoD, Foreign Service officers, and members of the intelligence community are excluded from the program because their parent organizations already have developmental programs. Secondly, participation in the program is voluntary for individuals, agencies, and departments, and to this point, few have signed up.[23] The NSPD initiative also includes a small integration office and is projected to include an education and training consortium in the future. However, since the NSPD was launched by a Bush administration executive order and still has no actual legislative mandate, it struggles for this reason, as well.[24] More recently, a proposal has gone before Congress that would authorize State to place personnel temporarily in an administrative holding area while the agency participates in this developmental experience.

Increasing Non-DoD Agency Capabilities.

A second set of proposed solutions to these national security problems focuses upon increasing the capabilities of agencies outside the DoD. Examples of these initiatives include the ongoing effort to create a Civilian Response Corps within State, as well as other proposals to scrap DoD's geographic combatant command structure altogether in favor of a set of functional interagency commands. A perceived advantage of this approach would be its de-emphasis of the military's role in nation-building or similar activities, while simultaneously enhancing the role of the ambassadors in each country and integrating all staffs at all levels.

In creating the Office of the Coordinator for Reconstruction and Stabilization (S/CRS), the primary goal was to give State an administrative and planning element capable of carrying out its statutory role as the lead federal agency for reconstruction and stabilization activities. In turn, S/CRS pushed for the creation of the Civilian Response Corps (CRC) and other related interagency coordinating teams, aimed at overcoming many of the parent agencies' statutory limits on the authority to deploy and operate outside the

United States. In order to surmount the inherent limitations on capacities and authorities among partner agencies and departments, S/CRS has also initiated a slate of training and educational opportunities aimed at increasing these other-than-DoD agency capabilities. Highlighted in the State internal report on reconstruction and stabilization improvements for 2009, the reconstruction and stabilization courses offered by S/CRS for the Civilian Response Corps include orientation training, annual training, pre-deployment training, in-theater continuity training, and reintegration training.[25] In many ways, this approach closely parallels the military's model for its own Reserve Component assets.

Similar non-DoD-centric proposals have included creating an altogether new independent government organization responsible for integrating civilian and military planning, or replacing the military-run geographic combatant commands with "regional Embassy-like teams with all agencies represented."[26] There are similar initiatives under consideration in many of the other agencies that are traditionally focused on domestic American operations but find themselves called upon to bring to bear their expertise in irregular warfare and nation-building operations overseas. Among these agencies are the U.S. Department of Agriculture, the Department of Justice, and a number of others. Seeking to achieve the benefits of the planning and operator culture that predominates in the DoD, State, and the U.S. Agency for International Development (USAID) have undertaken an effort to conduct organizational strategic planning in the form of a *Quadrennial Diplomacy and Development Review* (QDDR) patterned after the DoD's QDR.

At the same time, it is important to note that past efforts in this direction have frequently fallen short of their goals, often running into substantial obstacles in the form of dominant and resistant organizational cultural norms. As one high-profile example of such an outcome, Secretary of State Colin Powell attempted to introduce a more rigorous planning and operating culture at State during his tenure, but this effort ended with mixed and incomplete results upon his departure. Furthermore, to place the relative scope of these other-than-DoD changes into perspective, in 2004 S/CRS began with just a few staff members, and by October 2007, it still only had about 80 personnel assigned to it.[27] With about 200 personnel assigned to the office now, S/CRS stands in stark contrast to the tens of thousands of planners working at all levels of DoD. Of all of the proposals and potential solutions in this category, perhaps the most intriguing and promising variation on the theme has emphasized the need for increased on-the-job-training opportunities between DoD and non-DoD agencies. Representative of this idea, Lieutenant General William Caldwell of the U.S. Army's Combined Arms Center, created an exchange program in which mid-career Army officers are sent to work in other-than-DoD agencies, while their counterparts attend Army training at Fort Leavenworth, KS.[28]

Finally, it is also worth noting that juxtaposed against these calls for developing other-than-DoD agency and department capabilities, there is another line of thinking that would push in the exact opposite direction. That is, some other analysts argue that instead, the solution should be to give the DoD the nation-building mission altogether and to resource the department appropriately for it.[29] However, this approach would bring with it the various disadvantages already evident in the DoD's current resource and capability dominance. Or as counterinsurgency expert John Nagl puts it, "If the only tool you have in your toolbox is a hammer, all problems begin to resemble nails."[30] This concern holds true whether the issue is viewed from an interagency perspective, a national strategic viewpoint, or internally to the DoD itself.

In any event, the DoD has in fact developed new internal capabilities, among them; teams of agricultural development experts, Human Terrain Systems, and Human Terrain Teams, as well as other nontraditional areas of expertise. There is certainly room for further DoD innovations that will bring other value to the nation-building and irregular warfare mix, especially given the diverse skill sets of the military's Reserve Component troops and their varied civilian occupations. However, these ancillary uses also serve to divert those troops from their existing core military requirements and competencies. At the same time, for other practical reasons related to the department's ability to operate in non-permissive environments, the DoD is likely to remain the vehicle for enabling other agencies and departments to function within those environments.

Increasing Key Leader Engagement and Oversight.

A third category of commonly proposed solutions to these national security problems emphasizes largely unrealistic calls for heightened senior leader attention, or more centralized management of irregular warfare and nation-building operations at the national level of government. Examples of this line of thinking include a proposal that would create a czar for interagency —

or a Deputy National Security Advisor for Interagency Affairs—as well as a similar approach that would create Crisis Action Teams (CATs) for each irregular warfare mission.[31] Other proposals in this vein include proposals to expand the National Security Staff (NSS) of the NSC to give it a major role in managing the execution of these missions. Still other proposals call for increased leader emphasis and oversight, with some focusing on the role of the President and others highlighting the role of the Secretary of Defense. Proponents of this approach typically call for an increase in the priority given to these missions at the highest levels.[32]

In this same fashion, one recent response has been to assign responsibility for coordination and oversight of implementation of nation-building and irregular warfare operations to members of the White House staff. In the case of Afghanistan, Lieutenant General Douglas Lute served as an Assistant to the President and Deputy National Security Advisor for Iraq and Afghanistan.[33] Another current technique is to designate a lead federal agency for a particular operation or issue area, a somewhat flexible concept that designates one agency or department as the lead for coordinating the efforts of multiple agencies.[34] Along these lines, S/CRS has a permanent lead agency role for coordinating the planning and execution of complex reconstruction and stabilization contingencies.[35] However, there are a number of problems with this approach in the case of S/CRS, since the office is neither an agency nor a department. As such, even its own parent organization—State—has not embraced the S/CRS's leadership role.[36] As noted above, it is also not usually the case that reconstruction and stabilization operations occur in isolation, thus complicating the notion of S/CRS as a lead agency even further.

Other recent proposals along these lines have included the idea of creating a Deputy Assistant to the President or an NSC Senior Director with responsibility for coordinating and integrating national security operations.[37] Other similar proposals have called for the creation of a new Cabinet-level position and agency with direct control over modest resources to be used in common in the agencies with national security responsibilities.[38] However, recent experiences with the appointment of czars and other centralizing initiatives have been checkered at best, and most serious analysts of the executive branch dispute the feasibility of asking senior decisionmakers to add even more supervisory responsibilities to their already overcrowded plates.

Increasing or Enhancing Interagency Coordinating Venues.

This fourth set of recommended solutions generally assumes that the U.S. Government's national security problems are caused mainly by an inability of the key players to engage in constructive interagency dialogues. In this line of thinking, the lack of opportunities to coordinate and integrate agency efforts toward common ends occurs because of shortcomings in the bureaucratic mechanisms that facilitate that integration. Accordingly, this category of potential solutions usually focuses on creating or enhancing bureaucratic coordinating mechanisms to provide more and better venues for interagency coordination, or otherwise implementing enhanced (and usually more complex) rules for interagency interactions. As a prime example of this category of proposal, the *Interagency Management System* represents the most significant ongoing reform initiative aimed at providing additional and better interagency coordinating venues.

As the statutory lead federal entity for reconstruction and stabilization activities, State and its embedded S/CRS provided the impetus behind the initiation of the *Interagency Management System* (IMS). In its essence, the IMS is a negotiated interagency agreement that outlines the way in which U.S. Government departments and agencies should organize for reconstruction and stabilization planning and operations. The system consists of three interlinked elements, including a Washington-based Country Reconstruction and Stabilization Group (CRSG), the Integration Planning Cell (IPC) at the theater level, and the Advance Civilian Team (ACT) at the country level.[39] As part of this interagency agreement, S/CRS also touts the Civilian Response Corps (CRC), which "gives the American people another way to share their skills with people in need while serving their country."[40] The core of this new reconstruction and stabilization response capability consists of the Active Response Corps (ARC) and the Standby Response Corps (SRC), including active U.S. Government employees with development skills from USAID and other relevant agencies. In 2007, there were a total of 33 employees in the ARC, while the second-tier SRC—personnel requiring 30 to 45 days notice before deployment—had approximately 90 personnel assigned to it.[41]

To place the limited current scope of this initiative into perspective, the Reconstruction and Stabilization Civilian Management Act of 2008 (PL 110-417) expanded the CRC further, providing an initial $55 million in funding to establish its Active and Standby components.[42] The Fiscal Year 2009 (FY09) appropriations earmarked an additional $75 million for the development of the CRC, including $45 million to State and $30 million to USAID.[43] After the FY09 expansion, the funding supported a distribution of CRC-Active personnel that included a total of 250 personnel across State, Commerce, the Department of Justice, the Department of Homeland Security, the Department of Health and Human Services, the Treasury, USAID, and the Department of Agriculture.

In terms of its structure, the great majority of the CRC-Active personnel come from State, the Department of Justice, and USAID, with fewer than eight personnel coming from each of the other five agencies and departments represented in this element. For its own part, only 13 personnel from S/CRS itself are actually dedicated to the CRC initiative.[44] The CRC-Standby element was funded for 500 personnel in the Fiscal Year 2008 (FY08) supplemental and FY09 appropriations, with the ultimate goal being able to expand the CRC-Standby element to 2,000 personnel.[45] CRC members are assigned to one of the three IMS structures, and when they are not engaged in actual S/CRS missions, they return to their parent agencies to continue preparing for any future reconstruction and stabilization duties.[46]

Although certainly representing steps in the right direction, these initiatives fall short in several ways. Among other limitations, the actual number of experts is very small, and their deployability is contractually limited. Furthermore, these personnel typically have very limited experience in carrying out the broad and complex tasks of nation-building and irregular warfare. For example, a civilian police officer from the United States is likely to be skilled at law enforcement, but he or she is not also likely to be skilled at standing up the other required elements of a civil justice system. Nor is that civilian police officer likely to be able to direct the establishment of the administrative agencies needed to oversee each of those various elements. Reinforcing the magnitude of this challenge, the CRC task force identified 121 different sets of skills needed within its ranks.[47] Lastly, the CRC is also limited in the sense that this fledgling institution comes with all of the administrative, training, and logistical challenges inherent in maintaining a reserve element of any kind.

Not surprisingly, S/CRS has to fight to maintain both its resources and its relevancy. For one reason, while the S/CRS has in fact deployed personnel to Afghanistan in support of reconstruction and stabilization activities, these personnel have not been utilized in the ways envisioned when this element was designed. Rather than deploying as coherent teams in accordance with the IMS conceptual design, the S/CRS personnel have instead been used as individual staff augmenters. For example, about a dozen S/CRS personnel are assigned to the U.S. Embassy in Kabul, but these personnel serve as complementary staff, rather than holding significant authority over the reconstruction and stabilization activities. This use has dissipated the impact and viability of the S/CRS in at least two ways: its personnel are unavailable for other missions, and the office struggles to show its value.[48]

While the IMS is the most significant of the reform initiatives falling into this category of potential solution, there are other similar proposals that seek to enhance or formalize the existing interagency coordinating structures, as well. At the country level, the traditional model is the Country Team, centered on the U.S. embassies and falling under the authority of the Chief of Mission or Ambassador as the President's designated representative. Similarly, the various geographic combatant commands already have the Joint Interagency Coordinating Group (JIACG), serving as the "combatant command's designated lead organization for the interagency community, providing oversight, facilitation, coordination, and synchronization of agencies' activities within the command among."[49] In reality, most combatant commands have come up with alternate methods for managing their interagency coordination other than this mechanism, since the partner agencies typically cannot commit the personnel needed to staff the JIACG on a full-time basis.[50] At the operational level, the Provincial Reconstruction Team (PRT) and various boards, bureaus, centers, cells, and working groups (B2C2WG) already serve as the primary interagency coordinating venues.

With these existing interagency mechanisms in mind, other reform proposals include calls to standardize or enhance Country Team, JIACG, B2C2WG, or PRT structures, each with various goals in mind. Some of these goals include creating leadership opportunities for civilians; establishing guidelines that explain the roles, missions, and authority of team members; conducting significant joint pre-deployment and cultural awareness training; and, increasing civilian involvement on the teams.[51] Other horizontal integration proposals include giving greater authority to Chiefs of Mission, or aligning the geographical regions of the different departments and creating regional ambassadors that correspond to the current geographic combatant commanders' areas of responsibility. Still other proposals include the idea of strengthening the representation of civilian agencies within those commands.[52] Another similar approach that has been suggested would be to create teams of leaders — or commander leader teams (CLTs) — who would be empowered to exercise the authorities of their respective agencies while taking advantage of enhanced knowledge or information management.[53]

In similar fashion, a 2008 Rand study of Afghanistan suggested a need to develop reconstruction teams featuring military and civilian representatives from DoD, State, USAID, the Department of Justice, the Department of Agriculture, and other relevant agencies.[54] This study also recommended modifying the PRT structures by increasing the civilian developmental components of the teams and by lengthening their tours of duty. The study also recommended changes that would improve the cultural training of the teams, as well as increasing the number of teams in order to extend their reach.[55] Another recent and similar approach has been to advocate extra-agency bodies for interagency coordination, such as the National Counterterrorism Center, with the intent of bringing together experts from various departments and agencies to coordinate intelligence activities and planning.[56] In essence, each of these proposed reforms assumes that the major underlying obstacle to effective interagency integration is either a lack of venues for that integration, or a lack of bureaucratic rigor in managing the activities of the interagency participants.

Examined from a broader perspective, many of these ongoing reform measures and the other proposals for change represent significant and positive developments. However, each of them falls short of reorganizing the national security establishment in such a way that the key leaders are given the actual authority or resources needed to achieve success in nation-building and irregular warfare at the national, provincial, and local levels. Furthermore, none of these proposals really addresses the underlying lack of subject matter expertise that is needed to stand up viable economies, elements of the rule of law, national and local governing structures, and other required social and public institutions. Each of these components is needed to achieve success in these complex and demanding missions, and they represent capabilities not currently found in the various agencies or departments of the U.S. Government.

With all of these inherent limitations in mind, many of the currently proposed initiatives are promising in some respects, but they simply do not go far enough. That is, many of these reforms fall into the category of "necessary but not sufficient," in that they still do not overcome the numerous underlying and fundamental obstacles to coherent strategy formulation and effective interagency coordination. Nor do these potential solutions represent the robust resourcing of U.S. departments and agencies that is necessary to achieve success in these challenging nation-building and irregular warfare missions, given their scope and complexity. In this sense then, the various reforms and proposals under consideration really only nibble at the edges of the problem, as each rests upon a series of faulty and pervasive assumptions that will serve to undermine their ultimate prospects for success.

THE FAULTY ASSUMPTIONS

In spite of their potential merits, the most frequently proposed solutions to the U.S. Government's strategic and interagency problems depend upon the validity of a set of faulty assumptions that will likely undercut their prospects for success. In the process, these solutions generally fail to address the underlying root causes that have led to the strategic and interagency problems in the first place. In particular, there are seven major faulty assumptions that underpin these solutions, each of which has implications for any feasible and effective solutions to the problems.

Faulty Assumption #1.

Each of these solutions assumes away the major limitation that other-than-DoD agencies have in the fact that they cannot typically operate in non-permissive security environments. Even when escorted by military forces, experience in Afghanistan and Iraq shows that State, USAID, and other U.S. agencies are severely limited in their ability to operate throughout the theater of operations. This same limitation also extends to most contracted civilians employed by these agencies, because contracted personnel usually have caveats written into their contracts that prevent them from traveling outside the wire whenever threat levels indicate significant risk.

Faulty Assumption #2.

Proponents of these commonly proposed solutions also typically assume that using DoD in a leading and directive role will necessarily militarize U.S. foreign policy, leading to longer-term problems with international legitimacy and allied relationships. But the advocates of the "anybody-but-DoD" line of thinking miss the point that more often than not, irregular warfare and nation-building take place in non-permissive security environments. As a result, the U.S. military will almost always serve as the vehicle for providing security to other U.S. agencies in these types of operating environments, if not the actual lead agent for the delivery of other aspects of the reconstruction and stabilization operations. Circumstances and capabilities should dictate the mix of agency and departmental assets to be utilized for a particular mission, rather than any preconceived notions about departmental or agency suitability.

Faulty Assumption #3.

Proponents of these solutions often assume that other government agencies have the expertise that is relevant and necessary for the tasks required by nation-building or irregular warfare. These major tasks include creating the elements for the rule of law, enhancing or developing local and national governance, bringing about broad economic development, and other aspects of the development of civil society. Unfortunately, this assumption is not true. For example, the U.S. Embassy in Kabul and its associated State Department agencies were given the responsibility for overseeing the development of key Afghan national ministerial agencies and provincial governing institutions.

However, while the embassy personnel and their counterparts proved to be adept at their core competencies of strategic-level policy coordination, communications, and reporting, they were far less proficient at the task of developing Afghan governance. These shortfalls were obvious, whether the development of governmental institutions was viewed at the national, provincial, or local levels. Likewise, these institutional limitations were evident in the State mentoring effort, the quality of its operational planning, and the lack of resolution in the department's tracking mechanisms. The State core competency of conducting foreign policy clearly does not equate to the ability to build foreign governmental capacity, especially below the national strategic level. This same type of limitation also applies equally to other U.S. departments and agencies, including the DoD.

Faulty Assumption #4.

Another pervasive assumption that underpins the commonly proposed solutions to the U.S. Government's strategic and interagency problems is the idea that the lack of coordination is merely due to a lack of venues for coordination and dialogue. As this line of thinking goes, if we can just get all of the U.S. agencies to sit down together on a routine basis or if we give them just the right checklists or operating procedures, then they will likely arrive at a consensus regarding the actions to be taken and settle on a common vision for the desired strategic or operational end-state. Experience shows that this assumption is not true either, even within agencies with nominally hierarchical relationships, such as State and USAID. Instead, the more common scenario is for agencies to disagree over their visions, and to opt out when decisions are made that contradict those visions. Where there is no forcing function to compel cooperation or unified effort, it rarely occurs.

Faulty Assumption #5.

Another related assumption is the idea that if the various departments and agencies do in fact arrive at a common interpretation of the problem or at least a common vision for the operational end-state, they will then pool their resources and work together to contribute toward the accomplishment of the related tasks. Again, experience shows that without a forcing function to compel agencies to integrate their operations, it is more likely that the various organizations will merely continue to "do what they do," pursuing their own goals and objectives in accordance with their own operating procedures and internal organizational incentives. It is also often the case that interagency agreements at one level of the U.S. Government do not make their way to the operators lower in the organizational hierarchy. Even when these interagency agreements are understood by the operator-level participants, those agreements are often ignored. In sum, agency personnel do not typically pull together toward common objectives or a common vision without some strong incentive or mutual interest to do so, given a lack of statutory compulsion. Instead, everything is a negotiation.

Faulty Assumption #6.

The most frequently proposed solutions also assume away the problems associated with multiple points of entry into the U.S. Government in the operational theaters. Host-nation leaders, host-nation agencies, allies, intergovernmental organizations, and nongovernmental organizations each seek to exploit the seams between U.S. agencies. That is, the leaders of these organizations will often agency-shop from leader to leader or agency to agency until they get the answer or decision they want. Given the different agencies' independent resources and agendas, the currently proposed solutions to the U.S. Government's strategic and interagency challenges will not address this common problem directly. These external influences matter; the interagency process does not take place in a static environment.

Faulty Assumption #7.

Some of these solutions also assume that placing a senior leader from State or USAID into a geographic or functional combatant leadership position would somehow automatically enable that person to lead at the theater-strategic or operational levels. Instead, leaders from State, USAID, and other key departments and agencies will need formal training and relevant developmental assignments before they will be capable of exercising those major leadership responsibilities. For example, experience as a field operative in USAID is not the same as understanding the operational-level or strategic-level requirements of nation-building or irregular warfare. Likewise, bringing in ex-USAID contractors or current USAID employees to work toward those ends merely reinforces the status quo. In sum, the agencies' efforts are currently limited by organizational cultures and existing core competencies, which are not well matched with the broader requirements of nation-building and irregular warfare. In much the same way, the heavy reliance on contractors presents related challenges.

As one final systemic challenge to these proposed solutions to the U.S. Government's strategic and interagency difficulties, the congressional oversight mechanisms for interagency operations are typically very weak. In particular, the current system for oversight still focuses primarily on budget requests that come to Congress agency by agency, rather than coming to the appropriators holistically or systemically.[57] As a consequence of these institutional arrangements, even when the various actors' intentions are good, it is unlikely that the mission will be understood and executed uniformly by all of the players, given their options and incentives to act to the contrary. Viewed in the extreme, most of these potential solutions merely provide the opportunity for more dialogue, since none of them actually mandates coordination or enforces any resulting interagency integration. If the goals of national security reform are to achieve coherently formulated strategy and a unity of effort among the U.S. Government's departments and agencies, then these solutions do not go far enough.

THE BOTTOM LINE: POSITIVE BUT INSUFFICIENT STEPS

Taken together, these ongoing and proposed national security reform initiatives offer a variety of promising developments. For those agency personnel who have been involved in the execution of the interagency process at the operational level, however, it is hard to imagine that adding additional coordinating bodies, increasingly complex checklists and plans, or additional presidential directives will result in more effective interagency operations in the field. More pointedly, as long as agency personnel remain ultimately accountable to the home office instead of leaders on the ground, and as long as the agencies in question do not have the opportunities to develop the relevant operational level and strategic level expertise needed to carry out the complex and daunting challenges of nation-building and irregular warfare, these operations will remain disjointed and ineffective.

Put bluntly, the U.S. Government already has plenty of plans, checklists, directives, and coordinating mechanisms related to strategy formulation and the interagency process in place. However, there remains little bureaucratic incentive or statutory compulsion to "buy in" to the interagency agenda among the departments or agencies in the field. As a result, each of the currently proposed solutions represents more "hope" than they do "method," since history and human nature discount the notion that merely creating more venues for interagency dialogue will generate consensus or more effective integration. Instead, this basic assumption not only misreads history and human nature, but also ignores the practical experience gleaned from Afghanistan, Iraq, and other recent national security operations.

Even more directly, the realities of the existing organizational cultures of key agencies, their levels of expertise in the areas relevant to nation-building and irregular warfare, their comparative levels of resources in budgets and personnel, and the core tasks that currently define the central activities of these agencies all represent structural impediments that will prevent the commonly proposed solutions from succeeding. Consequently, any truly effective solution will necessarily involve revising agency mandates, consolidating lines of authority, building relevant expertise and resources within the appropriate agencies, aligning incentive structures, and decentralizing authority and execution. Consistent with this view, any feasible and effective solutions to the U.S. Government's strategic and interagency difficulties will have to address the specific root causes of the strategic disjointedness and disunity of effort that have led to the problems in the first place. In their essence, these root causes include:

- The failure of the current processes of strategy formulation to identify and link interests, ends, ways, means, and risks, either within any one national security operation or across the spectrum of global threats to U.S. national security;

- A fragmented and ineffective task organization that fails to provide key leaders with the statutory leverage needed to direct other agency resources and personnel, a situation that renders the existing structures and processes for interagency coordination and integration ineffective;
- A serious mismatch between the capabilities, resources, and expertise required for nation-building and irregular warfare and the existing capabilities, resources, and expertise of the departments and agencies of our government;
- A similar mismatch between existing agency and departmental organizational cultures and the requirements of nation-building and irregular warfare;
- An inability of other-than-DoD agencies and departments to operate effectively, if at all, in the non-permissive security environments typical of most nation-building and irregular warfare operations;
- Misaligned professional and career incentives within many agencies and departments that promote and reward in-house assignments at the expense of interagency assignments;
- Misaligned incentive structures within national-level coordinating bodies, as national-level budgetary and policy debates focus upon jurisdiction and resource allocation rather than broader strategic or operational concerns;
- Bottom-up interagency coordinating processes at the national, theater, and operational levels that engage key leaders late in decisionmaking processes, thus diminishing the focus and effectiveness of interagency coordination;

- A lack of sustained institutional political, economic, and cultural awareness and understanding, including any enduring institutional subject matter expertise tied to national, regional, or transnational actors;
- A major disproportionate allocation of resources among the various agencies, a situation that reinforces DoD dominance at the operational level while also leading to a corresponding disproportionate focus on security operations to the detriment of other key nation-building and irregular warfare objectives;
- A lack of formal developmental education and training opportunities for agency and departmental personnel charged with interagency planning and operational responsibilities;
- A lack of key and developmental operational and planning assignment opportunities for other-than-DoD personnel charged with senior supervisory and management responsibilities in nation-building and irregular warfare;
- Inadequate controls and supervision over contractors, as well as poorly written contracts that pay for process rather than outcomes or results;
- Generally centralized budgetary and operational approval processes that place the ultimate authority for budget execution and operational design in Washington, thus limiting the flexibility and responsiveness of local operators and their ability to tailor operational solutions to conditions on the ground;
- Inadequate national-level executive branch planning and oversight structures that yield ineffective national strategies and operational directives, while also failing to set clear objectives

and to enforce compliance and accountability; and,
- Inadequate and ineffective congressional structures and processes for authorizations, appropriations, and oversight, a system that reinforces the schisms between the various agencies and departments of the U.S. Government while failing to set and enforce measures of mission progress.

In closing, it is possible that the U.S. Government's Cold War-era national security structures and processes may have been sufficient to provide cookie-cutter responses to relatively homogenous Soviet-era threats. However, the U.S. Government's current institutional arrangements are not nearly agile or flexible enough to provide the measured and tailored responses that will be needed to confront the full spectrum of threats that our nation is likely to face in the 21st century. Outlining this same sentiment in testimony before the House Armed Services Committee in 2007, S/CRS leader Ambassador John Herbst called for a Goldwater-Nichols-like approach to achieve true unity of effort across the U.S. Government—3 years after S/CRS came into existence.[58] Yet, several years later, it is still the case that nobody is truly in charge, even as the end-state vision for these missions continues to drift, with little in the way of accountability mechanisms to force or gauge compliance among the various actors. Accordingly, the bottom line here is that as long as any planned or proposed reform measure fails to address these significant root causes of our strategic disjointedness and interagency disunity, those reforms will remain likely to fail to overcome either problem.

ENDNOTES - CHAPTER 8

1. *The 9/11 Commission Report, Official Government Edition*, Washington, DC: U.S. Government Printing Office, 2004, p. 399.

2. Quoted in Seth G. Jones, *Counterinsurgency in Afghanistan*, Santa Monica, CA: Rand Corporation, National Defense Research Institute Press, 2008, p. 132.

3. U.S. Joint Forces Command, *Commander's Handbook for the Joint Interagency Coordination Group*, Norfolk, VA: Joint Warfighting Center, March 1, 2007, p. II-2. Portions of this chapter first appeared in the author's "Filling Irregular Warfare's Interagency Gaps," *Parameters*, Vol. 39, No. 3, Autumn 2009, pp. 65-80. The author is grateful to *Parameters* for the permission to reprint portions of his arguments here.

4. Catherine Dale, Nina Serafino, and Pat Towell, "Organizing the U.S. Government for National Security: Overview of the Interagency Reform Debates," *Congressional Research Service (CRS) Report for Congress*, RL34455, Washington, DC: CRS, April 18, 2008, p. 2.

5. *The 9/11 Commission Report, Official Government Ed.*, Washington, DC: U.S. Government Printing Office, 2004, pp. 399-400.

6. *Ibid.*

7. Catherine Dale, "Building an Interagency Cadre of National Security Professionals: Proposals, Recent Experience, and Issues for Congress," *Congressional Research Service (CRS) Report for Congress*, RL 34565, Washington, DC: CRS, July 8, 2008, p. 9.

8. Project on National Security Reform, *Preliminary Findings*, Washington, DC: Center for the Study of the Presidency & Congress, July 2008, pp. 69-90.

9. *Ibid.*, p. 33.

10. *Ibid.*, pp. 30-31.

11. *Ibid.*, pp. 48-49.

12. Project on National Security Reform, *Turning Ideas into Action*, Washington, DC: Center for the Study of the Presidency & Congress, September 2009, p. ix.

13. *Ibid.*

14. Dale, Serafino, and Towell, p. 3.

15. Thomas S. Szayna, Derek Eaton, and Amy Richardson, *Preparing the Army for Stability Operations*, Santa Monica, CA: Rand Corporation, 2007, p. xv.

16. John E. Pulliam, "Lines on a Map: Regional Orientations and U.S. Interagency Cooperation," *USAWC Strategy Research Project*, Carlisle, PA: U.S. Army War College, March 2005.

17. *Report to Congress on Implementation of Title XVI of P.L. 110-147, The Reconstruction and Stabilization Civilian Management Act of 2008*, Washington, DC: Department of State, May 9, 2009.

18. Discussion with Colonel Mike McMahon, who suggested this point.

19. *Report to Congress on Implementation of Title XVI of P.L. 110-147*.

20. Dale, p. 4.

21. *Ibid.*

22. *Ibid.*, p. 9.

23. *Ibid.*, pp. 11-12.

24. *Ibid.*, p. 13.

25. *Report to Congress on Implementation of Title XVI of P.L. 110-147*.

26. Stephen J. Flanagan and James A. Schear, eds., *Strategic Challenges: America's Global Security Agenda*, Washington, DC: Institute for National Security Studies (INSS)/National Defense University Press, 2008, p. 303.

27. John Herbst, Coordinator for Reconstruction and Stabilization, in prepared testimony given before the Subcommittee on Oversight and Investigation of the House Armed Services Committee on October 30, 2007, p. 2.

28. This program was identified to me by Colonel Mike McMahon.

29. John F. Troxell, "Presidential Decision Directive-56: A Glass Half Full," Chap. 2 in Joseph R. Cerami and Jay W. Boggs, eds., *The Interagency and Counterinsurgency Warfare: Stability, Security, Transition, and Reconstruction Roles*, Carlisle, PA: Strategic Studies Institute, U.S. Army War College, December 2007, p. 26, available from *www.StrategicStudiesInstitute.army.mil*.

30. John A. Nagl, *Learning to Eat Soup with a Knife: Counterinsurgency Lessons from Malaya and Vietnam*, Chicago, IL: University of Chicago Press, 2005 Ed., p. 203.

31. Flanagan and Schear, eds., p. 303.

32. *Ibid.*, p. 321.

33. Dale, Serafino, and Towell, p. 9.

34. *Ibid.*

35. *Ibid.*

36. Colonel Mike McMahon made this observation.

37. Dale, Serafino, and Towell, p. 14.

38. *Ibid.*

39. Herbst, p. 3.

40. *Ibid.*, p. 6.

41. *Ibid.*, p. 5.

42. *Report to Congress on Implementation of Title XVI of P.L. 110-147.*

43. *Ibid.*

44. *Ibid.*

45. *Ibid.*

46. *Ibid.*

47. Herbst, p. 6.

48. Colonel Mike McMahon related this background information pertaining to the S/CRS to me.

49. *Joint Warfare Center (JWFC) Pamphlet 6: Doctrinal Implications of the Joint Interagency Coordination Group (JIACG)*, Norfolk, VA: Joint Warfare Center, June 27, 2004, p. 5.

50. Colonel Mike McMahon provided this background information to me.

51. Carlos Hernandorena, "U.S. Provincial Reconstruction Teams in Afghanistan, 2003-2006: Obstacles to Interagency Cooperation," Chap. 5 in Joseph R. Cerami and Jay W. Boggs, eds., *The Interagency and Counterinsurgency Warfare: Stability, Security, Transition, and Reconstruction Roles*, Carlisle, PA: Strategic Studies Institute, U.S. Army War College, December 2007, pp. 145-154, available from *www.StrategicStudiesInstitute.army.mil*.

52. Dale, Serafino, and Towell, p. 14.

53. Zeb B. Bradford, Jr., and Frederic J. Brown, *America's Army: A Model for Interagency Effectiveness*, Westport, CT: Praeger, 2008, p. 211.

54. Seth G. Jones, *Counterinsurgency in Afghanistan*, Santa Monica, CA: Rand Corporation's National Defense Research Institute Press, 2008, p. 130.

55. *Ibid.*, p. 131.

56. Dale, Serafino, and Towell, p. 9.

57. *Ibid.*, p. 13.

58. Herbst, p. 2.

CHAPTER 9

ESSENTIAL ELEMENTS OF ANY FEASIBLE AND EFFECTIVE SOLUTION

> A government ill-executed, whatever it may be in theory, must be, in practice, a bad government. . . . The ingredients which constitute energy in the executive are unity; duration; an adequate provision for its support; and competent powers.
>
> Alexander Hamilton,
> The Federalist #70[1]

Overcoming the U.S. Government's strategic disjointedness and disunity of effort will require much more than cosmetic changes. In fact, any truly feasible and effective solution to the U.S. Government's strategic and interagency problems will need to include a variety of essential, substantive elements in order to succeed — elements corresponding directly to the underlying structural causes that are at the root of these problems. Aimed at achieving the twin goals of strategic coherence and the true "whole of government" approaches needed to address the emerging threats to America's national security, these reforms will ultimately require policy changes, shifts in resource allocation priorities, and organizational structural changes in order to be truly effective. Chief among these desired changes will be shifts in jurisdiction and organization that will create a true unity of command. As history shows, while there have been many attempts in the past to make fragmented executive authority work, few of these arrangements have ever succeeded, and then, never for long. More directly, U.S. national security is too important to rely upon the hope that an executive-by-committee will yield a common vision or unified execution of that vision. Nevertheless, that is the de facto system that currently exists.

At the same time, achieving unity of command will not be enough by itself. American national security is also too important—and too complex—to allow one national instrument of power to predominate, whether that dominance comes as a consequence of remarkably disproportionate resourcing or as a result of an overreliance on the military's far superior planning and operating capabilities and its mission-oriented organizational culture. Once again, history illustrates that when the different elements of the U.S. Government are given the latitude to pursue their own visions, agendas, or interests, it is a rare case in which those agencies and departments see things the same way or act in concert. Given the American military's incredible advantage in resources and organizational capabilities, it typically does not matter very much whether the other-than-Department of Defense (DoD) agencies and departments see things differently, anyway. Our system is clearly out of balance, and any feasible and effective solution to the U.S. Government's strategic and interagency problems will have to enhance the resources and capabilities of the other-than-DoD agencies and departments to enable them to meet the demands of these challenging missions.

With each of these ideas in mind, achieving success in future nation-building and irregular warfare operations—as well as other emerging national security challenges for that matter—will require substantial changes to the U.S. Government's organization. These essential elements of change will necessarily stretch across the whole of the national security apparatus, encompassing a set of broader institutional changes as well as specific reforms at the strategic, theater-strategic, and operational levels. At the same time, any package of reforms will also have to be structured and implemented in such a way as to enable those changes to overcome likely political resistance to their adoption and the practical obstacles to their implementation. This final proposition represents no small challenge in of itself.

FIRST PRINCIPLES: THE THEORY AND PRACTICE OF THE UNITARY EXECUTIVE

As careful students of history who had also experienced the British government's abuses of political and military power firsthand, America's Constitutional Founders were primarily concerned with creating a system of separated, shared, and fragmented powers that would ultimately minimize the potential for abuse of authority. At the same time, the Founders were also experienced practitioners of government themselves, and had similarly witnessed firsthand the major failures of the fragmented colonial executive structures that were a fairly common feature of that era. The Constitutional Convention had convened largely for the purpose of amending or replacing the ineffective Articles of Confederation, an arrangement that allowed the nominal national governmental leaders to set policy without giving them any corresponding resources, leverage, or statutory authority to enforce compliance. Abandoning the toothless Articles and their original mandate altogether, the Founders sought to craft a workable alternative framework for a U.S. Government that would protect against the potential abuse of authority while also enabling the government to govern effectively.

In the Founders' view, and one supported by the lessons of history and their own governing experience, the safest course of action was to fragment the legislative authority severely. This first principle has translated into the modern U.S. Congress's bicameral structure of 100 senators and 435 representatives. However, the Founders very clearly drew the line at fragmenting executive authority. Rather than dividing the executive branch in any way, they wisely created a unitary executive instead, intentionally vesting the executive authority in one person. This single executive would exercise the powers of the office in accordance with the limits provided and enforced by the legislative branch, retaining broad and largely unconstrained executive authority in the vaguely worded Article II of *The U.S. Constitution*. As Alexander Hamilton noted in *The Federalist* #70, many colonies and other egalitarian societies of the past had implemented various organizational schemes that sought to divide executive power among different actors within government. However, none of these schemes had ever succeeded. Hamilton pointedly observed that whatever one of these fragmented executive arrangements might have been in theory, all had uniformly failed in practice. He further noted that these schemes had ultimately failed, regardless of the good intentions of the designers or the particular details of the fragmented structures had been implemented.[2] So in a framework for governance that otherwise placed a premium on the separation and fragmentation of power, the Founders drew the line at the executive. They knew that any system that divided executive authority would be inefficient and ineffective.

In making this argument, Hamilton analyzed the structure needed for an effective executive branch, and he applied empirical evidence gleaned both from a close reading of the failures of fragmented executive leadership over history as well as an observation of the struggles among the colonies to make his case. Specifically, Hamilton identified four essential elements needed in order to realize energetic—or effective—executive leadership. These four essential elements include: (1) unity; (2) duration; (3) an adequate provision for support; and, (4) competent powers.[3] *Unity* in this case refers to mathematical unity. Reviewing history, the Founders concluded that the only effective executive is one person, ultimately responsible for exercising the executive authority but also able to exercise the powers as he or she sees fit, within prescribed limits.

In addition to unity, *duration* refers to the idea of a fixed period of executive authority and responsibility, along with the features of periodic scrutiny, performance review, and accountability by higher authority. An *adequate provision for support* refers to both the emoluments of office, as well as a sufficient supporting staff, to enable the executive to succeed. The element of *competent powers* refers to the idea of providing the executive with sufficient authority to carry out the specific responsibilities of the office, without circumscribing or limiting those powers in a way that prevents the mission from being accomplished. In sum, Hamilton argued that history discounts the notion, or the hope, that merely creating enough venues for dialogue will generate consensus, more effective coordination, or any effective execution of complex governmental operations.

In the modern case, every current U.S. Government manual or set of guidelines tiptoes around the fragmented executive authority that is characteristic of the

American government's organization for national security. Although once anticipated as a document that might potentially make inroads into this major organizational limitation, the Obama administration's *Presidential Policy Directive (PPD)-1* of 2009 established (or reestablished) Interagency Policy Committees, but the guidance gives no real authority or leverage to those committees. Likewise, not one of the reform initiatives currently underway actually changes any statutory relationships in any substantive way.

Of course, the Founders' vision for national security was one that included the President actually marching in the field as commander in chief of the nation's military when needed, much as President Washington actually did in response to the Whiskey Rebellion in western Pennsylvania in 1794. Given the scope and reach of the U.S. Government's executive branch today, the President's modern designated national security executors must be given the same leverage and authority originally intended for the executive to be effective. At the same time, these executive agents must be subject to the due dependence on the people—the Congress and the President—that the Founders identified centuries ago as the keys to effectiveness and accountability. Although the technology and the scope of the work have changed, human nature has not.

Examining these same issues in a more modern context, renowned political scientist (and former naval officer) James Q. Wilson tried to identify why some bureaucratic agencies successfully carried out their missions while others failed. Scrutinizing armies, schools, and prisons as representative bureaucratic organizations, Wilson attributes the success of the German army against the French in World War II to an organizational culture that combined universally understood objectives with decentralized operational planning and execution.[4]

Citing military historian Martin van Creveld's careful analysis, Wilson attributes the German army's success against the French to the Germans' mission-oriented command system. This mission-focused command system was one in which higher commanders expressed their intent in an unmistakable way, after which they afforded their subordinate commanders wide latitude in making personnel, resource allocation, and operational planning decisions. In this way, these commanders were able to take advantage of their subordinates' proximity to the situation and their better understanding of circumstances on the ground.[5] In turn, these subordinate commanders also stressed independent decisionmaking, decentralizing authority down to the lowest levels, while also holding subordinates strictly accountable for the consequences of their actions and punishing them severely for infractions.[6]

These concepts of clearly articulated guidance and decentralized command are clearly relevant to the current problems with the U.S. Government's organization for national security. It is essential that the U.S. Government unify its own operational effort by decentralizing operations after aligning them with clear strategic goals that are both plainly defined and universally understood. With this goal in mind, relevant first principles for any effective reforms include achieving unity of effort through operational-level unity of command, after centralizing and operationalizing a more robust and coherent strategic planning effort at the national level.

At the same time, the resulting strategies must acknowledge the realities of available agency and departmental capabilities, and national-level resource decisions must be aligned with both current and projected requirements. The U.S. Government must get back in the habit of explicitly and rationally linking vital interests to ends, ways, and means, all while placing these elements of national strategy into the context of risk. Once those strategic choices are made, the authority for operational-level decisionmaking must be decentralized, along with control over resource utilization. From an institutional perspective, the various departments and agencies must be given adequate opportunities for education, training, professional development, and the other elements needed to achieve success. To achieve these ends, a bottom-up review of the U.S. Government's national security apparatus should be undertaken, with a primary goal of inventorying and cataloguing roles, functions, resources, and capabilities in U.S. Governmental agencies and departments. Every office of the U.S. Government must clearly understand its role and requirements, whether functioning as operators, planners, capabilities-providers, enablers, or sustainers. Every player must understand his or her role.

ESSENTIAL ELEMENTS: THE BROADER INSTITUTIONAL REQUIREMENTS

These relevant first principles should serve as the general guidelines to frame any feasible and effective reforms of the American government's national security apparatus. However, the actual specific changes needed to operationalize those guiding principles will ultimately require various essential elements of reform at each of the different levels of national security activity if those reforms are to succeed. Beginning at the broader institutional level—and acknowledging

the realities of the key organizations' existing mandates, cultures, expertise, resources, and career incentives—there are a variety of essential elements of reform that will need to stretch across all of the relevant departments and agencies and occur at all levels of activity. From this broader institutional perspective, any feasible and effective package of national security reforms will need to feature elements that enable all of the agencies and departments with national security responsibilities to achieve a number of key outcomes, including:
- The development of the organic nation-building, irregular warfare, and interagency expertise needed to meet each organization's responsibilities;
- The creation of professional career incentives and opportunities for interagency service, with demonstrated effectiveness in those assignments leading to promotion and advancement into senior positions of responsibility;
- The reorganization, development, and maintenance of organizational staffs to provide adequate personnel depth to meet the requirements of the interagency operations and functions;
- The creation of mechanisms for training and professionally educating key leaders and staff in interagency, nation-building, and irregular warfare responsibilities, along with mandating participation in that training;
- The establishment and support of an interagency and irregular warfare center for lessons learned, an initiative that is actually underway within S/CRS;

- A statutory redirection of agency and department incentives from their internal processes, agendas, and goals to national security goals;
- The creation of immersion training for other-than-DoD personnel in settings that will provide the opportunities needed for those agencies and departments to develop the operating and planning culture common to DoD;
- The creation of on-the-job training (OJT) in the specific tasks required of interagency coordination, nation-building, and irregular warfare, including the development of institutional expertise in the development of social, political, economic, and security institutions;
- The realignment of the geographic areas of responsibility and operational and functional subdivisions of all agencies and departments of the U.S. Government with national security responsibilities to create a common operating picture and functionality;
- The development and maintenance of enduring professional expertise among the various agencies and departments corresponding to that geographic and functional realignment, including in-house subject matter expertise related to the key countries, regions, transnational actors, functions, and operations;
- The redirection of sufficient resources to enable other-than-DoD agencies and departments to carry out their nation-building and irregular warfare functions;
- The decentralization of budget execution, giving funding control to leaders at levels directly in contact with the problems being solved, subject to strict oversight and accountability and severe sanctions for fraud, waste, or abuse;

- The implementation of true unity of command, ceding operational control of personnel and resources to the leaders of all agencies and departments charged with meeting operational objectives;
- The development and adoption of administrative mechanisms that afford other agency leaders the ability to contribute directly and substantively to the performance evaluations of the other agency personnel assigned to their operational control;
- The revision of job descriptions and employee contracts to give other-than-DoD agencies and departments the ability to assign certain key and essential employees to serve in overseas postings and in non-permissive security environments when designated for such service, after adequate training and preparation; and,
- The adjustment of standard operating procedures within the interagency coordinating bodies at the various levels of national security activity and organizational guidelines to require agency and departmental participation while also balancing the bottom-up activities of those groups with top-down direction from the key leaders.

ESSENTIAL ELEMENTS: THE NATIONAL STRATEGIC LEVEL

At the national strategic level of activity, any feasible and effective package of national security reforms will need to feature elements that enable the U.S. Government to achieve a number of other equally important outcomes, among them:

- The creation of far more robust national strategic planning capabilities;
- An operationalized national security strategy, or the creation and wide dissemination of a precise, concise, and complete statement of national strategic intentions, priorities, and objectives—a document that formally links U.S. national security interests with ends, ways, means, and risks while outlining specific organizational responsibilities, capabilities, and resources;
- The modification of national strategic planning processes and structures to enable those structures to generate orders that provide agencies and departments with clear, task-driven, and unmistakable strategic-level statements of intent, responsibility, authority, objectives, and measures of success;
- The decentralization of operational control over personnel and resources to subordinate leaders, while also holding those subordinate leaders directly accountable for progress in achieving clearly defined operational objectives;
- The establishment of binding and universally understood mechanisms of accountability, making those metrics more robust and comprehensive;
- The creation of theater-specific playbooks, including sets of objectives and metrics that will get agencies and departments pulling toward the same ends; and,
- The reorganization of congressional oversight, focusing on specific metrics and objectives, as well as agency performance and required capabilities.

ESSENTIAL ELEMENTS: THE THEATER-STRATEGIC AND OPERATIONAL LEVELS

Similarly, at the theater-strategic and operational levels of activity, any feasible and effective package of national security reforms will need to include elements that enable the key leaders at those levels to achieve effective interagency performance and a whole of government approach to planning and operations. Among other important outcomes, any reforms should enable:
- The integration of other agency personnel throughout all geographic and functional combatant commands;
- Key leaders to exercise operational control over other agency personnel to realize true unity of vision and effort;
- The development of leaders in other-than-DoD agencies and departments for senior interagency and leadership responsibilities, including experience in planning, management, oversight, and the interagency process;
- The development of a deep bench of nation-building, irregular warfare, and interagency specialists on the embedded staffs of all the relevant agencies and departments operating at the theater and operational levels, a process that will take years to bring to fruition;
- The development of theater- and operational-level one-stop shopping for strategy and operational guidance, a concise but complete document that lays out the broader goals and specific objectives and is required reading for all personnel assigned to the theater or operational headquarters; and,

- The development of enduring cultural expertise, language capabilities, and other social, political, and economic knowledge in each of the headquarters.

ESSENTIAL ELEMENTS: PRACTICAL AND POLITICAL CONSIDERATIONS

In order to be adopted and implemented, any solution to the U.S. Government's strategic and interagency problems must also include features that will enable the package of reforms to overcome likely practical and political obstacles. Among other functional considerations, the practical obstacles to this proposal center largely on the glaring lack of relevant expertise among the agencies and departments needed to carry out the demands of nation-building and irregular warfare tasks. These shortfalls are also coupled with the existing DoD-centered combatant command structure and its limits on career incentives and senior leadership opportunities for non-DoD personnel. In other words, non-DoD personnel do not currently have significant opportunities for developing the operational and strategic planning or operating experience that becomes second nature in DoD's culture. Nor are there currently many career incentives to develop this professional experience in the other-than-DoD organizations. Accordingly, any package of reforms will have to balance the goals of increasing other-than-DoD agency capabilities and leader development opportunities with the practical realities of current limitations in personnel, expertise, and other resources in those agencies.

From a political perspective, with bureaucratic politics and organizational cultures being what they are, any attempt to reduce or change the roles, responsibilities, and resources of any of the agencies and departments involved in nation-building and irregular warfare will be likely to result in bureaucratic pushback that will undermine the effort from the start. Therefore, to enhance the prospects for successful adoption and implementation, any solutions to the strategic and interagency problems must be additive to all organizations concerned. That is, successful organizational changes generally must be additive in the sense that the changes do not threaten the existing functions and organizational culture within the organizations affected. Political scientist James Q. Wilson found that these types of changes are the ones most likely to succeed, given bureaucratic and political realities.[7] It is likely that organizational cultures within these agencies and departments will change over time to conform more closely to the interagency expectations, much as the different branches of the U.S. military have come to embrace jointness in the years since the passage of Goldwater-Nichols in 1986. In any event, balancing the need to be additive with looming resource constraints will require a deft political touch as well as a serious and candid discussion that differentiates between wants and needs.

In terms of other potential political obstacles to significant reforms, there may also be resistance to any proposals that are seen as enhancing the military's resources or capabilities beyond the status quo, consistent with critics who have already expressed concerns about the militarization of U.S. foreign policy. In a book published in 2004 that was influential within Washington, DC, circles, journalist Dana Priest asserted a mismatch between the "culture and mission" of the demands of reconstruction and stabilization operations and the U.S. military's mindset.[8] Highlighting the expansion of the military's role in the conduct of foreign policy and the acceleration of that trend in the 1990s, Priest noted that the Clinton administration gave the military responsibilities for demining, drug interdiction, anti-terrorism, disaster relief, and other unconventional missions.[9] Priest went on to assert that the demands of the so-called Global War on Terror (GWOT) exceeded even the broad capabilities of the military and stretched the military thin while requiring skill sets that do not exist within the military at this point.[10] Priest also claimed that the use of the military as the primary vehicle for the democratization that was at the center of the Bush-era national security strategy is a poor fit, given that the administration failed to link social welfare and economic development resources to the GWOT military effort.[11] Along similar lines, any changes may require zero-sum choices or even budgetary reductions in light of the U.S. Government's current budget challenges, meaning that each increase in structure will likely need to come with an offsetting bill payer.

A VISION OF COHERENCE FOR U.S. NATIONAL SECURITY

As the 21st century unfolds, this period has already been marked by the emergence of a wide variety of diverse and unconventional security threats—threats that fall across the spectrum of conflict while calling for both military and nonmilitary responses. As such, the U.S. Government no longer has the luxury of allowing its component agencies and departments and their own competing organizational agendas, interests, and methods to get in the way of measured and effective national security responses. A major first step will involve undertaking the heavy work of reorganizing those organizations to achieve a true unity of effort through operational-level unity of command. However, any effective reforms of the national security apparatus must also include establishing national security structures and processes at all levels that enable policymakers to give unmistakably clear orders, with comparably clear objectives, authorities, and measures for gauging progress. These changes must also realign the career incentives and developmental opportunities for leaders, planners, and operators with the U.S. Government's national security goals. Finally, these reforms must be undertaken in such a way as to build upon the strengths of the existing organizational cultures, rather than trying to impose changes in spite of them.

Although it may seem farfetched to compare the two activities, in western Pennsylvania there is a high school football team that wins championship after championship in spite of the fiercely competitive programs that surround it. What sets this program apart from all of the others is the fact that every player in the school district, regardless of age, uses the same formations, the same plays, and the same terminology, even as they learn the same drills and techniques from that same early age. So when a player has been learning the same drills and playbook since he was 5 years old, he does not even have to think about technique when it comes time to execute the plays in high school. Instead, his reactions are synchronized and instinctive, and he is free to focus all of his energy on achieving success on that play. Although the U.S. Government's organizational structures for national security are far more complex and diverse than the Thomas Jefferson

High School's football program, the analogy is an apt one. In a similar way, the goal of these reforms is to get the various agencies and departments of the U.S. Government reacting in a synchronized and coherent way, thus enabling our government to succeed equally well in responding to the various threats and opportunities that our nation will encounter in the years ahead.

ENDNOTES - CHAPTER 9

1. Alexander Hamilton *et al.*, in Charles R. Kesler and Clinton Rossiter, eds., *The Federalist Papers*, New York: Penguin, 1999, p. 422. Some of the themes of this chapter first appeared in the author's "Filling Irregular Warfare's Interagency Gaps," *Parameters*, Vol. 39, No. 3, Autumn 2009, pp. 65-80. The author is grateful to *Parameters* for the permission to reprint portions of those arguments in this book.

2. *Ibid.*, pp. 421-429.

3. *Ibid.*

4. James Q. Wilson, *Bureaucracy: What Government Agencies Do and Why They Do It*, New York: Basic Books, 1989, pp. 15-18.

5. *Ibid.*, pp. 16-18.

6. *Ibid.*, pp. 16-17, 25.

7. *Ibid.*, pp. 225.

8. Dana Priest, *The Mission: Waging War and Keeping Peace with America's Military*, New York: Norton and Company, 2004, p. 19.

9. *Ibid.*, p. 45.

10. *Ibid.*, pp. 396-397.

11. *Ibid.*, pp. 403-404.

CHAPTER 10

A WAY AHEAD — THE NSC, COMBATANT COMMANDS, AND USRADCOM

> Why do U.S. Government agencies distribute assignments in ways that seem to minimize the chance for key employees to become expert in their tasks?
>
> James Q. Wilson
> Bureaucracy: What Government Agencies
> Do and Why They Do It, 1989[1]

To succeed in future nation-building and irregular warfare operations, and in any other major national security undertakings for that matter, the United States must adopt reforms that encompass all of these essential elements if they are to be effective. Of course, formulating and implementing reform measures that incorporate all of these essential features will require major organizational changes, along with a concurrent redistribution of increasingly scarce resources. Nevertheless, any reform measures that encompass these essential elements offer the ultimate advantage of directly addressing the fundamental, underlying causes that have led to the U.S. Government's strategic disjointedness and its disunity of effort in the first place. As daunting as some of these prospects might seem, there is a set of potential reforms that would accomplish each of these goals, while doing so in such a way as to mitigate the practical and political obstacles that usually attend bureaucratic changes of any real magnitude.

In their essence, these recommended reforms consist of four major components. The first two components call for major restructurings of critical organizations at the national and theater-strategic levels of activity—specifically the National Security Staff (NSS) of the National Security Council (NSC) and parts of the Department of Defense (DoD) combatant command structure. The second two components of this package of reforms involve a set of complementary changes that are aimed at our national security institutions and the U.S. Congress more generally, including a bottom-up review of our national security apparatus. Given their scope and reach, implementing these changes will require both executive orders and enabling legislation, and implementing them will also undoubtedly require heavy lifting from both political and bureaucratic perspectives. However, the shifting and dangerous nature of the 21st century security environment—when coupled with looming draconian budget cuts that will likely stretch laterally and vertically across the American government—will provide both an impetus and an opportunity for the consideration of changes beyond the normal pale.

When viewed holistically, these proposed changes are more likely than any other recent or ongoing reform initiatives to resolve the U.S. Government's considerable strategic and interagency difficulties. Likewise, these reforms would bring with them a direct and tangible means of bridging the gap between the increasingly complex demands of the modern national security environment and corresponding shortfalls in existing U.S. governmental systems and capabilities. At the same time, these measures would also take major steps toward achieving a more coherent process of strategy formulation, thus aiming to bring U.S. agency and departmental efforts into better alignment with the more robust strategic and operational objectives that would result from an increasingly rational, comprehensive, and integrated planning process.

Finally, when considered collectively and contemplated across a longer term, these prospective reforms would also create positive and persistent organizational pressures that would likely result in the modification of a variety of entrenched and adverse agency and departmental cultural norms over time. In turn, these resulting changes in organizational culture will yield professional and institutional incentives for interagency engagement and integration that would eventually help to bring agency and departmental processes and products into better alignment with one another. These reforms also offer the potential for realizing clean lines of authority, better focused capabilities, improved leader development, effective accountability mechanisms, and other attributes that are required to enable the U.S. Government to achieve genuine strategic and interagency coherence in the modern era. In sum, these changes will also enable the United States to take major steps toward achieving the agility, flexibility, and economy in our national security apparatus that is so vitally needed for the 21st century.

THE STRATEGIC LEVEL CENTERPIECE: REDESIGNING THE NSC'S NATIONAL SECURITY STAFF

At the strategic level of national security activity, any serious reform effort must address a host of deficiencies within the U.S. Government's national-level strategic and interagency structures and systems, none of which are addressed directly by ongoing initiatives. Chief among these major concerns is the fact that the

U.S. Government currently fails to make clear and rational linkages between its vital interests and the ends, ways, and means needed to advance those interests. Any truly serious reform effort should first enable the U.S. Government's national strategic organizational structures to conduct genuine and effective strategy formulation, making this missing linkage of interests, ends, ways, and means—placed in the context of risks and costs—a systematic and routine feature of our national strategies. Of course, this result can only occur after the completion of a corresponding and thorough inventory of existing U.S. agency and departmental capabilities and resources as an essential first step. This inventory of capabilities and resources would then serve as the baseline for a rigorous set of national-level policy discussions and decisions aimed at yielding more capabilities-based and holistic policy recommendations and strategic guidance that incorporates presidential (and congressional) priorities into a comprehensive whole. Clearly, the current national-level structures and processes fall well short of this standard, since the center of gravity of the national security activity at the national level remains within the individual agencies and departments rather than with national strategic body or interagency process.

To achieve these primary goals, this package of modifications at the national level of planning structures and processes must also feature the changes required to overcome and resolve the disproportionate allocation of resources that favor one instrument of national power at the expense of the others. Likewise, any reforms would also need to improve interagency coordinating and integrating processes—processes that are currently largely "bottom up" rather than "top down" and generally engage leaders too late for key decisions, while also failing to mandate participation at the lower levels. Any reforms would therefore need to provide sufficient staff resources to meet current planning, operational oversight, and long-range strategic assessment and planning requirements, among other critical capabilities that are needed at the national level of national security activity. Associated reform measures should also include a plan to develop sufficient and enduring subject matter expertise at the national level, organized by region, function, transnational threat, or presidential priority, with strong interagency representation holding sufficient authority among other-than-DoD agencies and departments to overcome the disproportionate emphasis on security-centered operations that has dominated in recent years at the national level.

At the same time, these reforms must also be aimed at achieving the ability to generate detailed and comprehensive national security objectives, tied to existing resources and capabilities, to be used to drive corresponding theater-specific objectives. These robust national and theater-specific objectives would be expressed both through a more detailed and coherent national security strategy, as well as through an equally specific set of strategies for each theater, each major national security threat, and other significant or distinct national security concerns. Ultimately, these enhanced national-level executive systems and processes should be clearly and directly linked to matching congressional oversight structures. These linkages and the corresponding organizational realignments within the parent agencies and departments can be organized by geographic region, functional responsibility, or presidential priority, with each organizational structure tied to its associated national security objectives.

Ideally, these modified national-level planning and oversight mechanisms would enable Congress and the President to define and monitor equally detailed measures of progress toward those objectives. These more robust and detailed measures of progress, or metrics, can then be used to enforce accountability and compel compliance among the various agencies and departments and their leaders. Likewise, these comprehensive metrics will also help those organizations to achieve a common understanding of the problem and to generate their own supporting objectives. These forcing functions and benchmarks would also subsequently serve as the organizational framework needed to shift the center of gravity in strategic deliberations at the national level from their current emphasis on turf and resource protection to discussions focused more on mission objectives and required capabilities.

The evidence from Afghanistan and in other systematic reviews of U.S. governmental performance clearly illustrates that our existing national security structures and processes are falling well short of accomplishing these desired outcomes. Placing the current bureaucratic arrangements into perspective, the organizational alignment of the NSC and its staff—at least nominally sitting at the center of the American national security effort—does not match either the functional and geographic alignment of the DoD combatant command structure or State Department (State) comparable organizational subdivisions, though it does reflect many current presidential priorities. In any event, a serious observer is hard pressed to see any logical connection or jurisdictional overlap between the various key players, let alone any commonality in form or function from one agency or department to the next. This interorganizational disjointedness stretches across the linkages between the NSC staff and the corresponding congressional structures and executive branch analogues, as well. For example, the Barack Obama administration's NSC staff—now known as the National Security Staff (NSC/NSS)—has separate Afghanistan and Iraq deputies, along with partitions for Strategic Communications and Global Outreach, International Economics, Global Democracy Strategy, and Combating Terrorism Strategy, a structure that is clearly at odds with DoD and State subdivisions.

Furthermore, this disjointedness is exacerbated by the fact that the Interagency Policy Committees (IPC), intended at least in part to bridge these gaps, do not exercise any real budgetary authority. Likewise, the White House's Office of Management and Budget (OMB) is represented in the NSC itself but does not have a substantive role in the budgeting for capabilities or the distribution of resources, since agency and departmental budgets are ultimately controlled by the parent organizations and reviewed by Congress from department to department. Additionally, the current NSC/NSS and the various working groups are typically bottom-up models, where issues that cannot be resolved at the lower levels bubble up to a level at which they can be resolved. While this model manages workload for the senior officials, it also has the adverse consequence of engaging senior officials late in the decisionmaking process, and often interagency partners opt out at the lower levels without serious consequence.

The evidence of this national-level disjointedness is also apparent in the goals of the various agencies and departments, as well. That is, given the typically vague nature of the various strategic policies and documents created by the White House and the NSC/NSS, agency and departmental goals can be, and are, interpreted variously among the different players in accordance with their own organizational cultures and the central tasks that they have already defined for themselves. For example, for a long time, DoD interpreted irregular warfare as a nearly conventional security operation—though this perspective has clearly changed—and State, the U.S. Agency for International Development (USAID), and other agencies interpreted these operations in ways consistent with their own existing organizational cultures. Political scientist James Q. Wilson talks to this central challenge of bureaucracy, noting that, "The State Department has goals, but they are so general that no executive can derive from them a clear definition of the department's tasks."[2]

For its own part, the NSC/NSS is already greatly overworked and understaffed for its scope of responsibilities, and as a result the leaders and staff of the NSS typically spend the majority of their time putting out fires rather than carrying out the fundamental advisory and integrating functions for which the council was constituted in the first place. Addressing this point directly, the 9/11 Commission concluded that the NSC and its staff were consumed by near-term requirements at the clear expense of longer-term and broader strategic planning. Specifically, the Commission noted that the NSC staff was "consumed by meetings on day-to-day issues (while) trying to coordinate everyday operations," leaving the staff with "less capacity to find the time and detachment needed to advise a president on larger policy issues."[3]

Largely determined by presidential preference, over its history the NSC staff has varied in size from administration to administration, but in nearly every case it has been small when compared with the scope of its responsibilities, a fact that holds particularly true today. Juxtaposed against the tens of thousands of planners and strategists assigned across the breadth of DoD, the personnel strength of the NSC staff has ranged from a low point of about a dozen personnel in the John Kennedy administration to about 100 staff members altogether in 2008.[4] It is modestly larger today. Of particular note, the Dwight Eisenhower model of the NSC staff contained a Planning Board of senior officials who thoroughly reviewed each issue before it came to the principal members, as well as an Operations Coordinating Board that monitored and reported on the implementation of the subsequent policy decisions.[5]

In any event, the centerpiece of any feasible reform package at the national level should include a major redesign of the NSC/NSS. The primary goal of this redesign would be to create a stronger NSS in terms of its ability to formulate plans and strategy, its resident institutional expertise, and its ability to generate specific accountability metrics and timelines, rather than any play-by-play oversight. That is, it is not the goal of these reforms to attempt to build the NSC or its staff into an organization with the mandate of managing the actual execution of national security operations—a move that would further centralize the handling of irregular warfare operations and other complex national security challenges that do not lend themselves readily to deterministic or cookie-cutter solutions anyway. Instead, the goal is to reorganize the NSC/NSS to match the requirements of the contemporary national security environment, partly in the style of the Eisenhower-era operations and plans cells, but with far more robust strategic planning, integrating, policy analysis, and advisory capabilities. As a strong and effective extension of the President's vision and guidance for national security policy, the NSS could then provide the President with "one-stop shopping" for thorough strategic and interagency planning of recurring and emergent national security challenges, establishing the foundation for the balanced application of the various instruments of national power and framing objectives, resources, and accountability mechanisms for presidential decisions.

To achieve this vision, this reform recommendation suggests adopting an Eisenhower-style redesign of the NSS, but with a far more vigorous interagency flavor. This redesign will therefore involve realigning along regional, operations, and functional lines. Rather than creating ad hoc crisis action teams that typically operate in a vacuum, the goal is to create structures and substructures that enable the NSC/NSS to achieve a proportional sense of the whole of national security concerns. Ultimately then, the goal is to enable the NSS to achieve a more holistic understanding of the impacts of strategic and operational choices on U.S. national security interests and global risks and threats. As part of this NSS redesign, the executive branch leadership and the relevant agency leaders must also create more robust interagency coordinating mechanisms, beginning with the NSC/NSS itself and the Joint Interagency Coordinating Groups (JIACG) at the theater-strategic level, but eventually carrying this emphasis through to the operational level.

As another essential feature of the NSC/NSS reforms, the resulting reorganized NSS interagency structures and processes must also enable the council to provide clear, task-driven, strategic-level statements of intent, responsibility, and authority for presidential ratification. Most current strategic documents emphasize vague goals that sound more like rhetorical platitudes than guidance. As Wilson notes, "When agency goals are vague, it will be hard to convey to operators a simple and vivid understanding of what they are supposed to do."[6] In essence, a primary related goal of the redesign is to create a streamlined but effective organization that is able to execute effective strategy formulation, with resulting policy products that include realistic, achievable ends linked to existing and adequate resources, in consideration of broader global threats and risks. Likewise, the NSC/NSS must be resourced to enable it to provide staff support to the President for both long-range strategic planning, as well as near-term crisis action planning. The NSC/NSS as currently configured is consumed by crisis action planning at the clear expense of longer-term strategic planning.

Collectively, then, the key features of the recommended NSC/NSS redesign will need to include expanding the council beyond its current level of about 100 personnel to meet the revised requirements of its planning and oversight functions, without doing so in such a way as to create a sprawling bureaucracy that would only serve to counteract the positive effects of the increased capabilities. As another key element of this reform, the U.S. Government must also reorganize the components of the national security apparatus to bring the DoD geographic and functional combatant command structures, DoS's separate subdivisions, and the structures of the other relevant agencies and departments into functional and geographic alignment. These reforms should also include equipping the NSC/NSS with a similar structure to the the DoD's "J-Staff," to enable the NSC to carry out all of those related functions and for commonality of operating practices with the U.S. Government's executive arms, the combatant commands. Expanding and reorganizing the Eisenhower model to meet the current U.S. national security demands would require a redesigned NSC/NSS that can perform the following *statutory* and *emergent* functions:

1. (*Statutory functions* under the National Security Act of 1947, as amended):
    - Advise the President with respect to the integration of policies related to national security;
    - Enable the military services and other agencies/departments to cooperate more effectively;
    - Assess and appraise objectives, commitments, and risks in relation to the use of military power, and make recommendations to the President in connection therewith;
    - Consider policies on matters of common interest to the agencies and departments concerned with the national security, and make recommendations in connection therewith;
    - Make recommendations, and such other reports to the President as it deems appropriate, or as the President may require;
    - Conduct specific reviews and reports related to foreign intelligence activities, transnational threats, weapons of mass destruction, and other directed topics; and,
    - Carry out other functions as the President may direct.[7]

Additionally, the evidence of history and the "best practices" of past Presidents suggest that the NSC and

Presidents are best served when the NSS is also prepared to carry out the following *emergent functions*:
- Serve as the impartial "honest broker" for policies, strategies, and resources;
- Serve as the primary interagency analysts of intelligence and national security threats;
- Serve as the primary interagency coordinators, integrators, and orders preparers;
- Set the conditions for exercising of presidential authority;
- Propose and independently analyze strategic options, and offer recommendations when requested, rather than serving as a policy advocate;
- Conduct a thorough analysis of strategic options, rather than serving as the agent to build consensus among competing departments and agencies;
- Integrate proposed and approved strategic plans and policies;
- Conduct medium- and long-range strategic planning, separately from current operations or crisis and contingency planning;
- Facilitate "whole of government" responses to national security challenges, including homeland defense and the application of soft power;
- Conduct contingency planning and monitor current operations;
- Oversee and monitor accountability among the implementing departments and agencies, specifically to assess compliance with presidential orders; and,
- Serve as the primary national-level capabilities planner, as the interagency organization that best understands the capabilities and limits of

the U.S. instruments of power, in the fashion of the National Security Resources Board that was part of the original National Security Act of 1947.

Of course, it is generally accepted that the NSC and NSS should stay out of the business of actually conducting or implementing operations.

With these statutory and emergent functions in mind, the NSC's NSS should be reorganized to include these sections:

- An intelligence section to analyze global threats, interests, and risks;
- A separate section to cross-walk, integrate, and manage intelligence;
- Strategic plans and guidance sections corresponding to regions, functions, and presidential priorities;
- A current operations integration and oversight section;
- A future operations planning section;
- An information and knowledge management section;
- A strategic and interagency lessons learned activity;
- A top-down interagency coordination and integration section;
- A "President's special action" section; and,
- A section that catalogues existing capabilities and forecasts requirements.

All in all, there are a number of major benefits to be gained from this redesign, chief among them the creation of robust national strategic planning capabilities and the corresponding establishment of binding and universally understood measures of success, including comprehensive and robust metrics for their measurement. This NSC/NSS redesign can also result in the creation of specific playbooks reaching across all agencies to provide common objectives and consolidated lists of appropriate and relevant metrics to help align agency and departmental effort. The redesign can also yield a scrub of actual agency and departmental capabilities, because the NSC could be staffed and equipped to inventory agency resources and their potential contributions to national security, with the ultimate goal of building on that inventory of existing skill sets and resources to make recommendations to Congress and the President regarding needed capabilities and potential resource redistributions.

Along similar lines, this redesign could also give the NSC/NSS the ability to influence and realign the various agency and departmental career and professional incentives as a secondary effect of the coherent strategic guidance, likewise helping senior leaders to hold those agencies and departments accountable for the results of their efforts, even while continuing to allow for decentralized execution. This redesign would also equip the NSC/NSS with sufficient staff resources and expertise to enable it to rewrite the National Security Strategy and complementary documents to make the linkages of objectives, roles, responsibilities, resources, and authorities explicitly clear. The NSC/NSS would also be better positioned to address the identification, definition, and mitigation of risks, thus achieving more balance in the use of scarce agency and departmental resources. From the start, this redesign would help to develop and reinforce an operator and planner mindset at the NSC/NSS, a mindset that will eventually carry through to the component agencies and departments of the U.S. Government.

In summary, the primary benefits that will result at the national strategic level from this NSC/NSS redesign will come in the form of clear-headed policy advice and operationalized plans that link interests to ends and means, including the delineation of specific organizational responsibilities, required capabilities, and dedicated resources. This NSC/NSS redesign will also provide our national decisionmakers with the staff expertise and capabilities needed to inform strategic decisionmaking more effectively, thus enabling our senior leaders to make clear their unmistakable intent after having made decisions informed by the best possible sense of the strategic context. To succeed in the complex, uncertain, and dangerous national security environment of the 21st century, the national leadership must create and clearly articulate one vision for each national security requirement, a vision articulated using one common language that also clearly defines specific tasks to be accomplished and assigns equally specific responsibilities and authorities. To achieve this end, the NSC staff must be redesigned and properly resourced in order to make this rational, ordered, integrated, and coherent outcome not only possible, but routine.

THE THEATER AND OPERATIONAL LEVEL CENTERPIECES: USRADCOM AND COMBATANT COMMAND REDESIGN

In addition to the national strategic level challenges, there are also a number of key concerns and challenges at the theater-strategic and operational levels of national security activity that also must be addressed by any serious reform effort. Among other major issues, obstacles to effective interagency integration and operational effectiveness at these levels include the fact that the key leaders at the theater and operational levels have no statutory leverage to direct other agency personnel and resources. This situation exacerbates the impact of the significant mismatch between the demands of modern national security operations and the U.S. Government's current capabilities, as well as the skewed distribution of resources. Other major challenges at the theater-strategic and operational levels of activity include the adverse effects created by mismatches between modern missions and the predominant norms of the organizational cultures of key agency and departments, as well as misaligned career and professional incentives in many agencies that fail to provide any real incentive or mandate for the personnel within those agencies to seek developmental interagency assignments.

As a further hindrance to interagency and operational success, the typical bottom-up interagency processes—with participation not mandated and evaluations handled by the parent agency or department—appear at the theater and operational levels as well and serve to undermine the possibility for unified effort. These effects are then magnified by the lack of sustained, relevant, and enduring institutional subject matter expertise tied to regional, national, or transnational actors and cultures. Of course, the disproportionate allocation of resources to DoD also leads to an equally disproportionate focus on security operations, resulting in a lack of key and developmental assignment and educational and training opportunities for other than DoD personnel in general, and rising senior non-DoD leaders and senior staff in particular. Adding another challenge to the mix, the contractors hired to make up for these shortfalls are more often than not paid for process rather than results, just as the ultimate budgetary approval authority resides in Washington with parent organizations. Taken together, these factors combine to prevent key leaders on the ground from being able to set and enforce unmistakably clear priorities, objectives, operating practices, and metrics of accountability.

With all of these challenges as a backdrop, the first major element of the recommended national security reforms at the theater-strategic and operational levels is the creation of a U.S. Reconstruction and Development Command (USRADCOM). Consistent with its name, USRADCOM would serve as a new joint, interagency command, with the strategic and operational responsibilities for reconstruction and development missions. Eventually led by a senior executive from USAID or State, the new combatant command would resemble the United States Special Operations Command (USSOCOM) in several ways. For example, just as USSOCOM has the functional responsibility for developing, maintaining, and providing U.S. special operating forces, USRADCOM would have a similar responsibility for developing, maintaining, and providing interagency expertise on reconstruction and development operations. In particular, USRADCOM's subject matter experts would include those trained and experienced in economic development, the building or rebuilding of the institutions for the rule of law, and the development of local and national governance, among other areas. In turn, the existing geographic combatant commands would retain the operational responsibility for carrying out routine short-term stability operations (and irregular warfare) as part of their execution of full spectrum operations.

Additionally, just as USSOCOM has evolved into a combatant command that now carries out operational missions within the areas of responsibility of the geographic combatant commanders when ordered to do so, USRADCOM would similarly carry out reconstruction and development missions in conjunction with the geographic combatant commanders or independently, as directed. As a newly created functional, interagency combatant command, USRADCOM would be responsible for the integration and development of personnel from all of the key agencies, while enabling State, USAID, and the other agencies to build operational and planning expertise at strategic, theater-strategic, operational, and tactical levels. Ultimately to be headed by a four-star equivalent civilian leader from USAID or State, this interagency command would also provide a developmental track for aspiring planners and operators in USAID and State, as well as promotion opportunities and career incentives for the most talented leaders and staff from those and other agencies involved in reconstruction and development missions. As envisioned, movement back and forth from USRADCOM to mainstream State and USAID (or other agencies) will also cross-fertilize those organizations with elements of the operational and strategic-level planning cultures, while performing the same function for DoD and the other combatant commands, as well. In any event, it has become clear in Afghanistan and Iraq that the U.S. Government does not currently possess much-needed reconstruction and development expertise and capabilities. This shortfall would be filled by USRADCOM.

As the second centerpiece of the major reforms at the theater-strategic and operational levels, the establishment of this new combatant command would be coupled with an interagency-driven restructuring of the geographic and functional combatant commands of the DoD. The goal here would be to achieve true interagency integration by permanently staffing the combatant commands with personnel from the whole of the U.S. Government; with individual personnel rotating back and forth from their parent agencies. In some ways, this change would merely represent an expansion of a trend that is already underway, as the recent tendency has been toward equipping many of DoD's combatant commands with interagency capabilities. For example, USAID personnel currently serve in five combatant commands, and the United States Africa Command (USAFRICOM) was designed from the start with a more robust interagency flavor in mind. Similar to the USAFRICOM in this respect, it will be appropriate to provide a deputy from the DoD in USRADCOM, and to integrate DoD personnel at all levels of that interagency command. As a distinct political and bureaucratic advantage, creating this interagency command would also basically maintain intact the existing organizational cultures and basic capabilities and structures of the key organizations, while also helping to "de-militarize" the face of American foreign policy in reconstruction and development operations. Likewise, this integration would enhance the interagency process, and giving nation-building and other development and similar development missions a better chance of succeeding.

    As an added benefit, this new structure would also involve creating a cadre of trained specialists in nation-building and development tasks, with particular emphasis upon the interagency components of those processes. At the same time, complementary measures should include placing deputies for economic development from USAID and experts on governance and diplomacy from State in each of the other interagency commands as appropriate to their circumstances, similar to the mix that has already been put into place in USAFRICOM. As part of the development of the expertise required for these missions, USRADCOM might have a newly created combat advisory corps assigned to it as suggested by strategic thinker John Nagl. This organization would establish a body of dedicated professionals with the skills needed to develop the security forces of the host nation, but who would also have the training, expertise, temperament, and rank to advise the indigenous leaders at the national administrative level.[8]

Among many other benefits to be gained from this strategic restructuring, senior leaders from State, USAID, and other key agencies with a role in this area of national security would gain an opportunity to realize a culminating assignment as an interagency commander under this structure. Accordingly, the leadership and professional development opportunities represented in USRADCOM, as well as the interagency postings in the other combatant commands, would increase the incentives of non-DoD personnel to commit to the interagency track, in contrast to the current arrangements that often primarily incentivize home office assignments in their parent agencies. Upon integrating other agency personnel as appropriate throughout all of the combatant commands, and after providing the key leaders with the statutory authority needed to direct those other agency personnel, theater- and operational-level leaders will then be able to achieve a true integration of other agency perspectives, expertise, and resources, thus creating a true unity of vision and effort.

Approaching this idea from the Founders' perspective, Madison noted in *The Federalist* #51 that in order for the various departments of the government to function effectively, "Ambition must be made to counteract ambition," in this context meaning that departments must be given similar outlets for talented individuals to pursue opportunities for leadership and development.[9] Consistent with this principle, the reform of the combatant command structure and the creation of USRADCOM will also provide rising senior leaders and managers from all of the key agencies opportunities to hold important responsibilities for planning, operations, management, and oversight. Corresponding changes would also need to afford these non-DoD personnel the opportunity for the developmental education and training needed to equip them to carry out those responsibilities. In the process, these shared interagency experiences, when coupled with appropriate formal institutional training and education, will enable the U.S. Government to develop a deep bench of career professionals in all agencies, reinforcing the trend by promoting and rewarding this interagency service and by providing the mechanisms for key operational and planning leaders to evaluate other-agency personnel formally.

As a separate advantage of this reform, this option will also help the combatant commands to develop the much-needed cultural and language expertise that is lacking across the various arms of the U.S. Government. In particular, USRADCOM will serve to develop and then sustain the expertise in the areas of social, governmental, economic, and security development that is sorely needed in all of the relevant agencies and departments holding responsibilities for nation-building, irregular warfare, and even humanitarian relief. The idea of earmarking individuals to develop and specialize in these areas is entirely feasible, given the immense size of our executive branch.

Another direct benefit of this major change would be to create on-the-job training opportunities for national security planners and operators from all relevant agencies, likewise establishing a foundation for the cross-fertilization of organizational cultures and expertise and enhanced interagency effectiveness at all levels of planning and execution. In the same way, this shift would bring other agency perspectives into the planning, resourcing, and operational processes in each command and ensure that each agency had the opportunity to have its viewpoints heard. As an added political benefit, the restructuring of the geographic and functional combatant commands, the fact that USRADCOM would be led by a senior executive from USAID or State should also shift the primary focus from security force-centered operations to citizen-centered ones. This move would also be consistent with some of the basic governmental reform themes laid out by reform advocates David Osborne and Ted Gaebler in *Reinventing Government* in 1992.[10]

In standing up this new organization, for several reasons, it would be prudent to ensure that the first USRADCOM commander is a senior military leader, rather than a senior civilian. This senior military leader would be more capable of establishing the operating and planning culture that the new command's organizational culture must embrace, and a senior military leader would understand how to establish the training and education programs needed to stand up the new capabilities required in the command. Ideally, this first USRADCOM commander would be someone coming from the military side of the civil-military equation, but having extensive experience with operating in interagency settings and in dealing with the nonmilitary instruments of power. Examples of such individuals might include: former Secretary of State, Colin Powell; former USCENTCOM commander, General Anthony Zinni; or perhaps a currently serving senior three- or four-star general officer having had substantial experience with reconstruction and development in the Afghan or Iraqi theaters of operations. In one sense, we would be looking for the modern day equivalent of an Eisenhower or George Marshall to initiate this new organization and its required nation-building capabilities, to pave the way and set conditions for success for the subsequent leader from State or USAID. Since the USRADCOM position would be a command position, this restructuring would also require accompanying legislation that would authorize a member of State or USAID to exercise command authority.

To achieve each of these desired effects, there are a number of related and concurrent operational-level changes that would also be required. For one, commanders should be given streamlined access to funds that have a direct, significant, and visible impact on the lives of average citizens within the theater of operations. Nagl identifies the Commander's Emergency Response Program (CERP) as one such vehicle.[11] More typically, State and the other key non-DoD agencies have retained the ultimate approval for spending decisions, meaning that too often funding decisions are centralized thousands of miles away in Washington, DC—far from the operational theaters. Likewise, contractor specifications are sometimes generated at the theater-level and operational headquarters, and so employment contracts civilian contractors must be written to make them results-based rather than merely time-based, another move consistent with the governmental reforms suggested by Osborne and Gaebler.[12]

In a sense, taking these steps to decentralize operational decisionmaking and personnel control will take advantage of the benefits of our broader system of federalism, in which the key decisions that affect operations locally are made by the leaders closest to the situation. These changes would also build upon two operational and tactical level interagency success stories from the past—including the Marine Corps Combined Action Platoons and the Civil Operations and Revolutionary Development Support (CORDS) program—both of which achieved significant interagency success in Vietnam.[13] Again, these changes are also consistent with the themes outlined in Osborne and Gaebler's recommendations on streamlining and decentralizing decisionmaking.[14]

In any case, the implementation of these interagency coordinating mechanisms at the lower levels could be ad hoc in nature at the start, but ultimately the goal would be to impose statutory guidance mandating the organizations while simultaneously providing more leverage, resources, and authority to the interagency participants. Currently, the interagency working groups that do exist at the operational and tactical levels are often information-sharing organizations, rather than decisionmaking ones. Finally, to succeed in these complex operations, we will need to develop a nation-building playbook similar to the Army's *Field Manual (FM) 100-11: Force Integration*, which provides a checklist of requirements and the systems and processes for building a viable, doctrine-based Army.[15] The doctrinal guidance covers the means for creating doctrine, organization, training and education, materiel, leadership, personnel, and facilities, often known as DOTMLPF.

Finally, some thinkers and practitioners have suggested that it is time to scrap the DoD-centered combatant command structures altogether in favor of interagency commands. In an insightful article in *Joint Force Quarterly*, which laid out this argument in detail in 2009, Brigadier General Jeffrey Buchanan of the U.S. Army, Captain Maxie Davis of the U.S. Navy, and Colonel Lee Wright of the U.S. Air Force assert that this change would offer at least three benefits. In their view, these benefits would include an increase in unity of effort across agencies, improved professional development across all of the organizations, and a heightened willingness of some foreign partners to work with the U.S. Government.[16] However, for a variety of practical reasons, the unified command plan and the DoD should remain the primary vehicles for the delivery of American national power. The DoD is the U.S. Government's primary operational arm, equipped by culture, resources, and operational and planning capability to carry out operations across the full spectrum of activity. Unlike other agencies and departments, the DoD features the capability to operate in any security environment. Lastly, from a political perspective, it is hard to imagine a scenario in which lawmakers dismantle the combatant commands to hand broad authority to agencies or departments without that same capability, except in some limited cases, such as reconstruction and development, in which the required capabilities are not a natural fit with the DoD warfighting function. Instead, any reforms should augment and build upon the strengths of the existing unified command structures, while taking full advantage of DoD's operational and planning culture and the department's already robust capabilities.

COMPLEMENTARY REFORMS: BROADER INSTITUTIONAL MEASURES

From a broader institutional perspective, there are a number of associated and complementary measures that will be necessary to achieve the broader goals of this reform effort. From the start, any feasible and desirable interagency solution must give leaders in the field operational control over interagency personnel and the subject matter experts that each agency develops, during the period in which they are assigned to that command. At the same time, other complementary reforms will have to overcome the general inability of other-than-DoD agencies and departments to operate in non-permissive environments, as well as the lack of the formal education and training opportunities for key leaders in other-than-DoD organizations, and the lack of decentralized budget authority, or the authority to direct other agency personnel and resources. Likewise, these complementary reforms will be aimed directly at overcoming the lack of interagency promotion and career service incentives among many agencies and departments, along with the lack of statutory leverage of those agencies and departments to compel that service.

From a broader institutional perspective, these complementary reforms will also need to change the mindset and practice of national-level interagency interactions that are focused on budget share and jurisdiction, as well as the disproportionate distribution of resources that limits the effectiveness of other than military instruments of national power, while overemphasizing the military instrument of power. As another facet of these challenges, changes at the broader institutional level must also shift contractor contracts that pay for process into more effective contracts that require results or specific outcomes. Agencies and departments must also revamp their centralized budgetary execution and approval processes, both to give more latitude to leaders in the field and to bring those processes more in line with the capabilities needed in the field. Along these same lines, the broader institutional reforms must feature the implementation of coherent, complete, and precise forcing functions, or measures of progress, for the enforcement of accountability.

Perhaps not surprisingly, given congressional control over budgeting, authorizing, and the appropriations processes, the primary vehicle for achieving any rebalancing of resources or the concurrent enforcement of accountability for results will need to focus on reforms of the congressional oversight structures and processes. In addition to reorganizing their own internal committee structures to make them more holistic and interagency-centered in form and function, these committees would also be more effective if the corresponding subcommittees mirrored the alignment of their executive branch equivalents by function, geography, and (possibly) presidential priority. Along similar lines, the national leadership must also identify and assign specific goals for improved interagency performance and then hold those agencies accountable for achieving these goals.

Specifically, the first step in this process will be for the executive branch leadership—most importantly the President—to place major leader emphasis on the goal of achieving cooperative unity of effort, but it is clear from the results of previous presidential policy directives in that vein that command emphasis by itself will not be enough. Instead, a related complementary reform will have to give agencies operational control over other agency personnel if the U.S. Government is to realize true unity of vision and effort, just as each agency and department must be directed to develop the organic interagency, nation-building, and irregular warfare expertise needed to meet each organization's responsibilities in these areas.

At the same time, concurrent complementary reforms will need to involve the creation of professional career incentives and opportunities for interagency service, with demonstrated effectiveness in those assignments leading to promotion and advancement into senior positions of responsibility. Agencies and departments will have to undertake some reorganization and development within their staffs to provide adequate personnel depth to meet the requirements of these interagency operations and functions. Not the least of these developmental requirements will involve the creation of mechanisms for training and professionally educating key leaders and staff in interagency, nation-building, and irregular warfare responsibilities, along with mandating participation in that training.

More broadly, complementary reforms will also need to include a statutory redirection of agency and department incentives from their internal processes, agendas, and goals to national security goals. Likewise, these reforms will also need to bring about the realignment of the geographic areas of responsibility and operational and functional subdivisions of all the agencies and departments of the U.S. Government, with national security responsibilities, to create a common operating picture and common functionality. Additionally, each agency and department will have to be directed toward the development and maintenance of enduring professional expertise among the various agencies and departments corresponding to that geographic and functional realignment, including in-house subject matter expertise related to the key countries, regions, transnational actors, functions, and operations.

Speaking of this need in particular, the USJFCOM commander—formerly the senior DoD leader for interagency study and development—notes, "The joint force will need patient, persistent, and culturally savvy people to build the local relationships and partnerships essential to executing irregular warfare."[17] The same is true for all agencies and departments with significant roles in these affairs. Accordingly, these complementary reforms must also include the redirection of sufficient resources to enable other-than-DoD agencies and departments to carry out their nation-building and irregular warfare functions. In the same way, the reforms must achieve a decentralization of budget execution, giving funding control to leaders at levels directly in contact with the problems being solved, subject to strict oversight and accountability and severe sanctions for any fraud, waste, or abuse.

Likewise, these complementary reforms must also include the development and adoption of administrative mechanisms that give other agency leaders in the field the leverage that comes from contributing directly and substantively to the performance evaluations of the other agency personnel assigned to their operational control. Another complementary reform should include the revision of job descriptions and employee contracts to give other-than-DoD agencies and departments the ability to assign certain key and essential employees to serve in overseas postings and in non-permissive security environments, when designated for such service, after adequate training and preparation. Other complementary reforms will need to include the adjustment of standard operating procedures within the interagency coordinating bodies at the various levels of national security activity and organizational guidelines to require agency and departmental participation, balancing the bottom-up activities of those groups with top-down direction from the key leaders.

Ultimately, any real transformation to create unified action will have to include "right-sizing," or reapportioning resources to give overmatched agencies such as State the chance to participate effectively across the breadth of activities relevant to our aggressive foreign policy objectives. Strategic thinker Joseph Cerami also suggests the need for systematic training and an education program for interagency professionals, along with a requirement for formal interagency knowledge management processes—including data bases, online courses, simulation networks, pre-deployment training and certification, leader development, subject matter networks, and an interactive center for interagency lessons learned.[18] Other careful observers of American government have also suggested a wholesale need to restructure contractor contracts to make them outcome-driven rather than input-driven.[19] To facilitate the sharing of interagency and irregular warfare lessons learned across agencies, it will be wise to create a national security clearinghouse for interagency lessons learned similar to the Center for Army Lessons Learned (CALL) in the Army. The S/CRS is the lead for creating such a knowledge center, but it is probably more appropriate to include this function in the NSC redesign, to avoid any potential agency parochialism.

While some of these types of professional developmental initiatives are already underway in some cases, almost all of them are wholly voluntary in nature and very limited in scope. We clearly need to take more of a hands-on approach if we are to solve problems. In fact, this reform effort will require creating significant career incentives, ranging from promotions to awards to financial incentives and professional educational opportunities, for the deployable personnel from the DoD and the other key agencies who become the cadre of specialists in nation-building, irregular warfare, interagency planning and operations, and humanitarian assistance and development. Of course, achieving this organizational change will not be an easy task. In fact, Wilson observes that U.S. agencies typically move in the opposite direction in their personnel practices. Due to promotion considerations, a desire for balanced experience throughout the force, and a perceived need to distribute opportunities fairly, Wilson notes, "U.S. agencies distribute assignments in ways that seem to minimize the chance for key employees to become expert in their tasks."[20] However, if the U.S. Government is to become more effective and efficient in these increasingly common tasks, we must do the heavy lifting required to make those changes happen.

IMPLEMENTATION: ENABLING LEGISLATION, EXECUTIVE ORDERS, AND A BOTTOM-UP REVIEW

In a very broad sense, there are essentially three strategic approaches that the United States could take in seeking to improve its strategic and interagency performance in national security affairs. The first of these, and the one that is most likely to occur from a political perspective, given entrenched bureaucratic and political interests, basically represents making largely cosmetic changes to the status quo. These approaches emphasize enlightened leadership, periodic and typically modest presidential reorganizational initiatives—usually without any serious redirection of resources—and equally modest increases in capacity, such as the creation of superimposed bureaucratic structures to continue to muddle through the application of the instruments of national power.

Another approach would entail more radical changes—changes that would reach aggressively into the existing agencies and departments to redirect resources, change mandates, and start from scratch. As likely to occur as the first status quo option is, this radical change option is just as unlikely to occur. Though seemingly radical in some respects, the package of reforms recommended here actually represents a more incremental, though still substantial, approach. This is an approach that would not be easy to enact, but does preserve most of the existing organizational resources of the component agencies and departments. This approach, which represents significant yet largely additive changes while emphasizing cross-fertilization and building organizational incentive and capability, provides the possibility of real and substantive change while mitigating some of the likely sources of political and bureaucratic opposition, as well as some of the practical obstacles to feasibility.

From a historical perspective, changes of this magnitude are somewhat rare, but not without precedent. Just as Goldwater-Nichols redefined the relationships among the services without altering the basic organizational structures of the component branches of the military, this reorganization will have to confront some outright opposition but stands a similar chance of adoption and successful implementation. The original reconfiguration of the American national security apparatus in the National Defense Act of 1947 faced its own challenges, and, of course, it will not be easy to make these changes happen either. In any event, this package of major reforms will have to be realized both through enabling legislation and presidential executive orders.

At the beginning of the Cold War in April of 1950, the United States published a 58-page document titled *NSC 68: U.S. Objectives and Programs for National Security*, outlining the specific objectives, organization, and resources directed toward meeting the security requirements of that time.[21] In addition to a new NSC-68, legislation will be required to equip the agencies with the personnel and funds to achieve the new strategic and interagency requirements while also compelling the other changes in those agencies that are needed to accomplish the other goals of the reforms. Ideally, these major changes will be implemented concurrently in order to achieve all of the intended effects, but this outcome may be too difficult to achieve.

As one model from an interagency perspective, the domestically-oriented Stafford Act directs federal Cabinet-level departments to "plan, prepare, and execute implementing operations," and there is currently no comparable act or directive that compels similar cooperation in foreign operations.[22] Clearly, however, any feasible way forward must fall within the bounds of practical and political constraints, obstacles, and limits. With all of the practical and political obstacles to successful implementation of this proposal in mind, creating USRADCOM—led by State or USAID—would actually help to overcome many of these bureaucratic and political impediments, as well as some of the practical questions of feasibility. Along similar lines, these reforms will likely be more palatable to other-than-DoD agencies and departments if the developing interagency talent is homegrown rather than imported. In other words, rather than bringing in a Colin Powell to lead State, these reforms will face less internal opposition if, instead, talented career diplomats with nation-building and humanitarian development and relief operations experience are selected for these key leader positions.

As a practical matter, a tricky part of the implementation of these proposals will involve the need to make them additive to the agencies and departments, while also confronting the reality of the Federal Government's massive budget deficit and the need to economize across the board. This challenge is certainly a significant one, but for any reform to have a realistic chance of achieving the coherence and integration that is needed with the U.S. Government, we will have to find a way to satisfy both requirements. Put another way, the national security budget is likely to be a zero-sum game, or worse, given the massive budget deficit and mounting U.S. debt. But from another perspective, this reality gives us even more reason to push to become more efficient. Secretary Robert Gates's recent decision to dismantle USJFCOM is an example of this need.

Accordingly, with all these considerations in mind, it will be necessary to conduct a bottom-up review of all of the agencies and departments involved in national security, with three related goals in mind. First, to achieve coherence in the process of generating strategy, it is necessary to understand exactly what capabilities and resources the various agencies of the

U.S. Government bring to the table. Second, to stand up any new structures or capabilities, it will likely be necessary to identify bill payers within the national security agencies to be able to afford the USRADCOM, the reconstruction and development experts, and the full-time interagency staff, who will be assigned to the combatant commands. Finally, if the U.S. Government is truly committed to achieving strategic coherence and unified effort among its component agencies and departments, this bottom-up review will serve another important purpose. As a result of this review, the roles and functions of each activity (and its assigned personnel) should be defined clearly as operators, planners, capabilities-providers, enablers, or sustainers—all corresponding directly to the specific capabilities required by the U.S. Government to exercise its instruments of national power. The question to be asked of the agencies and departments and their personnel is this: "How, exactly, do you contribute to U.S. national security?" Armed with the results, national-level decisionmakers can then craft feasible and coherent national strategies, while simultaneously making the hard choices needed to allocate our national resources in an efficient and sustainable way. As Admiral Mullen has noted, the status quo is not viable.

ACHIEVING STRATEGIC COHERENCE, BALANCE, AND UNITY OF EFFORT

Over the last several decades, the U.S. Government has strengthened its military instrument of national power at the clear expense of the other instruments of national power—diplomacy, information, and economic means. The major reform initiatives suggested in this book would reverse that trend, not in some arbitrary fashion but rather by providing systems and processes that will focus attention directly on creating the capabilities required to meet the emerging security threats of the 21st century. It is hard to argue against the fact that the U.S. military will remain the right vehicle for delivering American hard power in the non-permissive environments in which most nation-building and all irregular warfare operations occur, but equipping the military to achieve success in that mission cannot come at the expense of other soft power applications. Moreover, the package of reforms and the governmental reorganization suggested in this monograph would go a long way toward achieving a more balanced, coherent, and rational U.S. national security effort, enabling the American government to work more effectively and efficiently.

Without any doubt, this package of reforms will need to overcome a variety of political and practical obstacles to its implementation. At the same time, restructuring the geographic and functional combatant commands—coupled with the creation of a new functional interagency command with operational responsibility for reconstruction and development, led by a senior executive from USAID or State—will help to overcome some of the practical and political obstacles. However, we must find a way to get these reforms done. History and recent experience confirm that regardless of any claims or theories to the contrary, the only feasible path to a true interagency unity of effort is actual unity of command. Put even more directly, there is no feasible or effective substitute to executive authority than a unitary executive, expressing a clear statement of the commander's intent and holding the leverage of command authority to implement it. If our nation is to meet the dangerous and emerging threats of the 21st century, we must undertake the heavy lifting needed to reform our national security institutions to reflect this immutable and fundamental truth.

Finally, from the perspective of effective strategy formulation and interagency integration, the bottom line here is that incremental approaches similar to those taken since September 11, 2001 (9/11) will not succeed, because superimposed bureaucratic structures with all of the responsibility and none of the authority are likely to fail. Our nation ignores the basic and immutable principles of executive leadership outlined by Alexander Hamilton and others at its peril—principles that clearly apply in the nation-building and irregular warfare missions that will be increasingly prominent in the years to come. Complex schemes may sound attractive in theory, but they will not succeed in practice. Instead, effective interagency coordination and execution requires clear lines of authority, coherent systems, appropriate capabilities, and a common understanding of the tasks and objectives across the spectrum of agencies and departments.

ENDNOTES - CHAPTER 10

1. James Q. Wilson, *Bureaucracy: What Government Agencies Do and Why They Do It*, New York: Basic Books, 1989, p. 171.

2. *Ibid.*, pp. 31-49.

3. The 9-11 Commission, *The 9-11 Commission Report*, Washington, DC: U.S. Government Printing Office, January 26, 2004, p. 402, available from *www.9-11commission.gov/report/911Report.pdf*.

4. Project on National Security Reform, *Preliminary Findings*, Washington, DC: Center for the Study of the Presidency, July 2008, p. 52.

5. Catherine Dale, Nina Serafino, and Pat Towell, "Organizing the U.S. Government for National Security: Overview of the Interagency Reform Debates," *CRS Report for Congress*, RL34455, Washington, DC: Congressional Research Service, April 18, 2008, pp. 10-11.

6. Wilson, p. 95.

7. Cody M. Brown, *The National Security Council: A Legal History of the President's Most Powerful Advisers*, Washington, DC: The Project on National Security Reform, 2008, pp. 111-116.

8. John A. Nagl, *Institutionalizing Adaptation: It's Time for a Permanent Army Advisory Corps*, Washington, DC: Center for a New American Security, 2007.

9. James Madison et al., in Charles R. Kesler and Clinton Rossiter, eds., *The Federalist Papers*, New York: Penguin, 1999, p. 319.

10. David Osborne and Ted Gaebler, *Reinventing Government*, New York: Penguin, 1993, Chap. 6.

11. John A. Nagl, *Learning to Eat Soup with a Knife: Counterinsurgency Lessons from Malaya and Vietnam*, Chicago, IL: University of Chicago Press, 2005 Ed., p. xiii.

12. Osborne and Gaebler, Chap. 5.

13. Nagl, *Learning to Eat Soup with a Knife*, pp. 138-165.

14. Osborne and Gaebler, Chap 9.

15. See *Field Manual (FM) 100-11, Force Integration*, Washington, DC: Department of the Army, January 1998.

16. Jeffrey Buchanan, Maxie Davis, and Lee Wright, "Death of the Combatant Command? Toward a Joint Interagency Approach," *Joint Force Quarterly*, No. 52, 1st Quarter 2009, p. 96.

17. *Irregular Warfare (IW) Joint Operating Concept, Version 1.0*, Washington, DC: Department of Defense, September 11, 2007, p. 1.

18. Joseph R. Cerami, "What is to Be Done? Aligning and Integrating the Interagency Process in Support and Stability Operations," Chap. 17 in Joseph R. Cerami and Jay W. Boggs, eds., *The Interagency and Counterinsurgency Warfare: Stability, Security, Transition, and Reconstruction Roles*, Carlisle, PA: Strategic Studies Institute, U.S. Army War College, December 2007, pp. 562-564, available from *www.StrategicStudiesInstitute.army.mil*.

19. Osborne and Gaebler, Chap. 5.

20. Wilson, p. 171.

21. Zeb B. Bradford, Jr., and Frederic J. Brown, *America's Army: A Model for Interagency Effectiveness*, Westport, CT: Praeger, 2008, p. 205.

22. Scott R. Feil, "The Failure of Incrementalism: Interagency Coordination Challenges and Responses," Chap. 9 in Joseph R. Cerami and Jay W. Boggs, eds., *The Interagency and Counterinsurgency Warfare: Stability, Security, Transition, and Reconstruction Roles*, Carlisle, PA: Strategic Studies Institute, U.S. Army War College, December 2007, p. 294, available from *www.StrategicStudiesInstitute.army.mil*.

A BRIEF EPILOGUE: CONTEMPLATING THE CONTEXT AND FUTURE OF "NATION-BUILDING"

> In preparing for battle I have always found that plans are useless, but planning is indispensable.
>
> President Dwight Eisenhower[1]

Regardless of the eventual outcome of the mission in Afghanistan, there is no question that the United States must reflect carefully upon the lessons to be learned from our strategic and interagency struggles to build an Afghan nation. But while some readers might interpret this book as a warning against engaging in these operations under any circumstances, that is not the intent. Instead, the first point here is that our foreign policy decisionmakers must think longer and harder before committing to any future nation-building or irregular warfare operations, given their exhaustive scope, length, and expense. Likewise, policymakers cannot fail to address legitimate, first-order questions about the basic feasibility of nation-building operations in each unique set of circumstances, since the outcomes of these tough missions are by definition uncertain, even in the best of cases.

But even if the United States never takes on another nation-building mission—and that prospect is highly unlikely, given America's history—it is still imperative that we take the major steps needed to synchronize the effort and capabilities of the various organizations that comprise our national security system. Put another way, it is hard enough to operate in the international or coalitional settings that are increasingly common features of our foreign interventions, before adding any internal strategic and interagency impediments. So we must get our own house in order in any case, but this need becomes even more pressing if the United States intends to continue to try to "fix failed states."

If we accept history as our guide, it is more likely than not that we will again intervene in other countries' social, political, military, and economic affairs in the future, as foreign interventions on a larger or smaller scale have been a fairly routine feature of past American foreign policy. In fact, to put this type of mission into context, past large-scale irregular warfare or nation-building operations in the post-World War II era alone have included Germany, Japan, Somalia, Bosnia, Kosovo, Afghanistan, and Iraq.[2] Other missions of these types on a smaller scale have included relative successes in Panama and Grenada, as well as failures in Cambodia and Vietnam. Still other failed operations of this kind during the 20th century include: the Dominican Republic (twice), Cuba (three times before World War II), Nicaragua, Haiti (twice), and another pre-World War II operation in Panama.[3] In light of emerging global trends, analysts from the Institute for National Strategic Studies predict that it is likely we will undertake other similar nation-building and irregular warfare missions fairly commonly in the future.[4] But as significant as these endeavors are, we still have not yet created workable processes for strategy formulation and interagency integration that will routinely lead us to success.

At the same time, we must not forget that irregular warfare and nation-building are only part of the story. From a broader perspective, our nation must also be prepared for national security operations across the full spectrum of conflict. The world is rapidly becom-

ing a more dangerous and unpredictable place, and one in which the international system and its nation-state actors only constitute part of the relevant national security framework. Among other complicating factors, dangerous global trends include:
- A widening disparity of resources between the global rich and poor;
- Fluid and contested territorial boundaries and poorly secured or unsecured borders;
- The rising importance and threats associated with transnational terrorists, radical fundamentalist groups, and increasingly sophisticated criminal elements;
- Major demographic and environmental challenges, especially within the developing world;
- Increasing worldwide demand for food and fresh water;
- The likelihood of increasing proliferation of weapons of mass destruction;
- Pandemics and other public health crises;
- Our own growing reliance and dependence on cybertechnology;
- Unsustainable fiscal policies and mounting national and international debts; and,
- The declining resilience and reach of the institutions of the rule of law within many failing or failed states.[5]

All in all, these developments are not only cause for concern, but they also call into question the basic premise that the United States should engage in nation-building in the first place, given the diverse and transnational nature of modern security threats. Put another way, in this age of growing and more dangerous transnational threats that are just as or more dangerous that those posed by nation-states, it is not clear that the return on that strategic option is worth the cost or risk. We do not want to succeed in nation-building somewhere, only to fail from a broader strategic perspective somewhere else.

Likewise, we cannot forget the significant opportunity costs and strategic risks that come with using military power, among them considerations of economic strength, international goodwill, and political capital. Given that the ultimate outcomes in nation-building are uncertain—as evidenced by Afghan President Karzai's willingness to deal with Iran when unhappy with U.S. actions—we must define realistic and attainable objectives entailing calculated and acceptable risks. To succeed in any future nation-building and irregular warfare operations, we must choose carefully, understand the problem, commit the appropriate resources, and convince the American people and our allies of the necessity and desirability of the nation-building option. Policymakers must set national security objectives that match the realities of the situation, after careful analysis of the problem. The United States cannot do everything everywhere, so we must tailor our national security objectives to the "necessary" and "feasible," rather than the "desired" and the "optimal." In this sense, we need to get back into the habit of doing means- and risk-constrained strategy, rather than making ideologically driven or hastily considered policy choices that entail long-term commitments and exorbitant costs.

Similarly, although the United States has a clear interest in promoting democracy and our other core values, we must revisit the "liberal democratic peace theory" that currently underpins our foreign policy and our national security strategy. It has become clear that we cannot afford to achieve these outcomes solely by force of arms, just as we have found ourselves both unprepared to absorb the high costs of these lengthy missions and lacking in the right balance of resources and capabilities needed to succeed in them. In one sense, we need to work smarter and more selectively rather than harder, and it is important that we enter into these missions only after taking a more realistic long-haul approach, rather than assuming away problems or accepting challenges that are nearly intractable in some cases. We must be both smarter and more efficient, or we risk achieving success in building other nations, only to undermine the health of our own.

At the same time, while our nation has run into major challenges in its attempt to use the military instrument of national power to impose a democratic solution to regime problems in Iraq and Afghanistan, there are still a number of evident advantages to democracy promotion that argue for its inclusion as a central and durable component of U.S. policy. Liberal international relations theories hold that democratic regimes are inherently more stable and peaceful than authoritarian systems.[6] As an extension of this line of thinking, democratic peace theorists assert that democracies may go to war as often as other nation-states, but that they are far less likely to fight one another.[7] A corollary to this school of thought focuses on economic interdependence. Other scholars challenge the theory's validity on the basis of limited long-term evidence and a potential influence of post-World War II neorealists and anti-Soviet free-state coalition building among democratic countries.[8] However, this theory promises attractive advantages for democracy promotion as policy, if the theory, in fact, survives empirical scrutiny intact.

Similarly, democracy promotion holds the potential to help create viable middle classes within the successfully reforming countries, thus making the odds of political moderation and peace more likely, in accordance with democratic peace and economic interdependence theory. Democracy promotion could also help to achieve basic civil rights for religious and ethnic minorities, women, and other disenfranchised or persecuted segments of Middle Eastern and Central Asian societies, an outcome that clearly would be consistent with stated U.S. foreign policy objectives and U.S. national interests. This strategy could also foster democratic debate and deliberation within governments in the region, thus affording these countries better opportunities to achieve representative and public interest-minded policy choices.

Conversely, however, there are also potential disadvantages associated with democracy promotion as a central component of U.S. policy. Since Islamists tend toward nonsecular, religion-centered governance, the resulting Islamic democracies may resemble Iran's de facto theocracy. These quasi-democracies place the real power of government into the hands of Islamic religious leaders, often those least likely to seek constructive ways to work out differences with the United States. The demographic challenges of the average Middle Eastern or Central Asian country and their Islamic cultural norms also might make them especially susceptible to Tocqueville's "tyranny of the majority," or the routine abuse of minority interests and human rights at the hands of the dominant majority.

Such a tyranny sets the conditions for continuing civil unrest and unstable regimes. Or, as strategic thinker Larry Goodson points out, "Real elections in the region produce Islamist governments."[9] Accordingly, we must "be careful what we wish for," as currently secular or stable authoritarian governments can become extremist through democratic reforms that result in radical Islamic control and anti-American demagoguery. Furthermore, heavy-handedness on our part could open the door for energy competitors, such as China, the European Union, Japan, and India to strengthen their relations with the countries of the region at our expense. So democracy might be currently incompatible with the existing authoritarian social and political cultures of the Middle East and Central Asia, especially given the prevalent norms of patriarchy and the ideology of Islam.[10] Along these lines, Iran provides another clear example of the limits of democracy promotion as a panacea for the protection of U.S. interests in the region.

Expanding on this theme, Iran's government is nominally democratic, but it is really a quasi-democratic theocracy, with the real power in the country in the hands of religious leaders unfriendly to the West. Iran's popularly elected President and Parliament are ultimately checked in their ability to govern by the controlling Shiite clergy.[11] Furthermore, the public face of the Iranian democracy is President Ahmadinejad, who came to power on the basis of his hard-line conservative views.[12] Ahmadinejad is well known for his inflammatory, anti-American rhetoric, which has served him effectively as a domestic political tool to rally Iranian public opinion around his hard-line policies. Iran is another largely homogenous society, dominated by its nearly 90 percent Shiite faction. Described as pluralistic rather than democratic, Iran represents a logical form of democracy for an Islamic country, with modest democratic institutions dominated by the Islamic religious leadership.[13] Iran also demonstrates the potential longer-term dangers of supporting even moderate authoritarian regimes, as the United States suffered a backlash in the aftermath of the Iranian revolution of 1979 when the U.S.-backed Shah was removed from power. Applying a longer-term perspective, however, the democratic governing mechanisms in Iran, though impotent, may offer an opportunity for engagement and leverage in bringing about a favorable relationship in the future. The recent U.S. and North Atlantic Treaty Organization (NATO) assistance to the Libyan rebels provides another potentially successful model.

Viewed in the aggregate then, democracy promotion may in fact represent a viable longer-term strategic objective, but in some cases it may not be either wholly feasible or completely consistent with U.S. interests in the short- and medium-terms. For example, analyst James Russell has identified a wide variety of potential economic, environmental, and geopolitical risks associated with hard power regime change strategies, among them oil shocks, major budget deficits, fresh water problems, and international terrorism.[14] Given the inherent complexity of nation-building, as well as the wide variation in regimes, interests, demographics, and existing political cultures, the United States should use its full range of instruments of national power to protect its interests, but take a long-range and less-aggressive approach to democracy promotion. We can apply informational, diplomatic, and economic pressures gently but firmly — and consistently and in a measured way — to achieve this long-term strategic objective, doing so in ways that will not adversely affect other aspects of those strategic relationships.

In closing, we must embrace and acknowledge

the lessons of history and the realities of human nature and human organizations, if we are to succeed in these incredibly complex, challenging, and vitally important missions. There will likely come another time when U.S. policymakers, having carefully weighed the interests, risks, opportunities, options, and costs of the situation, decide that nation-building—whether limited or comprehensive in scope, and whether by force of arms or not—is consistent with U.S. national security interests. When that time comes, we must be prepared to carry out these missions more efficiently and more effectively than we have to date, in order to achieve a higher probability of success. We simply cannot afford to maintain the U.S. Government's disjointed and disunified status quo.

ENDNOTES - EPILOGUE

1. Quoted in Richard M. Nixon, *Six Crises*, New York: Doubleday Publishing, 1962.

2. Hans Binnendijk and Stuart E. Johnson, eds., *Transforming for Stabilization and Reconstruction Operations*, Washington, DC: National Defense University Press, 2004, pp. 4-5.

3. *Ibid.*, p. 117.

4. Stephen J. Flanagan and James A. Schear, eds., *Strategic Challenges: America's Global Security Agenda*, Washington, DC: Institute for National Security Studies (INSS), National Defense University Press, 2008, p. 142.

5. For analysis of these trends, see *The Joint Operating Environment (JOE) 2008*, Norfolk, VA: U.S. Joint Forces Command, November 25, 2008.

6. Stephen M. Walt, "International Relations: One World, Many Theories," *Foreign Policy*, Vol. 110, Spring 1998, p. 32.

7. *Ibid.*, p. 39.

8. *Ibid.*

9. Larry P. Goodson, "Things Change and Things Stay the Same," Text of a U.S. Army War College Presentation, Carlisle, PA: U.S. Army War College, 2006, pp. 1-7.

10. Graham E. Fuller, "Islamists in the Arab World: The Dance Around Democracy," *The Carnegie Papers*, Washington, DC: Carnegie Endowment for International Peace, 2004, pp. 4-5.

11. Robin Surratt, ed., "Iran," *The Middle East*, 11th Ed., Washington, DC: CQ Press, 2007, p. 235.

12. *Ibid.*

13. *Ibid.*, p. 239.

14. James A. Russell, *Regional Threats and Security Strategy: The Troubling Case of Today's Middle East*, Carlisle, PA: Strategic Studies Institute, U.S. Army War College, 2007, p. 5.

BIBLIOGRAPHY

"A New Strategy for Afghanistan and Pakistan," *The Briefing Room-The Blog*, blog post on White House public site posted March 27, 2009, available from *www.whitehouse.gov*.

Afsar, Shahid, Chris Samples, and Thomas Wood, "The Taliban: An Organizational Analysis," *Military Review*, May-June 2008.

Appathurai, James, *Afghanistan Report 2009*, Brussels, Belgium: The North Atlantic Treaty Organization (NATO), 2009.

Ashraf, Khalid, *The Tribal Peoples of West Pakistan*, Peshawar, Pakistan: Peshawar University, 1962.

Ayoob, Mohammed, "Political Islam: Image and Reality," *World Policy Journal*, Vol. 21, Fall 2004.

Bacevich, Andrew J., *The Limits of Power*, New York: Holt and Company, 2008.

Barno, David W., "Challenges in Fighting a Global Insurgency," *Parameters*, Summer 2006.

Barron, Bryton, *Inside the State Department: A Candid Appraisal of the Bureaucracy*, New York: Comet Press Books, 1956.

Bartholomees, Jr., J. Boone, ed., *U.S. Army War College Guide to National Security Policy and Strategy*, 2nd Ed., Carlisle, PA: Strategic Studies Institute, U.S. Army War College, June 2006.

Bebber, Robert J., "The Role of Provincial Reconstruction Teams in Counterinsurgency Operations," *Small Wars Journal* online, posted on November 10, 2008, available from *smallwarsjournal.com*.

Belasco, Amy, *The Cost of Iraq, Afghanistan, and Other GWOT Operations Since 9/11*, Washington, DC: Congressional Research Service, RL33110, May 15, 2009.

Benjamin, Daniel, and Steven Simon, *The Next Attack*, New York: Holt, 2006.

Binnendijk, Hans, and Stuart E. Johnson, eds., *Transforming for Stabilization and Reconstruction Operations*, Washington, DC: National Defense University Press, 2004.

Blanchard, Christopher M., *Afghanistan: Narcotics and U.S. Policy*, Washington, DC: Congressional Research Service, CRS 7-5700, August 12, 2009.

Blank, Stephen, "The Strategic Importance of Central Asia: An American View," *Parameters*, Vol. 38, No. 1, Spring 2008.

Blood, Peter R. ed., *Afghanistan: Past and Present*, Los Angeles, CA: IndoEuropean Publishing, 2007.

Bradford, Jr., Zeb B., and Frederic J. Brown., *America's Army: A Model for Interagency Effectiveness*, Westport, CT: Praeger, 2008.

Brown, Cody M., *The National Security Council: A Legal History of the President's Most Powerful Advisers*, Washington, DC: The Project on National Security Reform, 2008.

Buchanan, Jeffrey, Maxie Davis, and Lee Wright, "Death of the Combatant Command? Toward a Joint Interagency Approach," *Joint Force Quarterly*, No. 52, 1st Quarter 2009, p. 96.

Bush, President George W., *National Strategy to Combat Weapons of Mass Destruction*, Washington, DC: U.S. Government Printing Office, December 2002.

Butler, Desmond, "U.S. to Subsidize Afghan Training for Years," *The Pittsburgh Post-Gazette*, September 7, 2010, p. A-3.

Cancian, Mark, "Contractors: The New Element of Military Force Structure," *Parameters*, Vol. 38, No. 3, Autumn 2008.

Cerami, Joseph R., and Jay W. Boggs, eds., *The Interagency and Counterinsurgency Warfare: Stability, Security, Transition, and Reconstruction Roles*, Carlisle, PA: Strategic Studies Institute, U.S. Army War College, December 2007, pp. 289-290, available from *www.StrategicStudiesInstitute.army.mil*.

Chairman, Joint Chiefs of Staff, *Joint Publication 1-0: Doctrine for the Armed Forces of the United States,* Washington, DC: Joint Chiefs of Staff, May 14, 2007.

Chandrasekaran, Rajiv, "A New Plan for Afghanistan," *The Washington Post Weekly,* June 29, 2009.

Chandrasekaran, Rajiv, "General Petraeus Says Afghanistan War Strategy 'Fundamentally Sound'," *The Washington Post* on-line edition, August 16, 2010, available from *www.washingtonpost.com.*

Chandrasekaran, Rajiv, "Nobody Wants to Tell Us Anything," *The Washington Post National Weekly Ed.,* March 23-29.

Chandrasekaran, Rajiv, "Sticker Shock," *The Washington Post National Weekly Ed.,* October 12-18, 2009.

Chayes, Sarah, *The Punishment of Virtue: Inside Afghanistan After the Taliban,* New York: Penguin, 2006.

Cole, August, "U.S. Adding Contractors at Fast Pace," *The Wall Street Journal* on-line edition, December 2, 2009, available from *www.wsj.com.*

Coll, Steve, *Ghost Wars: The Secret History of the CIA, Afghanistan, and Bin Laden, From the Soviet Invasion to September 10, 2001,* New York: Penguin, 2005.

Collins, Joseph J., *Choosing War: The Decision to Invade Iraq and Its Aftermath,* Washington, DC: National Defense University/Institute for National Strategic Studies, April 2008.

Collins, Joseph J., *Understanding War in Afghanistan.* Washington, DC: National Defense University Press, 2011.

Constable, Pamela, "A Modernized Taliban," *The Washington Post National Weekly Ed.,* September 29-October 5, 2006.

Cordesman, Anthony H., "Afghanistan, Iraq, and Self-Inflicted Wounds," unpublished presentation, Washington, DC: Center for Strategic and International Studies, October 2007.

Cordesman, Anthony H., "The Afghan War--Part Three: Implementing the New Strategy," Burke Chair in Strategy publication from the Center for Strategic and International Studies, Washington, DC, September 8, 2010, p. 16, available from *csis.org/files/publication/100909_AfghanWarStatus-III_Strategy.pdf*.

Cordesman, Anthony H., "The Missing Metrics of 'Progress' in Afghanistan (and Pakistan)," unpublished manuscript from the Center for Strategic and International Studies, Washington, DC, November 29, 2007.

Council on Foreign Relations, *In Support of Arab Democracy: Why and How*, New York: Council on Foreign Relations, 2005.

Crews, Robert D., and Amin Tarzi, eds., *The Taliban and the Crisis of Afghanistan*, Cambridge, MA: Harvard, 2008.

Dale, Catherine, "Building an Interagency Cadre of National Security Professionals: Proposals, Recent Experience, and Issues for Congress," *CRS Report for Congress*, Washington, DC: CRS, RL 34565, July 8, 2008.

Dale, Catherine, Nina Serafino, and Pat Towell, "Organizing the U.S. Government for National Security: Overview of the Interagency Reform Debates," *CRS Report for Congress*, Washington, DC: CRS, RL34455, April 18, 2008.

Deeb, Marius, "In the Middle East, Oil Rules," *SAISPHERE*, 2005.

Dempsey, Gary, "The Folly of Nation-Building in Afghanistan," *CATO Institute On-line*, available from *www.cato.org*.

Department of Defense, *DOD Directive 3000.05: Military Support for Stability, Security, Transition, and Reconstruction (SSTR) Operations*, Washington, DC: Department of Defense, November 28, 2005.

Department of Defense, *DOD Instruction 3000.05: Stability Operations*, Washington, DC: Department of Defense, September 2009.

Department of Defense, *Irregular Warfare (IW) Joint Operating Concept, Version 1.0,* Washington, DC: Department of Defense, September 11, 2007.

Department of Defense, *Joint Publication 1-0: Doctrine for the Armed Forces of the United States,* Washington, DC: Department of Defense, May 14, 2007.

Department of Defense, *Joint Publication 3-0: Joint Operations,* Washington, DC: Department of Defense, September 17, 2006 with Change 1 as of February 13, 2008.

Department of Defense, *Joint Publication 3-08: Interagency, Intergovernmental Organization, and Nongovernmental Organization Coordination During Joint Operations, Vol. II,* Washington, DC: Department of Defense, March 17, 2006.

Department of Defense, *Joint Publication 5-0: Joint Operation Planning,* Washington, DC: Department of Defense, December 26, 2006.

Department of Defense, *Progress toward Security and Stability in Afghanistan: April 2010 Report to Congress in accordance with the 2008 National Defense Authorization Act,* Washington, DC: Department of Defense, April 2010.

Department of Defense, *Progress toward Security and Stability in Afghanistan: June 2009 Report to Congress in accordance with the 2008 National Defense Authorization Act,* Washington, DC: Department of Defense, June 2009.

Department of Defense, *Report on Progress Toward Security and Stability in Afghanistan and United States Plan for Sustaining the Afghanistan National Security Forces,* Washington, DC: Department of Defense, April 2011.

Department of the Army, *Field Manual 3-0: Operations,* Washington, DC: Department of the Army, February 2008.

Department of the Army, *Field Manual 3-24: Counterinsurgency Field Manual,* Chicago, IL: University of Chicago Press, 2007.

Department of the Army, *Field Manual 100-11, Force Integration*, January 1998.

DeYoung, Karen, "A More Nimble Approach," *The Washington Post National Weekly Ed.*, February 16-22, 2009.

DeYoung, Karen, "A Puzzle for Congress," *The Washington Post National Weekly Ed.*, December 7-13, 2009.

DeYoung, Karen, and Joby Warrick, "Change Comes to Pakistan," *The Washington Post National Weekly Ed.*, August 13-19, 2007.

Diamond, Larry, and Leonardo Morlino, "The Quality of Democracy: An Overview," *Journal of Democracy*, Vol. 15, No. 4, October 2004.

Dobbins, James F., *After the Taliban: Nation-Building in Afghanistan*, Washington, DC: Potomac, 2008.

Doyle, Richard B., "The U.S. National Security Strategy: Policy, Politics, and Problems," *Public Administration Review*, July/August 2007.

Elkins, Dexter, "For Afghans, a Price for Everything," originally published in *The New York Times* and subsequently reprinted in *The Pittsburgh Post-Gazette* on January 2, 2009.

Ewans, Martin, *Afghanistan: A Short History of Its People and Politics*, New York: HarperCollins Press, 2002.

Ewans, Martin, *Conflict in Afghanistan: Studies in Asymmetric Warfare*, London, UK: Routledge, 2005.

Fact Sheet: U.S. State Department Structure and Organization, available from *dosfan.lib.uic.edu/ERC/about/fact_sheets/950526str.html*.

Feaver, Peter, "Has Change Come to the National Security Council?" *Foreign Policy* on-line, May 27, 2009, available from *shadow.foreignpolicy.com*.

Flanagan, Stephen J., and James A. Schear, eds., *Strategic Challenges: America's Global Security Agenda*, Washington, DC: INSS/ National Defense University Press, 2008.

Fuller, Graham E., "Islamists in the Arab World: The Dance Around Democracy," *The Carnegie Papers*, Washington, DC: Carnegie Endowment for International Peace, 2004.

Gates, Secretary Robert M., *National Defense Strategy*, Washington, DC: Department of Defense, June 2008.

Gause III, F. Gregory, "Urgent: How to Reform Saudi Arabia without Handing It to Extremists," *Foreign Policy*, Vol. 144, September/October 2004.

Ghani, Ashraf, and Clare Lockhart, *Fixing Failed States*, Oxford, UK: Oxford University Press, 2008.

Giustozzi, Antonio, *Koran, Kalashnikov and Laptop: The Neo-Taliban Insurgency in Afghanistan*, London, UK: Hurst, 2007.

Gohari, M. J., *The Taliban: Ascent to Power*, Oxford, UK: Oxford University Press, 2000.

Goodson, Larry P., *Afghanistan's Endless War*, Seattle, WA: University of Washington Press, 2001.

Goodson, Larry P., "Things Change and Things Stay the Same," text of a U.S. Army War College presentation, Carlisle, PA, 2006.

Gray, Colin S. *Irregular Enemies and the Essence of Strategy: Can the American Way of War Adapt?* Carlisle, PA: Strategic Studies Institute, U.S. Army War College, March 2006.

Griffiths, J.C., *Afghanistan*, New York: Praeger, 1967.

Halliday, Fred, *Arabs and Persians: Beyond the Geopolitics of the Gulf*, Paris, France: French Associations of the Eastern Mediterranean and Turkish-Persian World, No. 22, July-December 1996.

Hamilton, Alexander *et al.*, in Charles R. Kesler and Clinton Rossiter, eds., *The Federalist Papers*, New York: Penguin, 1999.

Herbst, John, Coordinator for Reconstruction and Stabilization, prepared testimony given before the Subcommittee on Oversight and Investigation of the House Armed Services Committee, October 30, 2007.

Herbst, John, Prepared statement for testimony before the House Committee on Armed Services, February 26, 2008.

Hoagland, Jim, "Poppies vs. Power in Afghanistan," *The Washington Post Weekly*, January 20, 2008.

Irwin, Lew, "Filling Irregular Warfare's Interagency Gaps," *Parameters*, Vol. 39, No. 3, Autumn 2009.

Irwin, Lewis G., "Irregular Warfare Lessons Learned: Reforming the Afghan National Police," *Joint Force Quarterly*, Issue 52, 1st Quarter 2009.

Jalali, Ali A., "Afghanistan: Regaining Momentum," *Parameters*, Vol. 37, No. 4, Winter 2007-08.

Johnson, Charles Michael, Congressional testimony on GAO's "Afghanistan Security: U.S. Efforts to Develop Capable Afghan Police Forces Face Challenges and Need a Coordinated, Detailed Plan to Help Ensure Accountability," June 18, 2008, published as *GAO Report GAO-08-883T*, Washington, DC: GAO, 2008.

Johnson, Thomas H., and M. Chris Mason, "Understanding the Taliban and Insurgency in Afghanistan, *Orbis*, Winter 2007.

Joint Warfare Center, *JWFC Pamphlet 6: Doctrinal Implications of the Joint Interagency Coordination Group (JIACG)*, Norfolk, VA: Joint Warfare Center, June 27, 2004.

Jones, Seth G., *Counterinsurgency in Afghanistan*, Santa Monica, CA: Rand Corporation's National Defense Research Institute Press, 2008.

Jordan, Amos A. et al., *American National Security*, 5th Ed., Baltimore, MD: Johns Hopkins University Press, 1999.

Kaplan, Fred, "The Transformer," *Foreign Policy*, September/October 2010.

Katzman, Kenneth, *Afghanistan: Current Issues and U.S. Policy*, Washington, DC: CRS Report for Congress, RL30588, August 27, 2003.

Katzman, Kenneth, *Afghanistan: Politics, Elections, and Government Performance*, Washington, DC: CRS, CRS Report RS21922, August 28, 2009.

Katzman, Kenneth, *Afghanistan: Post-Taliban Governance, Security, and U.S. Policy*, Washington, DC: CRS, CRS Report RL30588, November 10, 2009.

Kerr, Paul, and Mary Beth Nikitin, "Pakistan's Nuclear Weapons: Proliferation and Security Issues," *CRS Report for Congress RL34248*, Washington, DC: U.S. Government Printing Office, January 14, 2008.

Kingdon, John W., *Agendas, Alternatives, and Public Policies*, 2nd Ed., New York: Pearson, 1997.

Lewis, Bernard, "The Roots of Muslim Rage, *The Atlantic Monthly*, Vol. 266, September 1990.

Maley, William, *Rescuing Afghanistan*, Sydney, Australia: University of New South Wales Press, 2006.

Matinuddin, Kamal, *The Taliban Phenomenon: Afghanistan 1994-1997*, Cambridge, UK: Oxford, 1999.

Mazzetti. Mark, and David E. Sanger, "Obama Expands Missile Strikes Inside Pakistan," *The New York Times*, February 21, 2009, available from *www.nytimes.com*.

McCaffrey, General Barry R., "After Action Report: Visit to Kuwait and Afghanistan, 10-18 November 2009," unpublished memorandum, West Point, NY: Department of Social Sciences, U.S. Military Academy, December 5, 2009.

McCaffrey, General Barry R., "After Action Report: Visit to NATO SHAPE HQ and Afghanistan, 21-26 July 2008," unpublished memorandum, West Point, NY: Department of Social Sciences, U.S. Military Academy, July 30, 2008.

McChrystal, Stanley A., *COMISAF'S Initial Assessment*, Kabul, Afghanistan: International Security Force Headquarters, August 30, 2009.

McMichael, William H., "Afghanistan Withdrawal in '11 Could Be a Problem, Critics Say," *The Army Times*, December 14, 2009.

Metz, Steven, "New Challenges and Old Concepts: Understanding 21st Century Insurgency," *Parameters*, Vol. 37, No. 4, Winter 2007-08.

Morgan, Matthew J., *A Democracy is Born: An Insider's Account of the Battle Against Terrorism in Afghanistan*, Westport, CT: Praeger, 2007.

Nagl, John A., *Learning to Eat Soup with a Knife: Counterinsurgency Lessons from Malaya and Vietnam*, Chicago, IL: University of Chicago Press, 2005 Ed.

Nagl, John A., *Institutionalizing Adaptation: It's Time for a Permanent Army Advisory Corps*, Washington, DC: Center for a New American Security, 2007.

Nawaz, Shuja, *Crossed Swords: Pakistan, Its Army, and the Wars Within*, Cambridge, UK: Oxford, 2008.

Naylor, Sean, *Not a Good Day to Die: The Untold Story of Operation Anaconda*, New York: Berkely, 2005.

Neufeldt, Victoria, ed., *Webster's New World College Dictionary*, 3rd Ed., New York: MacMillan, 1996.

Norland, Rod, "Afghan Strategy Shifts to Accent Civilian Projects," *The New York Times*, June 9, 2010, p. A1.

Norland, Rob, "With Raw Recruits, Afghan Police Buildup Falters," *The New York Times* on-line Ed., February 2, 2010, available from *www.nytimes.com*.

"Obama: Safety of World at Stake in Afghanistan," *CNN.com* report, available from *www.cnn.com*.

"Obama Seeks Record $708 Billion in FY11 Defense Budget," *Reuters* on-line Ed., available from *www.reuters.com/article/ idUSN0118167420100201*.

Office of the Coordinator for Reconstruction and Stabilization, "Preventing and Responding to Conflict: A New Approach," April 2009 presentation available from *www.CivilianResponseCorps.gov*.

Office of the Special Representative for Afghanistan and Pakistan, *Afghanistan and Pakistan Regional Stabilization Strategy*, Washington, DC: U.S. Government Printing Office, February 2010.

Office of the Spokesman, *Fact Sheet*, Kabul: U.S. Embassy, September 25, 2008, available from *kabul.embassy.gov/press_release_25_09.html*.

Osborne, David, and Ted Gaebler, *Reinventing Government*, New York: Penguin, 1993.

Peabody Newell, Nancy, and Richard S. Newell, *The Struggle for Afghanistan*, Ithaca, NY: Cornell University Press, 1981.

Pincus, Walter, "Up to 56,000 More Contractors Likely for Afghanistan, Congressional Agency Says," *The Washington Post* on-line, December 16, 2009, available from *www.washingtonpost.com*.

Priest, Dana, *The Mission: Waging War and Keeping Peace with America's Military*, New York: Norton and Company, 2004.

Project on National Security Reform, *Forging a New Shield*, Washington, DC: Center for the Study of the Presidency, November 2008.

Project on National Security Reform, *Preliminary Findings*, Washington, DC: Center for the Study of the Presidency, July 2008.

Project on National Security Reform, *Turning Ideas into Action*, Washington, DC: Center for the Study of the Presidency, September 2009.

Pulliam, John E., "Lines on a Map: Regional Orientations and U.S. Interagency Cooperation," *USAWC Strategy Research Project*, U.S. Army War College, March 2005.

Rashid, Ahmed, *Descent into Chaos*, New York: Penguin, 2008.

Record, Jeffrey, "Why the Strong Lose," *Parameters*, Winter 2005-2006.

Rhode, David, and David E. Sanger, "How the 'Good War' in Afghanistan Went Bad," *The New York Times*, August 12, 2007.

Rice, Secretary Condoleezza, Opening remarks before the Senate Foreign Relations Committee presenting the FY2009 International Affairs Budget Request, February 13, 2008, available from *www.state.gov/secretary/rm/2008/02/100726.htm*.

Roberts, Jeffery J., *The Origins of Conflict in Afghanistan*, Westport, CT: Praeger, 2003.

Rotberg, Robert I., ed., *Building a New Afghanistan*, Cambridge, MA: World Peace Foundation (and Brookings Institution), 2007.

Rubin, Alissa J., "Karzai's Increasing Isolation Worries Both Afghans and the West," *The New York Times*, June 8, 2010, p. A12.

Rumsfeld, Secretary of Defense Donald, *National Military Strategic Plan for the War on Terrorism*, Washington, DC: U.S. Government Printing Office, February 1, 2006.

Russell, James A., *Regional Threats and Security Strategy: The Troubling Case of Today's Middle East*, Carlisle, PA: Strategic Studies Institute, U.S. Army War College, 2007.

Schmitt, Eric, "U.S. Envoy's Cables Show Worries on Afghan Plans," *The New York Times* on-line, January 26, 2010, available from *www.nytimes.com*.

Sikorski, Radek, "Mujaheddin Memories," *National Review*, Vol. 56, No. 16, August 23, 2004.

Solana, Javier, EU High Representative for the Common Foreign and Security Policy. *Summary of the Intervention*, SO229/02, available from *ue.eu.int/newsroom*.

Suhrke, Astri, "A Contradictory Mission? NATO from Stabilization to Combat in Afghanistan," *International Peacekeeping*, Vol. 15, No. 2, April 2008.

Szayna, Thomas S., Derek Eaton, and Amy Richardson, *Preparing the Army for Stability Operations*, Santa Monica, CA: Rand Corporation, 2007.

Tan, Michelle, "Training Pays," *The Army Times*, October 20, 2008.

Tanner, Stephen, *Afghanistan: A Military History from Alexander the Great to the Fall of the Taliban*, Cambridge, MA: Da Capo Press, 2002.

Tellis, Ashley J., "Pakistan—Conflicted Ally in the War on Terror," *Carnegie Endowment for International Peace Policy Brief #56*, December 2007.

The 9/11 Commission Report, Official Government Ed., Washington, DC: U.S. Government Printing Office, 2004.

The President of the United States, *National Strategy for CombatingTerrorism*, Washington, DC: U.S. Government Printing Office, September 2006.

The President of the United States, *The National Security Strategy of the United States of America*, Washington, DC: U.S. Government Printing Office, March 2006.

The President of the United States, *The National Security Strategy of the United States of America,* Washington, DC: U.S. Government Printing Office, May 2010.

The Secretary of Defense, *Proliferation: Threat and Response,* Washington, DC: U.S. Government Printing Office, January 2001.

The White House, *National Security Presidential Directive- 1: Organization of the National Security Council System,* Washington, DC: The White House, February 13, 2001.

The White House, *National Security Presidential Directive- 44: Management of Interagency Efforts Concerning Reconstruction and Stabilization,* Washington, DC: The White House, December 7, 2005.

USAID, *About USAID: A Record of Accomplishment,* available from www.usaid.gov/about_usaid/accompli.html.

USAID, *About USAID: USAID History,* available from www.usaid.gov/about_usaid/usaidhist.html.

USAID, *At Freedom's Frontiers: A Democracy and Governance Strategic Framework,* Washington, DC: USAID, December 2005.

USAID, *Fragile States Strategy,* Washington, DC: USAID, January 2005.

USAID, *Provincial Reconstruction Teams in Afghanistan: An Interagency Assessment,* Washington, DC: USAID, June 2006.

USAID, *USAID Primer: What We Do and How We Do It,* available from www.usaid.gov/about_usaid/primer.html.

U.S. Department of State, *Strategic Plan: Fiscal Years 2007-2012,* Washington, DC: U.S. Government, May 7, 2007.

U.S. Department of State, *FY 2010 Mission Strategic Plan for Afghanistan,* Washington, DC: U.S. Government, May 12, 2008.

U.S. Department of State, *Doing Business in Afghanistan: A Country Commercial Guide for U.S. Businesses,* Washington, DC: U.S. Government, 2007.

U.S. Department of State, *Report to Congress on Implementation of Title XVI of P.L. 110-147, the Reconstruction and Stabilization Civilian Management Act of 2008*, Washington, DC: State Department, May 9, 2009.

U.S. Department of State and the Broadcasting Board of Governors Office of Inspector General, *Inspection of Embassy Kabul*, Afghanistan, Washington, DC: State Department, OIG Report ISP-I-06-13A, January 18, 2006, p. 1.

U.S. Government, *U.S. Government Counterinsurgency Guide*, Washington, DC: U.S. Government Interagency Counterinsurgency Initiative, January 2009.

U.S. Government Accountability Office, *Afghanistan Security: Afghan Army Growing, but Additional Trainers Needed; Long-Term Costs Not Determined*, Washington, DC: GAO Report to Congress, GAO-11-66, January 2011.

U.S. Government Accountability Office, *Afghanistan Reconstruction: Despite Some Progress, Deteriorating Security and Other Obstacles Continue to Threaten Achievement of U.S. Goals*, Washington, DC: GAO, GAO-05-742, July 2005.

U.S. Government Accountability Office, *Afghanistan Security: U.S. Programs to Further Reform Ministry of Interior and National Police Challenged by Lack of Military Personnel and Afghan Cooperation*, Washington, DC: Government Accountability Office, GAO-09-280, March 2009.

U.S. Government Accountability Office, *Report to Congressional Committees: Afghanistan Security*, Washington, DC: Government Accountability Office, June 2008.

U.S. Joint Forces Command, *Commander's Handbook for the Joint Interagency Coordination Group*, Norfolk, VA: Joint Warfighting Center, March 1, 2007.

U.S. Joint Forces Command, *The Joint Operating Environment (JOE) 2008*, Norfolk, VA: U.S. Joint Forces Command, November 25, 2008.

Wahib, Shaista, and Barry Youngerman, *A Brief History of Afghanistan*, New York: InfoBase Publishing, 2007.

Walt, Stephen M., "International Relations: One World, Many Theories," *Foreign Policy*, Vol. 110, Spring 1998.

Warrick, John, and R. Jeffrey Smith, "Outsourcing Assassinations," *The Washington Post National Weekly Ed.*, August 24-30, 2009.

"Wars Hinder Hunt for WMD," *Pittsburgh Post-Gazette*, August 28, 2010, p. A2.

Warwick, Donald P., *A Theory of Public Bureaucracy: Politics, Personality, and Organization in the State Department*, Cambridge, MA: Harvard University Press, 1975.

White, Philip L., and Michael L. White, eds., "What is a Nationality?" Chap. 1 of *Nationality in World History*, 2008, available from *www.nationalityinworldhistory.net*.

Williams, Brian Glyn, "Mullah Omar's Missiles," *Middle East Policy*, Vol. 15, No. 4, Winter 2008.

Williams-Bridgers, Jacquelyn, Congressional testimony on GAO, "Afghanistan and Pakistan: Oversight of U.S. Interagency Efforts," given on September 9, 2009, published as *GAO Report GAO-09-1015T*, Washington, DC: GAO, 2009.

Wilson, James Q., *Bureaucracy: What Government Agencies Do and Why They Do It*, New York: Basic Books, 1989.

Witte, Griff, "To the Warlords Belong the Spoils," *The Washington Post National Weekly Ed.*, June 22-28, 2006.

Woodward, Bob, "McChrystal: More Forces or 'Mission Failure,'" *The Washington Post*, September 21, 2009, available from *www.washingtonpost.com*.

Woodward, Bob, *Obama's Wars*. New York: Simon and Schuster, 2010.

Woodward, Bob, "Preventing Another Iraq," *The Washington Post National Weekly Ed.*, July 13-19, 2009.

Woodward, Bob, "The Case for Afghanistan," *The Washington Post National Weekly Ed.*, October 4, 2009.

Yarger, H. Richard, and George F. Barber, *The U.S. Army War College Methodology for Determining Interests and Levels of Intensity*, Carlisle, PA: U.S. Army War College, 1997.

Yarger, Harry R., *Strategic Theory for the 21st Century: The Little Book on Big Strategy*, Carlisle, PA: Strategic Studies Institute, U.S. Army War College, February 2006.

ACRONYMS AND ABBREVIATIONS

ANA/ANP	Afghan National Army/ Afghan National Police
ANSF	Afghan National Security Forces
CIA	U.S. Central Intelligence Agency
COCOM	Combatant Command
DEA	U.S. Drug Enforcement Administration
DoD	U.S. Department of Defense
DoJ	U.S. Department of Justice
IMS	Interagency Management System
ISI	Pakistan's Inter-Services Intelligence Directorate
ISAF	International Security and Assistance Force, Afghanistan
JIACG	Joint Interagency Coordinating Group
MOD	Afghan Ministry of Defense
MOI	Afghan Ministry of the Interior
NATO	North Atlantic Treaty Organization
NSC/ NSS	National Security Council/ National Security Staff
NSPD/ PPD	National Security Presidential Directive/ Presidential Policy Directive
NSS	National Security Strategy
PRT	Provincial Reconstruction Teams
State	U.S. Department of State
USAID	U.S. Agency for International Development
USDA	U.S. Department of Agriculture